# Refreshed

Dr Gary Franks

First published by Busybird Publishing 2023

Copyright © 2023 Gary Franks

**ISBN:**
Paperback: 978-1-922954-64-0
Ebook: 978-1-922954-65-7

This work is copyright. Apart from any use permitted under the *Copyright Act 1968*, no part of this publication may be reproduced, stored in a retrieval system or transmitted in any form or by any means, electronic, mechanical, photocopying, recording or otherwise, without the prior written permission of Gary Franks.

The information in this book is based on the author's experiences and opinions. The author and publisher disclaim responsibility for any adverse consequences, which may result from use of the information contained herein. Permission to use any external content has been sought by the author. Any breaches will be rectified in further editions of the book.

**Cover image:** Max Lissendon (Upslash)
**Back cover image:** Lyndal Salter
**Cover design:** Nathan Cairns / Busybird Publishing
**Layout and typesetting:** Busybird Publishing
**Illustrations:** Bev Hawkins
**Editing and proofreading:** Denise Henry, Carol Franks, Scott Vandervalk (Busybird Publishing)

Busybird Publishing
2/118 Para Road
Montmorency, Victoria
Australia 3094
åwww.busybird.com.au

**Proceeds** from the sale of this book will support a not-for-profit charity 'OnCourse' - lifting children, adolescents and women out of poverty through education and vocational training in Kenya.

For my beautiful wife Carol
and her lifetime of support.

For my much loved children and their partners
Justin and Katherine
Racquel and Joel
Luke and Travis.

For my adored grandchildren
who bring much happiness
Jack, Jai, Lilielle, Bodhe,
Lakyn, Pearl and Alaska.

For the love and care of parents and parents-in-law.

For my numerous medical colleagues, medical staff
and faithful patients who have supported me
throughout my career.

Thank you.

# Contents

Foreword     1

Preface     3

**CHAPTERS**

1. HERITAGE     12
2. 47 WEBB STREET     28
3. FAMILY OF ORIGIN     46
4. SCHOOLING     72
5. UNIVERSITY     88
6. HOSPITAL     108
7. GENERAL PRACTICE     118
8. MEDICINE AND MISSION     146
9. COVID-19     174
10. MEDICINE AND FAITH     210
11. MARRIAGE AND FAMILY     236
12. BALANCING LIFE WITH MEDICINE     262
13. THE GOODNESS OF GOD     282

    Appendix     297

# Foreword

I have known Gary Franks for over 40 years. He has been my doctor and my friend for all of that time. This is his story so far, unique and wonderfully well told. His story recounts life in the baby boomer years of Australia and extends to the present day challenges of a general practitioner who worked through the COVID-19 pandemic.

Gary has provided through his narratives how faith, medicine, family and his patients have helped him learn lessons that could be of benefit to others. It's not just a commentary on his career. He lays out before the reader the story of his calling in life and the love he has for his family. It comes with an array of emotions, from grief and sadness to frustration and disappointment, light-heartedness and humour.

*Refreshed* is Gary's story of a life lived with purpose. It is a written account of a humble Christian man for posterity. He tells his story with facts, details, evidence and rational logic interspersed with his Christian beliefs.

This story is about the power of God working in a man's life to guide and direct his ways to the benefit of all. This timeless story will be used as a guide to all that read it for generations to come. For Gary, this is about leaving a legacy 'snapshot' for his family as they reflect on what he values and cherishes, from his early informative years to this present time.

His writing challenges firmly held attitudes, opinions and prejudices. He highlights some ethical challenges about the inequality of the world's resources through the different aspects of his work.

It's an honour to write this foreword and I recommend *Refreshed* to you. Enjoy the read. I certainly did!

> 'The good physician treats the disease. The great physician treats the patient who has the disease.'
> – William Osler

**Andrew Scipione. AO APM**
**NSW Commissioner of Police (Retired)**

*'Memory is the diary we all carry about with us.'*

– Oscar Wilde.

# Preface

I was awake night after night writing farewell messages to my wife, children and grandchildren.

This was one experience for me in the early months of 2020, just as the COVID-19 viral pandemic started having devastating consequences in overseas countries. Medical and mainstream media were reporting stories of illness, suffering and escalating deaths, with concerning significant numbers of these amongst healthcare workers, including doctors.

And it was heading for Australia like a tsunami. My dad had made detailed lists and notes of where important documents were to be found after he died. I found myself undertaking the same preparation, even including details about my own funeral service!

The period from 2020–2023 were years to remember for so many unpleasant reasons (some would rather they be forgotten). Two thousand and twenty in particular was bookended by fires and the start of a pandemic, before flowing seamlessly into the further trials of 2021–2022. Like a grand final football commentator, adjectives flowed from the lips of many health professionals, media reporters, politicians, patients, friends and the general public – words like 'unprecedented', 'unique', 'uncertain', 'devastating'. For the majority of the Australian population it was a difficult time in our history with compounding crises of traumatic events – drought, bushfires, floods and to top it all off the health pandemic – a quadruple whammy!

Catastrophic and widespread bushfires caused incalculable losses to people, land and wildlife. The bushfires lasted for three months and affected large areas of all the Australian states. A map of Australia at night on the television looked as if the whole country was burning. These wildfires followed a prolonged and severe drought across the continent that had already caused hardship and suffering.

Partially to blame for the ferocity of the bushfires was climate change, which had caused temperatures to rise and the drying of bushland across our vast country. Water restrictions affected city folk too – with scenes of people watering plants and lawns via watering cans. A time-consuming endeavour on my part that I did not enjoy.

Individuals and churches prayed for, and most of the country hoped for, rain. The prayers were answered, the rain came, and then the floods, causing extensive damage to multiple towns and rural areas through much of 2022.

Just when we thought the situation was calming down from the earlier drought and wildfires over the Christmas/New Year period, warnings came in late January 2020 to general practitioners (GPs) – a novel virus causing respiratory complications and death had broken out in Wuhan, China. We were told to consider the possibility of infection if we consulted patients who had travelled to that area. Little did I know that this pandemic would be the greatest and most overwhelming challenge I would face as a GP of 40 years, and that this 'once-in-a-lifetime event' would wreak havoc across the planet, with billions of people infected and millions dying from an enemy that could not be seen.

These events all seemed to occur quickly. I was up late at night trying to absorb information from different sources. I found myself thinking, planning and praying about how I would be able to adapt and strategise to protect patients, staff and my family, yet keep the surgery open to offer medical care. It led me to diarise my experience, emotions and behaviour – these are expanded in a later chapter. The 'uncertainty' that this pandemic caused was a personal experience as well as an experience that affected the whole world, reaching every continent and country except Antarctica. The only certainty for me during this time was the assurance that God was in control and, therefore, I felt at peace and able to focus on the task I knew was ahead.

The goodness of God has become an overarching theme of my life, even if I may have not been aware of this in every circumstance at the time. This should become obvious to the reader through my stories and the transparency with which I relay them.

Two thousand and twenty, however, was also the year that I arrived at 42 years in medicine and 40 in general practice. Like the speed of the bushfires and the spread of the pandemic, these 40 years have come and gone too quickly. This was meant to be the year that I'd planned to try my hand at writing – also a 'unique and unprecedented' experience. When I commenced writing I was unaware that these years would become the most confronting of my life.

I had a desire to put pen to paper and write my memoir/autobiography – my life experience as a Christian, husband, father, brother, son, friend, doctor of medicine and proud grandfather. The latter was the predominant reason for writing. I was hoping that my three children, spouses and partners and, in particular, seven much loved grandchildren would be interested in reading about my life. I would therefore leave them with a legacy that might be remembered and, hopefully, provide for them a source from which to seek wisdom in their future lives.

So why write my story?

The answer is this: 'If I don't tell my story, then who would?'

It is a misconception to think if one is not famous then one's story is not necessarily interesting. It's not just a navel-gazing exercise.

Another reason for writing was that for decades I had come to know personally thousands of patients, often at deep levels, as they came to trust in my understanding of the more personal, private and confidential areas of their lives. Yet these same people knew very little about my life, other than the medical relationship I had developed with them.

An unexpected benefit of starting to write was that this helped me to remember past events and appreciate the many people in my life and the influences they have been to me. As we age, we tend to become more nostalgic. Our memories allow us to 'meet' ourselves and others again, and with sometimes challenging honesty. I desired for the lives and memories of those no longer with me to be brought to the pages of this book.

We need to be able to remember in order to write a memoir but it's true that 'we write in order to remember'. In other words, reflecting, studying, revisiting and seeking others' stories about my life helped me to remember, especially memories around growing up.

*'A memoir is how one remembers one's own life.'*
– **Gore Vidal.**

## History -a thing of the past?

According to Christian Theologian and Historian John Dickson, we are living in a contemporary, post-truth, ahistorical age where history and the past are considered irrelevant and having 'faith' is ignorance. We tend not to care as much about tradition and we are sceptical of the past. History is an academic discipline, based on facts, real events, stories and truth. It's how we make sense of the past and our engagement with it in such a way that passes down these stories and makes life meaningful. History can be an opportunity to value the good and learn from the mistakes of the past.

'History provides surviving evidence for what was once objectively real and true about the past, even though there is a human element that is open to interpretation. Inherited histories, stories and traditions that are passed down to teach and shape us, as well to help us understand who we are, and how we were formed. History is a vast treasure. If we steward it, tend to it and keep it, then it holds profound riches for us.' (Professor of History, Sarah Irvine-Stonebraker) 'Tending' means to uncover and cultivate the stories of the past that we actually know about - including stories that might sit uncomfortably with us.

The 'Baby Boomers' generation to which I belong, holds a special place in history as a generation that experienced significant cultural, social and economic changes. These included pay phones, going to drive-in theatres, enjoying vinyl records, changing a dial for TV channels, and enjoying peaceful Sundays with all shops closed. We have fond memories of simpler times unique to our generation and as we grow older we look back on our youth with nostalgia. From the perspective of younger generations however, the Baby Boomers have been criticised for squeezing others out of the housing market, straining the healthcare system, destroying the planet and causing economic inequality - just to mention a few. Possibly some of these may have been accurate undesirable outcomes, (even though not intentional) as I am sure there are similar unwelcomed outcomes of any past or future generation.

My perception of personal life experiences and that of my generation are unchanged and are still valid. Hopefully through this record of my life, I will have been a good steward of history which will be passed down to anyone interested in reading this book. A conservation of the past and a preservation of my cultural heritage, that was both individual and reflective of Australian society at this time in history.

## Refreshed

My favourite book in the Bible is Proverbs, and I will be making reference to this book to reinforce various parts of my story, as well as other quotations and writings that have inspired me from a variety of sources over the years – from favourite musicians, famous people I've admired, or just ordinary people I've met during my lifetime. I have created an appendix for further reading if desired by readers for expansion on certain references or content I mention.

Proverbs is based on the wisdom and life of King Solomon and is a memoir of his life, mistakes made and lessons learned.

In life, we can either learn from our own experiences (which can be difficult and challenging), or we can learn from those who have had similar experiences and avoid the mistakes they've made. Knowledge alone does not necessarily change behaviour, but knowledge is required to initiate the change. Wisdom can be defined as the correct application of knowledge, and we all need wisdom. The attainment of wisdom is a challenging goal, and errors will be made but it is a worthy pursuit.

The title of my story Refreshed is inspired by Proverbs 11:25. 'The generous prosper and are satisfied, those who refresh others will themselves be refreshed.' Or, as another translation explains it, 'The one who blesses others is abundantly blessed; those who help others are helped.' Helping others with their health, their lives, their growth – physically, emotionally and spiritually – was a goal I desired to achieve, both in my medical career as well as my personal life.

I observed and learnt the value of generosity from the example of my parents and those who were generous towards me. Although seeking to be generous in all aspects of my life, I've found the hardest time to show generosity is when you don't feel like it.

Queen Elizabeth II stated, 'I know just how much I rely on my own faith to guide me through the good times and the bad. Each day is a new beginning. I know that the only way to live my life is to try to do what is right, to take the long view, to give of my best in all that the day brings, and to put my trust in God.' Words that were put into action in her life and that inspired me to aim for similar.

My life experience has been, and still is, that this endeavour of helping others, in Australia or Africa, has brought me great satisfaction, purpose and joy. It has not always been easy, nor successful, nor perfect – often far from it. My stories will reveal this – the mistakes, the missed opportunities, the disappointments, the times overcoming difficulties, the times of celebration, and the times of answered prayer. But through it all, the realisation as I draw near to the end of my career and working life is that the goodness of God stands out to me and has had a profound influence on my life's direction.

Being as 'novel' to writing as the virus that inflicted itself upon us in 2020, I needed some guidelines and so studied others memoirs. A most helpful resource was *Writing the Story of Your Life* by Australian writer Carmel Bird. This author gave many exercises to undertake as homework to stimulate memories and writing, describing the exercises as 'looking in the mirror'. A memoir is like a self-portrait that needs to be frank, not glossing over the personal flaws.

I've learnt that the parts of the narrative, parts of my life that highlight the good times and good things are thrown into relief by the flaws, the cracks, the breaks, the specs on the mirror and the shadows in the corner.

Often a memoir contains a guiding metaphor that can be a theme or a word. My metaphor would be 'water', relating to not only the title of this book but also to many aspects of my life, including the enjoyment I've found in activities and sports that I've participated in and that I still love – surfing, fishing, waterskiing and, later, kayaking and swimming.

## Memoir or autobiography?

Carmel Bird suggests: 'Autobiography is writing that attempts to stay close to as many of the facts and feelings of the writer over as great a length of time as possible. A memoir is a completely individual construction designed to deliver to the reader some elements of the autobiography, some elements of the journal but moving at its own pace. Memoir is a freer medium in which the writer can engage perhaps more fully and creatively with the material of the life and memory, which can range across time and location. Ultimately the boundaries of one form blur nicely into the edges of the other.'

I relate to this definition and explanation of the differences. I desire to engage more fully with readers by not just recollecting facts and dates, but to portray my feelings, opinions, experiences, beliefs and worldview that may stimulate thinking and reflection in the lives of those who choose to read it. I will tell stories – some sad, many serious, and a number of humorous ones. I've attempted to remain open, transparent and honest in these stories, even though a few are so personal that I've never shared them publicly.

And so I commence my story, despite the warning of Simone de Beauvoir: 'Writing memoir is somewhat a rash adventure!' This may be true but I intend to enjoy the journey anyway.

# CHAPTER ONE

# HERITAGE

'The heritage of the past is the seed that brings forth the harvest of the future.'
– Wendell Phillips

'He who denies his heritage, has no heritage.'
– Khalil Gibran

# Hereditary traits

There are many traits that can be hereditary and so be traced back through their lineage of past generations. Some of these include physical appearance, medical conditions and diseases – often logical results of genetics. But some behavioural qualities can be passed on that are not so logical. It is considered that the way we behave and our personal preferences are mainly influenced by environment, lifestyle and experiences, but genetics may play a role. In my family, one of these behaviours may be likes and dislikes of food and its quality. For instance, I appreciate my meals being hot, not warm, not lukewarm, not cold – but hot. The temperature of the meal makes the taste much more enjoyable – that's what I think anyway.

The first descendants on my mother's side to make the arduous journey by sailing ship from the United Kingdom to Australia in 1855 must have been carrying the same genes to this peculiar malady. The Matthews family, consisting of two adults and six children, travelled by ship for at least three months. I was interested to read in research documents that the ship's log noted that 'they were outspoken and complained about the quality of the food on the voyage'.

The 'gene' for this trait seemed to remain dormant for a few generations since one of the great descendants, Shirley June Brown, my mother, was never outspoken nor complained about the quality or temperature of her food. Eventually, however, this trait seemed to have reemerged in the generation that followed her – namely myself!

# Franks

On 6 April 1859, Francis Franks from Shropshire, England, my great grandfather, married Susanna Elizabeth Jagger from Oxford, England. He was 31 years old (born in 1828) and she was 22 years old (born in 1837). Francis moved to New Zealand in 1857 and he and Susanna married in Kaiapoi. He was the first school teacher at Waikouaiti in 1861 with 20 pupils. Renowned as being a fine teacher, his teaching skills were appreciated until his resignation in 1864. He then, ironically, became a brewer, soap manufacturer and operated a 'bone factory' (a graveyard) until in 1870 the brewery burned down. The story has it that Francis won an annual New Zealand 'best beer' contest after a keg fell off a truck and then matured in a snow-fed creek.

The irony of that story came later, with his conversion to Christianity and joining The Salvation Army and commencing an alcohol-free life (something that lasted a number of generations in the Franks lineage). Francis resided in Temuka from 1874 and stood for parliament in 1884. Receiving only 20 votes, his political career was anything but lengthy. He died of apoplexy/cardiac failure (a commonly used diagnosis in the past on a death certificate) in 1905 and is buried in Temuka cemetery, which Carol and I visited nearly a century later.

Susanna, Francis's wife, had died some 15 years earlier in 1890 of 'chronic nephritis of two months' as suggested on her death certificate which seems erroneous and not chronic, rather acute. She's also buried at Temuka Cemetery. Together they had six boys and two girls. One of the boys became my deeply admired grandfather, George Washington Franks – a name alluding to a famous American president. Although not famous, my grandfather became synonymous as a loyal, humble servant of the people and of his family.

George Washington was born in Temuka in 1878, when his father was a spritely 51 years of age. George was converted to Christianity at the Eltham revival in 1903, which is on the west coast of the North Island of New Zealand. He initially worked as a grocer, but his life was radically transformed at this time and his desire to share his new faith led to him to attend The Salvation Army training college for officers (a theological college, rather than military college) in 1905.

In 1916, George was appointed as a chaplain in the First Australian Imperial Force (AIF) in World War I (WWI). He served the troops as a padre, particularly in the training area of Salisbury Plains in Central Southern England, a place that decades later would be used for training the D-Day landing troops.

He attended the Salisbury Salvation Army where he met a stunningly beautiful young lady by the name of Hilda Margaret Bartlett. She must have been just as beautiful in her character since he fell in love with this woman and they were married in 1919, a year after the Great War ended and the year that the Spanish flu pandemic (the last great pandemic before 2020) spread around the world killing 50 million –more deaths than from WWI. The Spanish influenza was actually wrongly labelled since it was thought to have originated (according to historians) in China – similar to the virus the world faced a century later.

George and Hilda's marriage photo shows my grandmother smartly dressed in a Salvation Army uniform and my grandfather in his military uniform.

They survived both war and pandemic and moved to Australia. My grandmother never entered training to become a Salvation Army officer, a very uncommon situation, perhaps an oversight due to the pandemic. Hilda was born in February 1895, daughter of William and Margaret Bartlett and lived in Rampart Road, Salisbury in a small two-bedroom semi, small enough that one of her sisters had to live with other relatives because there was not enough room for all the children.

In 2013, my wife Carol and I had the pleasure of visiting Salisbury and Salisbury Plains and in particular the unchanged semi where my grandmother spent her childhood. Although the eldest of nine, she described how 'although she did not have much of the world's goods, she had plenty of fun'. She talked about The Salvation Army band and songsters coming to play and sing carols at Christmas-time, never thinking that one day she would be joining them – a scenario repeated in Australia at Lewisham years later for my mother and future wife of Hilda's son (Ronald, my dad).

My grandparents served fruitful lives with their five children as Salvation Army officers in various field appointments in all Australian states except Western Australia. They offered much needed physical and spiritual support to the thousands of people they cared for especially through the years of the Great Depression. They retired in 1941 after my grandfather's health deteriorated.

My grandfather died suddenly of a presumed heart attack on 3 July 1945, aged 67, while reading the newspaper in his home at Kyle Bay in Sydney. Apparently he was reading an article that involved details of my dad's army regiment invading Borneo, understandably a worrying report for him to become aware of personally.

Dad and his brothers only became aware of my grandfather's death sometime after his funeral via a telegram while on active service in Papua New Guinea, too late to return to even support his grieving mother. My dad only had his father for 22 years, five of these while absent, serving in the war. I could relate to how my dad felt losing his dad at that age since I would only be 25 when my mother died.

Major George Washington Franks was 'Promoted to Glory' (The Salvation Army's terminology for one of its member's death), suggesting that after death as a Christian he would enter Heaven, and that transition was described as a promotion.

*The War Cry* was the weekly newspaper of The Salvation Army, and the heading that week said, 'Won in a Revival, Major George Franks never lost his zeal for souls'. At his funeral service, apparently there were moving tributes and descriptions of his character that were most inspiring – such as his uncalculating graciousness and unpretentious kindness, his faithful life and work and the intensity of the major's own religious fervour. The article went on to say, 'Another of The Salvation Army's devoted officers now dwells within the radiance of the Heavenly throne, the character and worth of his earthly influence bright in the minds and hearts of his comrades and loved ones.'

One regret of my life was that I never met or knew him in person, or had the benefit of appreciating this man's character and values. I think he would have been an inspiring grandfather and I would have loved to hear his life experiences and stories of how he endured the hardships of WWI and the Great Depression, and how his faith intersected with his life.

When I eventually became a grandfather myself (to our seven grandchildren), these memories stirred a deep desire to be the best grandfather I could. I wanted to not only show my grandchildren how loved and valued they each were but how keen I was to spend time with them, to have holidays and fun with them, and to have opportunities to encourage them. Developing a unique relationship with each grandchild was a definite aim I had, and still do.

Grandparenting has been one of the most enjoyable and rewarding experiences of my life. It has also been shown to be of significant importance and value to children and young people as they face life and all its challenges. Grandparents should be safe resources of trust, advice, love and time – something parents trying to balance busy lives can struggle with.

Hilda, my paternal grandmother, went on to live until 1965, 20 years after her beloved husband was 'Promoted to Glory'. She lived at Kyle Bay with Aunty Peggy and when we visited her she was warm and interested in her grandchildren's lives. She returned home to England a few times by ship to visit family and would always bring something back with her for each child from her journeys. I would have liked to have had more of her influence in my life, but the times we did see her were valued and enjoyed.

Mrs Major Hilda Franks was also 'Promoted to Glory' when I was 12 years of age and, although I don't remember the details of this first funeral service I attended, I do recall it was a mixture of a wonderful celebration of a worthy life, an assurance of eternal hope and yet an awareness of earthly grief.

George and Hilda had five children – Ken, Gordon, my father Ronald, Peggy and Arthur. The three oldest sons enrolled in the AIF for Australia during World War II (WWII). A photograph of them in uniform alongside their padre father supported by his wife, with high-waisted-white belts, khaki green uniform and slouch hats must have been a proud moment in family history and an important inclusion in their photo album.

Ken ended up fighting with the famously dubbed 'Rats of Tobruk' holding out against General Rommel and standing in the way of the German advance towards Egypt and the Suez Canal. Arthur, too young to enrol, later became the only member of the family to follow in his parent's footsteps by becoming a Salvation Army officer. For a number of years after the war, it was always enjoyable to attend family gatherings and to play and interact with our many cousins.

## Brown and Matthews

On my mother's side, my grandparents were Arthur (Cecil) and Nita Brown (nee Matthews).

My maternal grandmother has an interesting heritage. Her lineage dates back to 1631 in a small village in the United Kingdom called Woodborough in the county of Wiltshire, England, with an early record of the Matthews family and with Richard Matthews marrying Susanna Farmer in 1655. This village of quaint thatched-roofed stone houses was probably founded by the early Celts (where there was evidence of Saxon invasion in the sixth century).

Of circumstantial interest is that this village where my lineage on my mother's side commenced is just a few miles north of Salisbury, England where my paternal grandmother was born and raised.

The only church – St Mary Magdalene – built in 1280, was the site of many baptisms, marriages, worship services and funerals for the Matthews family, with burials taking place in the peaceful tree-shaded churchyard adjacent to rolling hills of green fields and grazing sheep. In 1766, one of the descendants, John Matthews, married Anne Blanchard in Woodborough, and they had three children, one of whom was Daniel Matthews who lived from 1768 to 1812.

Daniel had seven children, the youngest being Richard. Richard's date of birth was unknown. He married Sarah Bristow in 1835. They were the first descendants to make a courageous start in the new NSW colony after sailing from Southampton aboard the ship Lloyds on 8 May 1855, arriving in Sydney three months later. They had six children at the time of travelling, with another born in Australia. This was the family carrying the 'complaints about the food' gene.

Richard settled at Brisbane Waters near Gosford as a timber worker but soon caught the infectious 'gold fever' and tried his luck in the goldfields at Ballarat in Victoria, then finally settled in the mining area aptly named Goodrich, near what is now Yeoval, NSW. Richard had a tragic and sudden death in 1873 when he fell under a bolting horse and cart. He was 62 years old, and his wife unfortunately also died within the same year.

The fifth child of Richard and Sarah was Jacob Matthews, born in Woodborough in 1846 and was aged nine when he arrived in Australia. His lineage was the one that eventually led to my maternal grandmother Nita Brown (nee Matthews). His life turned out to be a very influential one in the development of rural NSW and, in particular, a town called Peak Hill, situated between Parkes and Dubbo on the Newell Highway.

Jacob married Mary Ann Higginbothams at Scotts Church Sydney in 1868, apparently starting married life with a horse and cart and a halfpenny. Following the goldfields, Jacob settled in Yeoval as well, and he built the Royal Hotel, raised stock and then sold the meat to miners through his butcher's shop. His old timber butcher shop is still standing on the main highway running through this small town in Western NSW, as is the Royal Hotel with some extra additions and renovations. Jacob cared about his community and, at a public meeting, he proposed that a public school be built – which was standing for about 150 years until 2020 when it had to be demolished after a fire.

When gold was discovered at Peak Hill, Jacob Matthews was one of the first on the field, taking up land in the appropriately named 'Struggle Street', opening a restaurant, building another Royal Hotel and a butcher shop. He cleared land three kilometres south of Peak Hill for grazing cattle on a property called 'The Farm'.

Jacob was active in the establishment of the first town council of Peak Hill in 1894, serving two terms as mayor in 1899 and 1902. Not resting on his laurels, he was instrumental in the railway coming to Peak Hill, being president of the Railway League. Unfortunately, he died in 1906 before the railway finally arrived in 1914. He was also a tireless worker in establishing the Peak Hill and District Hospital in 1892, simultaneously being an innovator and instrumental in the first wheat crop grown in the district.

He had a love and knowledge of horses and this was put to good use in his membership of the Stock Board. He kept building more for the community including the Matthews Assembly Hall – which still stands today. His incredible community achievements were obviously observed by governing bodies because he had the distinct honour of being invited by Edmund Barton (later prime minister of Australia) to represent NSW on the Federation Association.

While being an ambitious achiever and community leader, Jacob's priorities of family and faith were still paramount. His 12 children understood from their parents the value and importance of family and supporting each other as the need arose. The church and his faith in God held an important place in their lives. They worshipped and were active in St Stephen's Church of England, which has a commemorative plaque mentioning their names on the front stone fence.

His funeral and procession and the obituary in the *Peak Hill Express* on 10 August 1906 revealed the affection and sentiments all the residents of the Peak Hill district had for him:

'To the final day of his slow death he had the welfare of the town and district at heart. Peak Hill has lost its "father". His death will cause a void that cannot be filled. As a benefactor to his fellow man he was in the forefront, and scores will miss his practical sympathy.'

Jacob was survived by his widow and six sons and five daughters – most of them born on 'The Farm'.

# Convicts and bushrangers

Sidney Matthews, born 1882, was the seventh child of Jacob and Ann, and married Emily Mary Tyler of the same age and together had 11 children. Emily Mary was a daughter of Emily Elizabeth Hall whose father William Hall Jr was the brother of notorious bushranger Ben Hall, who is remembered in Australian folklore and who was shot dead by police in Western NSW aged only 27 years. Their father, William Hall Sr, born in England in 1804, was charged for stealing a small amount of clothing as a young man and sentenced to seven years in the colony of NSW. William Sr continued his criminal behaviour, becoming a well-known cattle and horse thief and spent a number of periods in jail. The woman he met on his three-month journey to Australia he eventually married, the service undertaken by the well-known historical figure – the Reverend Samuel Marsden.

Unfortunately, most of the male children of William Hall Sr also became criminals, the most famous being Ben Hall, whose notoriety came to fruition when he organised the successful theft of a large amount of gold being transported from the goldfields. That is, except one son – William Hall Jr. He became a Christian and ironically joined The Salvation Army, and with his wife was active serving in this organisation all his life. There are many photos of him in his Salvation Army uniform and there are many letters he wrote to his brothers explaining how he loved them and how he shared his faith with them. William Hall Jr wrote in one of the letters, 'We have spent many happy years in God's service and He (God) has watched over us, and kept us from all harm and spared us both to the present date.' Being a relative of criminals, his life must have been seen as significantly different from that of his family by those around him. People would most likely have had no doubt about his transformation. I found it quite astonishing that four generations later, with probably little knowledge of the life of a distant relative (William Hall Jr), that one particular Sunday decades later my mother would also be attracted to that same religious organisation and have a similar transformation and devote herself to serving others – as William did.

It appears from my mother's lineage, my extended family and children are related to convicts and bushrangers – a fact I inadvertently forgot to share with my wife until we were married! As well as the food fussiness gene that I found I'd inherited, it seems the gene for stealing a small amount of clothing was also passed on (explained in a later chapter).

The second child of Sidney and Emily Matthews (nee Emily Mary Tyler) was Nita Doris, known as 'Doss' who was to become my maternal grandmother. Nita was born and raised in the Peak Hill district, but after WWI she moved to Kensington, Sydney with her family because her father was interested in racehorses. In 1925, the family moved back to the original district when Sidney, like his father, took on the licensee of the Royal Hotel in Tomingley, 17 km north of Peak Hill, for a number of years before moving back to live in Coogee in 1940. Sidney died in 1943, and his wife Emily in 1946.

Nita died aged 56 in 1958 in Marrickville Hospital when I was five years old, so my recollections of her are shallow and were mainly developed through my older sister, Carolyn. I don't remember having a close relationship with my grandmother; however, she had a large family by all accounts, many of whom still lived in the Peak Hill area. Unfortunately, and sadly, I later learnt from my parents that she had an alcohol addiction, developed cirrhosis of the liver and died earlier than she should have.

The only relative of my grandmother I can recall having anything to do with was her much younger sister Merle, who married a farmer at Tomingely, interestingly named Tom (Hart) – a delightful tall and slim farmer who always made us feel welcome when we met him, either on their farm when we visited, or at the beach when they holidayed in Manly. In 2023, my sisters and I visited the farm that was once owned by Tom and Merle Hart, and we were invited into the old cottage there called Hart Cottage. The new owner made us a cup of tea and showed us the extent of the huge 80 acre farm that is still now producing wheat and wool. We were amazed to learn that a large part of the farm, which was originally 10 times that size, is now an open-cut mining excavation that has produced some of the largest gold deposits in NSW. Little did we know as small children rounding up sheep, nor did Uncle Tom know, that a few hundred metres below from where he was growing wheat and grazing sheep was a gold mine waiting to be found, containing the precious metal that attracted Jacob Matthews to the remote area over 150 years previously. Tom's daughter, Barbara Dunn, organised a large Matthews reunion at Peak Hill in 1994 and there was a large number of relatives in attendance.

Although I don't know where she originally met him, Nita Doris Matthews married Cecil Arthur Brown, a chartered accountant. They lived in a grand two-storey house on a corner block, which is still standing in the suburb of Lewisham, Sydney overlooking the railway line. This could explain why Mum was not perturbed when my dad bought a block of land to build their first home, which overlooked another railway line.

Mum was born at Hurlstone Park on 5 June 1928 and became a typist. Her sister Beverly was six years younger and became a secretary at the University of Sydney.

Cecil Brown was born in 1900 and died in 1988. Not much is known of his family heritage except his father was was Arthur Hayward Brown who died after throat surgery at the young age of 30 years. Arthur married Anne Edith Maling who was 16 years older than him. Anne died in 1963. Cecil had two sisters and one brother – little is known about them. Whilst writing, I realised the depth of my disappointment of not having a close relationship with the only grandfather that was alive when I was young. I would have cherished that. It seemed to my sisters and myself (as suggested by his behaviour ), that his self worth was determined by money and his wealth- a melancholic memory for each of us.

This makes me wonder how my dad ever convinced Cecil to let him marry his eldest daughter Shirley, being penniless after the war, and the son of Salvation Army officers, with little prospect of any inheritance. Whatever dad said or whatever his character portrayed seemed to have done the trick, as he married his sweetheart on his return from WWII.

My older sister called him 'Paw Paw' when she was a toddler instead of calling him Pa. This title stuck, with the rest of us referring to him as 'Paw Paw' or perhaps 'poor poor' – which had on hindsight, a particular ironic twist to it considering his emphasis on earthly wealth. This criticism however needs to be tempered with some empathy in that we did not know all the details of my grandfathers backstory, his upbringing at the start of the twentieth century and the consequences in his life of living through two world wars and the great depression.

As well as his Sydney house, Cecil owned two cottages at Pretty Beach on the Central Coast, one of which was mainly built by my father and provided many enjoyable Christmas holidays with family and friends. Paw Paw had a supercilious attitude and belief system that it was mainly direct family that really mattered, as Dad discovered soon enough.

In our world, materialism and greed can easily supersede personal relationships and become the seismic force that causes rifts and breakdowns in families. Generosity, selflessness, humility and love on the other hand can precipitate deep and fulfilling relationships and produce strong families, mend hurts and overcome difficulties – a wonderful legacy.

The words in the following two Bible verses seem an appropriate conclusion of this chapter and relate to the differences I experienced in my grandparents, because of their behaviour, values and relationships within our family as a child, and the generational outcomes I observed over time. I believe this opinion came from my observation that a faith in God radically changed one set of grandparents lives, bringing a focus on serving others that resulted in a transformed trajectory for future generations, for which I am personally indebted.

'Don't lose your grip on love and loyalty. Tie them around your neck; carve their initials on your heart. Earn a reputation for living well in God's eyes and the eyes of the people.'

'Don't store up treasures here on earth ,where they can be eaten by moths and get rusty…but store your treasures in heaven. Wherever your treasure is ,there your heart and thoughts will also be.'

# CHAPTER TWO

# 47 WEBB STREET

'A home is built by wisdom, and it is established
by understanding; by knowledge the rooms
are filled with every precious
and beautiful treasure.'

– **Proverbs 24:3–4**

# Herne Bay

In 1953 there were many outstanding world events that took place, which on hindsight seemingly intersected at later times with my life story. To name a few: Jonas Salk gave himself and his family the first polio vaccine, Queen Elizabeth II was crowned queen of England, Crick and Watson discovered the double helix of DNA, and Sir Edmund Hillary and Tenzing Norgay were the first to summit Mt Everest.

To many, the address I was brought home to after my birth in a Salvation Army hospital in Marrickville in May 1953 would have been considered rather lowly, undesirable, noisy and at the 'end of the line'. Not so much at the 'end of the line', but certainly opposite the line was accurate. The East Hills railway line (now called the Airport and Southern line) was established in 1931 to serve the south-western suburbs of Sydney.

Our home in Webb Street was situated alongside the railway line, the street stretching from Herne Bay shopping centre to Salt Pan Creek Bridge.

That same railway line with its initial steam trains, and later electric 'red rattlers' as they were called, became symbolic of the street. It certainly provided an amazing array of adventures growing up as a free-spirited boy. One adventure was lying on our backs under the bridge with our faces as close to the overhead rail lines as possible, while trains went over the top of us – a sort of an initiation feat to belong to a gang of young boys growing up together. In later years, the area we crawled into was cemented over, suggesting its risk not being acceptable to present councils – how times change.

Another adventure involved climbing through the wire railway boundary fence, racing to the railway tracks between trains, putting a large penny coin taped down on the track with the newly commemorated Queen Elizabeth II's face staring heavenwards, waiting for the impending assault. After hiding in bushes, the last part of this adventure was to dash out after the train to collect the elongated, defaced copper coin with the iconic face looking very distorted. This behaviour would also not be acceptable these days and not recommended for young readers of this book.

That railway line and its incredibly noisy steam trains provided numerous opportunities to observe the startled faces of visitors who were not expecting or were not conditioned as we were to the noise of trains. My bedroom, at the front of the house, was particularly lacking soundproofing, and visiting mates would invariably jump out of their bed and duck for cover since they thought the 2 am freight train was coming straight through the house.

## 'The Block'

The house that my dad single-handedly built at 'No. 47' ended up as a masterpiece for someone who was forced to learn as he went. I'm not sure of the exact build time – but it was long, and it was arduous. Dad would travel out by train after his day's work, carrying building materials (which were scarce after WWII) on his shoulders and on his pushbike. Fortunately, the walk or ride from Herne Bay station was downhill and only a few hundred metres. He was still employed at this time, but continued in spare time to work on the building of his own home.

Most nights of the week and most weekends except for Sundays (which was his church day), he would be pegging out boundaries, digging with pick and shovel, nailing hardwood and erecting fibro walls and concrete roof tiles. The bearers and joists were 4×2 (inch) hardwood and needed drilling by hand before nailing. Dad was such a detailed person and he would persevere until everything was correct.

My bedroom was a small sun-filled room at the front of our house and it was the best 'possie' to overhear conversations that took place just outside my window on the small patio entrance, especially when my older sister started dating her future husband!

Mum and Dad's bedroom was large, with wardrobes providing Dad with the ideal soundproofing for his nightly soprano cornet practice. He faced the bell of his cornet into his clothes to muffle the noise, but I could still hear the sweet high-pitched sound it made. There are many types of sounds that children listen to as they grow up – some pleasant, some not so. Fortunately, I didn't have to deal with the yelling and screaming of parents, nor the sounds associated with drunkenness, abuse and violence that too many children sadly experience as I increasingly became aware of as a general practitioner over the years. I feel blessed that what I remember was laughter, decent conversation and music from within our family home.

In the middle of the house was a large combined lounge and dining room, with a gas fireplace. It was a room where our family celebrated many events. This was the location where we annually left our Christmas stockings, which were filled on Christmas Eve. My room being closest to the action meant some premature investigations of wrapped presents in the early hours of the morning.

Mum managed to cook the best meals in a very small kitchen at the back of the house, and I still remember the smells and tastes of my favourite dishes, including chicken roasts, lamb chops and vegetables, and chilli con carne. The desserts she cooked have become my favourites, which include lemon meringue pie, pavlova and her classic ice box cake (which has been passed down in the family as a favourite celebration cake). Mum was a beautiful homemaker who created a warm and cosy atmosphere for all the family.

The rear kitchen of our home led to a concrete area behind the house, the future storage location for *Sally F*, Dad's prized 13 ft fibreglass runabout. There was a narrow covered walkway to one side of the outside laundry, fully equipped with the most modern hand-wringer and concrete tubs. We had an outside toilet, which was well positioned for summer but a reason to 'hold on' in winter.

Mum and Dad bought well – a good size block, long and adequate width, with a lengthy dual sectioned driveway up to a large garage that Dad had built and was still standing strong in 2020. It later became the storage area for all the variety of goods my dad sold in his self-started business called Ronita (coffee and milk bar equipment). Ronita was a combination of Ron (my dad's name) and Nita (his mother-in-law's name).

The large backyard had a home-built single swing, and a steel Hills hoist – a rotating clothes line built strong enough to hold a child on each corner hanging on for dear life as it spun around like an amusement park ride. There was a sandpit for the kids, filled with Cronulla sand after a few visits to the beach by Dad.

In later years, Dad built an above-ground pool about five metres long, which gave endless opportunities in summer, assembled with precision by Dad for his growing children and their friends. At the rear of the yard was an incinerator, a flat storage concrete area and some gardens, with sandstone borders and each child's name engraved in the concrete.

The front yard landscaping was a proud achievement for Dad, with the then fashionable dual driveway – two narrow concrete sections, one for each wheel with a garden in-between. The garden required filling in with concrete when my older sister was learning to drive most likely due to her not keeping on the concrete sections! Sandstone edges along the driveway became the border for Mum's rose garden and other floral choices – annuals and shrubs.

Dad thought it would be attractive to have the three-foot-high timber stakes supporting the roses painted the same colour as the expected flowers. It helped him to remember what was coming before they bloomed. Dad had difficulty affording the whole garden at once, so he was given rose plants as birthday and Christmas presents for a number of years until the bed was full. Mum and Dad loved their garden and I'm sure it brought them much pleasure, which as an older adult I could relate too. There were poppies, snapdragons, roses, cigarette bushes, black-eyed susans, red begonias, geraniums and a colourful collection of hydrangeas. This mini-nursery gave the three of us children many opportunities to woo our teachers with small bunches of flowers. I think Dad knew we needed all the credit points we could attract with our teachers!

When I was about 10 years old, when returning home from church on a Sunday evening, Dad used to let me hop out of the car at the top of Webb Street, sit on his lap, and then steer the car all the way down the street, leaning inwards as we veered around the bend halfway down and then up the driveway. Because I couldn't reach the pedals, he used to control the speed as a precaution to ensure I didn't run into our next door neighbour's fence (a great reassurance to Mum who was hanging on in the front for dear life).

Our front yard was surrounded by a small metal fence. There was a good-sized nature strip on both sides of the road that became a great area for kicking a football about, particularly in a popular game called 'Forcings Back'.

## Riverwood

The other side of the railway line was a notably different socio-economic location with many blocks of higher density living, originally war hospital accommodation, and later owned by the NSW Housing Commission.

In 1958, the following was announced in the newspapers and Council Chronicles:

'On this day 1 February 1958, the suburb of Herne Bay was to be known as Riverwood after the suburb developed an unsavoury reputation for poverty, overcrowding and violence, in large part to remove the stigma associated with living there. This helped to change the reputation of the area.'

'In November 1957, the Secretary for Railways advised Hurstville Council of departmental approval for the alteration of the name of Herne Bay Railway Station to Riverwood, based on the willingness of other authorities to adopt the name. Subsequent correspondence of postal authorities received at a Council meeting in January 1958 stated the name of the railway station and official post office at Herne Bay was to be changed to Riverwood as from 1 February 1958.'

Riverwood was a well-catered for suburb with many shops. It was divided in the middle by the railway line and station. We lived on the southern side, a five minute walk from the station. Belmore Road was the main thoroughfare through Riverwood, commencing at Canterbury Road Punchbowl and winding all the way to Lugarno. At the top of Webb Street there was a paddock on one corner that used to host visiting circus groups in their large tents. It was an unusual but exciting experience at times to see elephants and other wild animals as we turned the corner into our street.

We loved going to the picture theatre (also at the top of our street) when we were old enough to go on a Saturday afternoon by ourselves. Some 'local' lads worked out that if one of them paid to enter, he could then duck down to the rear of the theatre and open the EXIT door that opened straight out the back onto the paddock where there was always a group of youth waiting for their free access. I can't remember whether I entered via that route or whether I've just suppressed this misdemeanour! However, it could explain why I always had enough coins to cross the road to the milk bar at intermission to obtain more supplies of Jaffas! Having old wooden sloping floors in the picture theatre, it was the ideal location for the Jaffa roll from the rear row of seats – usually right in the middle of a quiet scene of the movie.

The milk bar was a popular location on the southern side of Riverwood. A place filled with the memories of the best chocolate milkshakes anywhere. They were only three pence, and they seemed to last forever – assisted by the repetitive blowing of air through the straw to froth the milk up again when it reached the last inch or so. This habit has persisted to the present, much to the annoyance and embarrassment of my wife when she hears the inevitable slurping noise generated by such action. Chocolate milkshakes are still my favourite, as they are for my two youngest granddaughters – Indiana Pearl and Alaska Rose. I've become a connoisseur of my favourite cold drink, rating and remembering the locations of the largest and best quality shakes since the Riverwood milk bar days.

On the other corner at the top of Webb Street was Trevors, a bike and sports store. It was a great shop for a young boy to visit, especially around the Queen's Birthday holiday weekend when it became the place to purchase all the fireworks required for one's arsenal, in particular the bungers (penny and tuppeny) and the penny skyrockets, which we launched in empty milk bottles.

Adjacent to Trevors was a takeaway store that was in a perfect position as I alighted the bus from Peakhurst High School at the end of each school day. Their superb hot chips at an incredibly low price were wrapped in white paper and smothered in salt and vinegar, a much enjoyed treat especially on a cold winter's day.

The local solo GP had small rooms next to Trevors at the top of Webb Street consisting of only a waiting room and consulting room. He was well respected and used to undertake home visits before and after day surgery on a regular basis, as was the custom of GPs in that era. Over my lifetime, these visits have largely faded out except for at aged-care facilities, although when I practised at Lugarno for 30 years they were still in demand and we gave the same service. I well remember some home visits that I wish this GP would have been too busy to perform when I went through a period of suffering from recurrent boils. I still recall the fear of the long needles of penicillin plunged into my buttock every few days for weeks.

Another visit to this doctor is still vividly recalled, when I had to urgently attend to have my lip sutured after standing too close to our next door neighbour's son who was chopping wood with an axe when he swung it over his shoulder and connected instead with my lip. I was driven up to the doctor's surgery by our other neighbour and my mother was not in a good state after observing the bloody wound. The doctor's calm and fairly painless suturing of my laceration had a positive influence on me. This situation was frequently recalled by me while I had to be on the other end of the needle and thread, suturing many facial lacerations on children over four decades, including some of my own children and grandchildren. This experience gave me plenty of empathy for the children I treated in my career with similar injuries.

On the other side of the railway station were a variety of shops including a popular Chinese restaurant, which was the favourite takeaway shop for Mum, even if it was the only takeaway in the area. It was a special time when we visited as a family and dined in. Also on this side of the line there were some of the best entertainment shops in Riverwood – the pinball parlour and the slot car track. It was a challenge to save up and lay-by my own slot car, but the fun of racing it on that large seven lane track was a treat.

There was a small, wooden police office adjacent to the railway station giving a good view of the happenings in Belmore Road. In the time I grew up in Riverwood, there was always a significant respect for police, usually male, a person of authority and any misbehaviour could invoke a clip over the back of the head, which I attracted on only one occasion.

Halfway along Webb Street on a corner was a good-sized park – the location of afternoon footy matches in winter after school. Dressed in our favourite team's jerseys (South Sydney for me), we would do battle that was full-on tackle. I was usually chosen as half-back but I had to make sure I was quick and knew how to offload the ball or do a punt or a grubber kick and follow through, or run the risk of injury.

## Adventures

Life in Webb Street as a young boy (and later teenager) produced many opportunities for adventure. There seemed to be greater number of boys in my street than girls (or at least that was my perception) and they were generally my friends, and we enjoyed wonderful escapades, some more mischievous than others. Two that stood out were the 'newspaper' and 'penny skyrocket' ambushes.

The former escapade was aimed at the man who delivered the weekly local newspaper, *The Propeller*, now knowns as *The Leader*, by driving down our street in his car and throwing them into every property. We knew, however, that he had to turn around at the bottom of the street and drive back, so we planned to attempt to throw the papers into his open window on his way back up Webb Street. What we had not counted on was the numbers of papers (about 20) flying back his way. We were always ready to split and hide after the aerial attack, as invariably he would slam on his brakes, reversing and yelling obscenities while getting out of his car. The launching area we chose was our neighbour's a few blocks down since it had dense trees and shrubs in which to become invisible – or so we thought.

The penny skyrocket escapade was planned for the Saturday night of the Queen's Birthday weekend – or 'Firecracker Night' as it was known. This was one of the highlights of our year. Every house would make a timber bonfire from scrap timber, which would not be lit until that night. It had to be watched and protected from marauding groups of youth from other streets, just like our metal letterbox, which became targets for tuppeny bungers that would decimate the box in one explosive blast.

Most houses had a bonfire except the house of 'Pop' Hughes and his daughter, who lived together two doors from us. As kids, we thought he was an old grump of a man who complained if we played football in front of his house. The two of them would sit and watch the street activities from their enclosed verandah and we called it their 'lookout'. The only things continually lit at their house were their cigarettes.

Every boy's role was to stock up on penny skyrockets from Trevors sports store, pack an empty milk bottle. At dusk, camouflaged as best as possible, we would enter the railway line precinct and quietly crawl on our bellies until reaching across the road from the Hughes place. The target was a brick bunker – Pop Hughes's verandah.

On a designated signal, multiple skyrockets would be lit and repeatedly fired, with allowance for angles, distance and windspeed. The chaos of this attack had to be seen to be believed, with the aim after running out of ammo to quickly retreat, hide all evidence in the bush and sneak back through the strung wires of the railway line. We would end up standing in front of our own bonfire acting as normally as you could, even with a racing heart and evidence of prickles stuck to our clothes. They never seemed to work out where the ambush had originated from, and we never found out if they knew!

Webb Street had a gradual slope from the top of the street, to just beyond our house where it became steeper until the bottom of the hill. The street was sealed with smooth tar and so became an ideal location for billycart derbies. Every boy in the street had a billycart fashioned with a basic hard seat, a long neck out the front, and a cross member at the front bolted on, which we steered with our feet. The four-inch ball-bearing wheels were very fast, unless poor driving led you into the dirt on the side of the road. This was an exhilarating time – everyone started on the same starting line, racing to the bottom of the hill, where we hoped to turn and avoid any cars coming around the bottom of the street under the railway bridge. My billycart was a hand-me-down and rather a slow machine, so my winning record was poor.

One night my dad called me up to the garage after dinner where he used to work packing orders for his business for the next day's delivery. I thought he'd been working there rather late recently and I soon found out why. He presented me with a brand new, handmade billycart that he'd been designing and building at night for a number of weeks. It was an amazing machine – slick, comfortable and fast, with large ball-bearing wheels on the rear and smaller ones at the front. The seat was large and comfortable and trimmed with aluminium beading useful as a precaution when others might have collided with me. It had a round front cross member for my feet (probably an off-cut of the timber stakes for the roses) and a rope assembly for steering.

I was overwhelmed to think Dad had been aware of the state of my old billycart and had designed and built a racing machine personally for me. As I reflect on this time, I've realised how much this was an act of sacrifice and unconditional love that I didn't have to earn.

My chest was protruding with pride when I wheeled it down to the derby that next afternoon. As I sat on my machine in the pits waiting for a race, my new cart attracted admiration for its speed, features and appearance. I can still feel the excitement when I think about the day I first drove that billycart that Dad had built for me.

## Neighbours and pets

There's fundamental importance in having good neighbours. The reliability of people who can help in times of trouble, the value of people whose behaviour does not cause undue conflict, people with some commonality in values, who maintain their properties for the good of everyone. We were very fortunate to have neighbours who respected each other and avoided causing disturbances with such things as barking dogs, drunkenness or loud parties.

Two doors up were Norma and Terry who had three daughters. As children, we used to be fascinated watching Terry roll his own cigarettes. Directly next door were Laurie and Elva. Laurie was a heavy smoker who spent much of his time at the lawn bowls club. Elva was a kindhearted neighbour but seemed to know everything about everybody. She was definitely a good talker. At my bedroom 'observation tower', I would often listen to prolonged conversations my mum had with Elva and I admired my mum for her patience and endurance.

On the other side of our six foot classic paling fence lived Alf and Betty with their three sons. The middle son, Michael, was more my age, but taller and heavier than me, which became a lot more pronounced when he started playing tackle football with us in the park. He was the 'axe swinger' who caused my lacerated lip that required suturing. He also struck me with a timber spear when he threw it over the fence. I had to duck a few arrows when we each received bow and arrow sets for Christmas one year. It was a tad risky having a neighbour like Michael.

Alf and Betty were kind and humble people. Alf's work involved making and servicing televisions and he made and sold us our first stereogram – a cabinet that contained three appliances in one. A black and white TV, a radio and a record player. This was ahead of its time, a wonderful piece of electronics that we enjoyed for years. Colour television was released in the USA the year I was born with a cost of US $1500 – a fortune at that time. Alf had a clever way of giving us a taste of colour TV – he joined three pieces of thin painted perspex – red, green and blue and stuck this over our TV screen. It was not until I was in England at the age of 20 that I saw what a real colour TV looked like and it was a vast improvement on our tri-colour perspex one.

As a family we had enormous enjoyment over many years from this entertainment unit. It was where we viewed in awe the TV show *Disneyland* every Sunday evening.

One of the other memories I have of watching TV was Neil Armstrong's moon landing – broadcast live. I'll never forget seeing him walk down the ladder onto the moon's surface and his unforgettable statement: 'That's one small step for man, one giant leap for mankind.' An unforgettable experience for a teenager.

Our family had a few pets – some I enjoyed, others I tolerated. My first and only dog was Patsy a cute but crazy black and white terrier. Being untrained as most dogs were in those days, he would run down to the bottom of Webb Street, jump into Salt Pan creek, roll in the mud then jump up onto people on the way back home. He disappeared one day – I'm not quite sure what happened to him but the neighbours seemed pleased. We had two cats at different times – one was named Tinker Bell, a quite obese cat, and the other Winkie. Their leisurely pace and lack of energy did not provide a great deal of excitement for me as an adolescent boy, rather a temptation to practise my slingshot technique.

# Revisit

In 2020, during COVID-19 times, I revisited Webb Street in Riverwood, my old neighbourhood. Reminiscing and stimulating my memory for writing this chapter, I watched the electric trains now travelling in both directions, walked along our street where I used to race my billycart and drive the car while on Dad's lap. I strolled through the park where I played some serious rugby league, and stood under the railway bridge while the trains rolled over the top of me.

When I reached No. 47 Webb St, the original house was still there. The only difference was the new owners had added another storey, suggesting that Dad's footings had met the requirements of structural engineers some seven decades later.

Riverwood was much busier and more multicultural, no longer just one Chinese restaurant. Rather, it was a feast of every taste and food from around the world. Mum would have been amazed in what was now a food extravaganza.

I was flooded with many wonderful and joy-filled memories of a happy and satisfying childhood full of love, adventure and security – the values of which all children should have the opportunity to experience. This place had been pivotal in my life – the location of my childhood and adolescence years, the home I had left to go to primary school and high school and then university. This was where I first began to court my wife to be, and celebrate important milestones like 21st birthdays and engagement parties. It was where I learnt to walk, graduated from billycarts and pushbikes, obtained my driver's licence, and purchased and repaired my first car. It was the home where my parents (notably my mum) taught me about God, and where I became clearly aware of my calling to be a doctor of medicine.

Both Carol and I had very different upbringings with regards to home and location. Carol and her family moved every three years, a vast contrast to my upbringing, living in a family home for 20 years. When Carol and I started our own family, it was our desire to live in one family home to provide stability and consistency for our children.

As I walked away after visiting my old home and reflecting on all of the above, I was thankful that Dad – with much sacrifice and hard labour – had built us a *house*, then Mum and Dad together had made us a *home* where our family had enjoyed an abundance of happy and memorable times together. Although this is a commonly used cliche, it was, thankfully, my experience. I felt a sense of deep gratitude to God for the parents he'd given me. I had been valued and loved unconditionally. That day I was also feeling the blessing that the legacy of my parents had left – examples of hard work, perseverance, generosity and godliness, all at 47 Webb Street.

# CHAPTER THREE

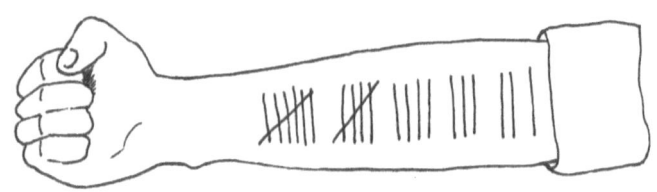

# FAMILY OF ORIGIN

'Memory can be a burden, but it can also be a blessing'
— **Douglas Murray**

'Grief is the price we pay for love.'
— **Queen Elizabeth II**

'When God took you back he said, Hallelujah, you're home.'
— **'Supermarket Flowers', Ed Sheeran**

# Count your blessings

My father was ahead of his time when he became aware that there was a benefit to having an 'attitude of gratitude'. Psychologists now understand that being thankful and expressing gratitude are positive ingredients for good mental health, especially when there are trials in life. Dad may not have realised or understood the proven benefit – he just did it and meant it. His trademark expression was based on the lyrics of an old Salvation Army song called 'Count Your Blessings', which he would have learned by rote as a child in Sunday school. The song states to 'count your blessings, name them one by one'. He often told us that he did this when growing up in a poor family during the Depression years, and then during the challenges and threats to his health and life during WWII.

My children often heard these stories as well on visits to Pa Frank's place. My youngest son, Luke, a psychologist, took the idea to the next level, when he had tattooed on his forearm a daily reminder to 'count his blessings'. Personally, I try to employ this simple strategy most mornings before getting out of bed, intentionally thinking of 10 things I'm thankful for.

My dad also had another method of being happy and positive. He simply did this by whistling tunes, smiling and telling corny dad jokes. This seemed so natural, and was based on his attitude of contentment in life. A well-known psychiatrist, Professor Ian Hickie, authored a book *Minding Your Mind* – one of his suggestions was to 'try to act happy'. In other words, even though we may not feel joy or happiness, we should try to be intentionally happy. Often this is difficult to do, but it can become natural and spontaneous.

# Dad

Dad was born 11 September 1923 at Breakfast Creek in Brisbane, Queensland to Salvation Army officers, Major and Mrs George and Hilda Franks. Dad was proud to be given George as his middle name, as I was to receive his name Ronald as my middle name, a tradition that waned when Carol and I didn't give our children middle names. His childhood was adventurous and full of interesting stories and challenging times. The family of seven lived close to the poverty line during the Great Depression, and they learnt to be resourceful, resilient, thankful and content – values Dad would draw on later in life.

His father taught him to play the cornet, which he loved, becoming a natural musician. When all the other children were similarly taught brass instruments, my grandfather had a ready-made band of five, providing musical backing for the church hymns. Over the years, Dad became a renowned player within the Australian Salvation Army band scene, with a reputation as the 'sweetest' sounding soprano player in Australia, with many tours with bands interstate and overseas, also playing cornet solos and duets. He was honoured to be selected as part of the Salvation Army All Stars band.

Dad did his best to teach me the cornet, but I didn't seem to inherit his ability to be a quality player, or perhaps it was because I was rather complacent in practising my scales. Whatever the reason, I didn't progress past the lowly position of second cornet. My father's patience and perseverance were exceptional, but my progress and prowess were painfully slow, and possibly a part of the causation of the duodenal ulcer he later developed! He eventually allowed me to play drums and percussion, which I enjoyed and still dabble in some 60 years later. Dad loved brass bands his whole life and we both continued to enjoy watching, then discussing the Edinburgh Military Tattoo every New Year's Day. Dad finally was able to see this live. My plans to do the same in 2020 were interrupted when it was cancelled due to the COVID-19 pandemic.

Because most Salvation Army officers only stayed in one country town or city suburb for one to two years, Dad had to attend many different schools as a child. Dad had to repeat sixth form and left school at 13 to find a job and support his parents financially. He held a number of positions, mainly as a junior grocer assistant and by the time he joined the military to fight in WWII for five years, he missed some of his later teenage years and also his education. He was determined to ensure that his three children would not miss out on their education or their adolescence.

He had just turned 18 when he enrolled for the military in late 1941, along with his two older brothers. Many young men and women had the desire to serve Australia, to maintain its freedom and prevent a threatened Japanese invasion. Dad's motives were altruistic, but there was a suppressed fear of never returning that he experienced along with all of his soldier friends. After only five months training in Bathurst, he was sent to Papua New Guinea (PNG) with the famous 2nd/16th Battalion.

Promoted to sergeant, he served mainly in PNG and Borneo and was present for the largest Pacific invasion at Balikpapan. Home leave occurred only once in five years of service, and consisted of 14 days, seven of which he spent in hospital with malaria. He remembers being surprised that his family home on the waterfront at Kyle Bay, Sydney was blacked out by paper taped on the windows, and all the boats in the Georges River were removed since there was concern that if there was an invasion they would use these as transport by any invaders to go up the river. Dad found there was strict rationing on food, clothing and petrol, with few cars on the road. Mothers at that time tried to avoid the postman in case they delivered a telegram containing the all too frequently bad news about their husbands, sons, daughters and fathers.

My dad's experiences and observations of the Japanese during the war caused him to despise them for most of his remaining life. He described them as being 'brutal, barbaric and exhibiting animalistic behaviour'. According to reports, they killed and captured Australian nurses, deliberately sunk hospital ships that were clearly marked, and starved to death thousands of Australian prisoners of war.

Dad knew as a Christian there was a need to forgive those who had killed many of his cobbers *(friends)* but it was difficult, and forgiveness took many years and was associated with many nightmares from the evil he had witnessed. Dad lived in the ambiguity and conflict of memories that had traumatised him yet with a faith based on the principle of forgiveness – this was challenging for him. The dilemma was helped by the fact that he strived for the rest of his life to put an emphasis on never forgetting the Aussies soldiers who didn't make it home. He celebrated them especially on Anzac Day, where their memory was honoured.

As well as witnessing many atrocities, deaths and the wounding of close mates, Dad suffered scrub typhus and repeated malaria and other tropical diseases. Although deeply scarred by the war, he was able to share some wartime stories with other veterans, friends and family for the rest of his life, which was helpful and therapeutic, even if he was not conscious of it. Many others were so traumatised that this sharing was not possible.

He recalled the saddest times were witnessing loss and injury to friends, and before going into action with the other five men in his tent needing to draw the mandatory 50 rounds of ammunition, two grenades and basic food rations of bully beef and tea for a week. He then had to pack his personal belongings into his kitbag for storage simultaneously thinking he may never see his friends again.

Dad described the happiest times in the war in three experiences. The first was when he found out the war was over while in his frontline foxhole with 30 other soldiers.

The second was nine months after the official cessation of the war, and being involved in the round-up and disarming of the Japanese in Celebes. He was travelling home on a troop ship to Brisbane. Standing on the crowded bow, he and his fellow troops could suddenly see the distant flickering lights of Cooktown in Far North Queensland. This caused an emotional outburst of widespread tears as the troops realised that they were finally home for good after surviving a horrible war.

When the ship arrived at the terminal in Brisbane there were no fanfares, no recognition, no parades and no counselling. After an overnight train journey, Dad arrived alone at Central Station in Sydney to an emotional welcome of tears of joy from his mother, and his wife to be, Shirley.

This was the third happy experience he described: the last son welcomed home by his mother. He received a discharge certificate from the army and an allowance to buy some clothes. His army days were over!

Dad always stated that veterans did not want to be applauded – just remembered, along with the approximately 30,000 lives lost bringing freedom to our country. Prime Minister Scott Morrison stated in 2021 that the WWII veterans were Australia's most important generation. That's something Dad would have loved to have heard.

On his return to civilian life, most jobs had already been taken, so he was only offered tailoring as a vocation, which he did not enjoy, but he tried his best for a year at Anthony Horden's tailoring factory. Desiring to work outdoors, he took on labouring for a bricklaying firm, where he learnt skills that were later needed to build his own house. After his bricklaying work, he started a wedding catering business with Mum and his mother-in-law, mainly working on weekends. While he was working in the catering business, he obtained full-time employment with Horlicks in 1951, selling their famous 'malted milk' to milk bars around Sydney, eventually becoming the NSW sales promotion manager. His success and reputation over 11 years meant that he was headhunted by a cafe catering equipment business to be their sales manager.

After years of experience and competency in the industry, Dad found himself a niche that he enjoyed for the rest of his life: in the establishment of his own business in 1963 – Ronita Milk Bar Catering Equipment.

Initially he was selling crockery and cutlery to milk bars, but quickly expanded to all manner of catering equipment to smaller businesses. He then imported Italian espresso coffee machines and later became an important supplier to newer corporations entering Australia – Pizza Hut, McDonalds and Kentucky Fried Chicken. He was good at customer service and was a highly respected businessman – he joined Rotary and served for years. He invented and manufactured a five-in-one milkshake mixer and a scoop for fries for McDonalds who even offered him a franchise, which he turned down for reasons he never shared.

In The Salvation Army, along with being an excellent brass musician, Dad held leadership positions in the band, as well as being the social organiser for the church even using his own boat to hold waterskiing days for anyone wanting to learn how to ski. Working alongside Mum, together they really valued the importance of strengthening relationships for everyone.

Dad had a long working life, retiring north to Hawks Nest in 1995. He was so dedicated to his business that he continued to commute for many years back to North Ryde where he worked. Finally, when he realised what the term 'retirement' meant, he turned his planning and organisational skills to projects in the Hawks Nest/Tea Gardens locality.

He joined the Returned Services League (RSL) and was later elected president. He saw the need to expand the Anzac Day memorial services and to move the memorial to a more prominent location. Using his learnt skills from the military and The Salvation Army, he set about involving the whole community in dawn services and the Anzac Day march. These attracted increasingly large crowds, involving not only returned service men and women, but also council officials, school children and voluntary organisations like the Life Saving Club, Rotary and Lions Club. Weeks prior to the Anzac Day march, he would go and talk to school children about their heritage of freedom, due to the sacrifices that many made in war.

On 25 April each year, Dad would march at the front of the parade behind the brass bands, proudly wearing his slouch hat and medals on his suit. As now president of the local RSL, Dad would lead the services in the most respectable and sensitive manner, never to glorify war, but more importantly to honour and remember those who had sacrificed their lives for our country. He cherished the virtue and value of freedom. As well as the crowd attending the services, there was the deafening noise of overhead jets giving an honouring salute of remembrance. He organised the whole day with military precision, and the services were often reported on local TV and in local newspapers.

This and other services throughout the year were held at the new and modern Anzac memorial, moved from the unseen spot in the backstreets of Tea Gardens to a prominent place on the river. Not surprisingly, Dad was involved in the planning, design, fundraising, building and opening of this functional monument of remembrance. The cenotaph consists of three tall pillars with figures representing air force, military and navy, surrounded by bench seats facing the river, where people sit and enjoy quiet reflection. In the middle of the three figures there was a tall flagpole carrying the Australian flag which flew at half-mast on the day of his death. There is still an automatic audio information stand and a rendition of 'The Last Post'. On the back of the benches are plaques of remembrance of past veterans placed by the RSL. It seemed to me to be rather a symbolic gesture that these men and women metaphorically had the backs of all Australians in wartime and also now practically.

Dad was also elected president of the University of the Third Age (U3A), ironic for someone who left school in sixth grade, and he later became president of the Lions Club, working for years to advance the needs of the community and the environment. He belonged to the local vintage motor car club, enjoying rides and outings and meeting much of the community. I don't know if he was ever tempted to, but if he was 30 years younger, I would not have been surprised to see him running for mayor!

Dad spent decades serving others – in his work, neighbourhood, especially with Rotary, and his involvement with The Salvation Army Red Shield Appeal. His years of community service at Hawks Nest/Tea Gardens were recognised when, on 26 August 2010, he was invested with the Medal of the Order of Australia (OAM) at Government House by the governor of NSW, her excellency Professor Marie Bashir, for 'service to the community of the Hawks Nest region through a range of voluntary roles'.

A brochure given on the day had written: 'The Australian Honour system celebrates the outstanding achievements and contributions of extraordinary Australians in a diverse range of fields and areas of endeavour. It is about recognising those people in the community whose service and contributions have had the effect of making a significant difference to Australian life or, more broadly, to humanity at large.'

This was a deeply moving day, honouring my simple and humble dad for a lifetime of voluntary work and selfless love for others. What matters most to God is shown in the Bible in two statements: 'Love God' and 'love others', and from my perspective he did his best at both. It was a poignant moment where we, his children and family, recognised that he had not just 'talked the talk but he walked the walk'.

He left a wonderful legacy for all who knew him. That day I reflected about his simple, no fanfare and lonely return from five years' war service, with no official recognition or welcome home from government or community.

Despite not seeking this award, he was finally given a hero's accolade and the recognition that he so deserved, from his family, his community and his country. He was rightly happy and proud of his achievements, his family and his country.

Dad died aged 91 on 24 September 2014, and we knew (as he did) that he was going to a better place. His physical health had been slowly deteriorating due to heart failure over a few years, but despite physical struggles, his mind remained extremely alert. He knew what he wanted, and that was to remain amongst his friends and community at Hawks Nest, and to avoid the need of placement in an aged-care facility. We respected his desires, but it unfortunately meant one day he was urgently admitted to the John Hunter Hospital in Newcastle. Although we were told he was stable, he suddenly and quietly passed away alone just before we arrived.

Dad's plaque was added to a bench seat at the Anzac Memorial, recognising all he'd done for both his community and country. It was obvious to the family that his main funeral service should be at the Dulwich Hill Salvation Army church, but we needed to organise a community service as well, at Tea Gardens Hawks Nest War Memorial. The community demonstrated their appreciation by their numbers and also their tributes. The family were so proud, and gave thanks to God for Dad. This location is very dear to myself and my extended family as a place of meaning and memories.

By now it would be obvious to the reader that Dad excelled in the gifts of planning and organising, which were evident in every stage of his life, and even to the extent of preparing for his own death. Although not quite meeting the definition of a hoarder, he certainly was a collector of notes, books, articles, memorabilia, tools and countless jars of screws and nails and so on. After his death, we found small handwritten notes all around Dad's unit at Hawks Nest, in bedroom drawers, in his bookshelf and behind framed photos, giving hints about who to share his belongings with and who to notify of his passing.

Reflective of his organisational skills, and his rascal-like sense of humour, we found an article that he'd kept on how to organise and sort through his valued items. It stated, 'Take time to allocate and sort items as this will allow you to feel a greater peace knowing you've done the best you can for that person.' The article has Dad's unmistakable handwriting, all in capitals with the clear message: HOUSE SORTING AFTER DECEASED – GOOD LUCK – DAD.

It was such a blessing to spend time with Dad on our many visits to Hawks Nest in his later years, but how I regret not having the same opportunity to do similar with my mum.

## Mum

My mum, Shirley June Franks, was a beautiful person: a friend to many; a devoted wife to my dad; and a dedicated mother to her three children. A worthy cliche applies in that 'She was just as beautiful on the inside as she was on the outside.' She was empathetic towards others who she knew were struggling, and she was warm and friendly. More an introvert than an extrovert, she was hospitable, especially to friends of her children, neighbours and friends. She shared herself, her home and her family with many and, in particular, her friends.

My memories of my mum are deeply flooded with a sense of being loved, supported and cared for. She was proud of her children and protected them as a mother should, balancing risks to our wellbeing against the increasing freedom a parent allows their child to have, as they move from childhood into adolescent years. She understood forgiveness and I cannot remember her yelling or acting in anger.

There was a time, however, when I pushed the boundaries of her love and forgiveness, all in the one act of foolishness. When I was 12 years of age, I went to Roselands Shopping Centre with a friend, and for some unexplained reason, I was obsessed with a blue terry towelling hat that was popular at the time. I didn't want to pay for it, so I just put it under my jacket and proceeded to walk out of the store. All of a sudden, I was shocked to realise that I had just been lifted off the ground. The cause was soon apparent when I saw out of the corner of my eye, that a burly plain-clothed policewoman had just lifted me up in one foul swoop by my collar, and was 'airlifting' me to the security room of the shopping centre to be interrogated. The character 'Strop' on *The Paul Hogan Show* in later years, wore this type of hat, representing his naivety and stupidity, both descriptors that applied to me on that day.

The embarrassment of becoming a 'strop' myself in front of shocked members of the public in the store, paled into insignificance with the embarrassment of seeing both my parents called up and interviewed in front of me by the store detective that apprehended me. Although understandably disappointed, and having to discipline me by confiscating my surfboard for two weeks (which I did not object to, as it was a fairly mild sentence), my parents, especially Mum, were very gracious to forgive me for my misdemeanour.

When writing this book, I realised how insignificant my penalty was, and how fortunate I was compared to my distant relative, William Hall Sr, who was sentenced to be banished to a new colony the other side of the world for similarly stealing one piece of clothing. I also reflected how this other young man, possibly as a result of the harsh consequences, went on to live a sad life of crime and how different this was to my outcome.

Mum grew up in Lewisham in a family of four, including her parents and a younger sister. They lived right next to the railway line, a convenient location, and she attended school in Dulwich Hill. I don't know as much detail about her childhood and upbringing as I did with Dad, nor her early interests, hobbies and sports, although some years later when Dad bought a boat, Mum learnt how to waterski.

One day, as a teenager, she heard brass band music out in the street, and discovered the Dulwich Hill Salvation Army Band playing nearby. She was invited at the age of 14 to sunday school and after attending, she soon decided to become a Christian. Being a Christian is not a commitment to a person or a church, but to a God who transforms people's lives. The Salvos are simply a community of people whose common feature is their love for God and their love for others. Their focus has always been looking outwards rather than inwards, and has been since the origin of the denomination by its founder William Booth.

For someone with no prior knowledge of church or the early Salvation Army, it would have taken a while for Mum to become accustomed to some of the Salvos' idiosyncrasies, like wearing a uniform, playing a tambourine, singing in the songsters (the choir) and marching behind a band. She became an enthusiastic member of this church, and she could recognise the significant changes that becoming a Christian made in her life.

Mum was a clever student and was getting good grades at school, but at that time girls usually left in third year of high school after completing their intermediary exams. Her father, an accountant, promised her anything she wanted if she did well in commerce. To his, and I think Mum's surprise, she became dux of the school in this subject, and her choice of reward was a Salvation Army bonnet.

Mum enjoyed attending events both on Sunday and also social nights, and it was at one of these that she met my dad, who was on leave from war service in PNG. They were both young, but there was obviously strong mutual attraction. They became serious in their relationship and Mum was welcomed into Dad's family. She wrote to Dad while he was away overseas and, with her future mother-in-law, welcomed him back home when he eventually returned for good in 1946. They married at the Dulwich Hill Salvation Army church later that year, so much in love, and gave their lifelong commitments to each other – Mum was 18 and Dad 23.

For years to come they were affectionately known as 'Ron and Shirl'. They were devoted to each other, their growing family and served alongside with many others in the community and the church.

After Dad worked as a brick labourer for a year, Ron and Shirley commenced a business doing mobile catering for weddings. Mum adored her mother, Nita, who was also a good cook. Nita had helped to develop my mother's culinary skills, and she joined the catering team as well. It was hard physical work. It even involved other female friends from church helping with the waitressing. Putting her commerce and organisational skills into good practice, Mum looked after the financial books, both for the business and the family household, and she did this for many years.

My older sister, Carolyn, recalls Nita being a doting, caring and hard-working woman. Mum was devastated when she died relatively young.

My mother was strongly compassionate. The Salvation Army owned and ran a maternity hospital in Marrickville called Bethesda, which was my birthplace. This hospital cared for both married and single mothers, and Mum's heart was for the singles and the struggle they would face in that era, particularly when a child would usually be adopted out. She became the president of the Bethesda Auxiliary, a group of women who raised finances to support these young women. Mum personally sewed babies clothes for them.

In 1974, Mum and Dad visited The Salvation Army Chikankata Hospital in Zambia to support my sister and her husband. Carolyn (my oldest sister) tells the story of Mum baking cookies and taking them to the many children of patients in the hospital leprosy settlement. Most people, when buying souvenirs at a market in an undeveloped country, would try to barter the price down. Because she had compassion for the vendors, Mum would offer more than the first negotiated price, much to their surprise and pleasure.

Mum was also a homemaker and, using her sewing abilities, produced handmade clothes for her children and her friend's children. She made all our curtains at Webb Street, and loved painting the house, including the stakes for the roses. When they both worked together to establish Ronita, Mum answered the landline phone at home, wrote out the invoices, and prepared the accounting for her father Cecil to audit. Mum especially excelled in the management of running the home. She was always there for her children, a decision the three of us are forever grateful for. Along with Dad, Mum encouraged and arranged annual family holidays for two to three weeks at Pretty Beach on the Central Coast in a holiday house Dad helped to build. These were fun times with long-lasting memories, and provided times of surfing, fishing and playing games and reading. Cool bucket showers to save water and an outhouse loo (complete with pan) helped us kids appreciate the luxuries of our Webb Street home.

There are two prominent letter 'S's on either side of the collar on a Salvation Army uniform. They stand for 'Saved to Serve' – and this is what Mum decided to do in the church. She taught children in Sunday school, and teenagers in Bible study groups. Mum was a great organiser and facilitated regular social nights called 'Men Versus Women'. As a child, I recall how these were such well-attended nights, full of fun, where there would be comedy and acrobatic and musical items performed by competing teams.

When her children grew past teenage years, Mum decided to return to work, catching the train into the city to manage the accounts for a shoe store. I would drop her at the train station in my Austin. The only trouble was when the battery was flat, I would need Mum in her work attire to help me push this heavy beast down the street to clutch-start it, much to her embarrassment.

## The phone call

Certain things that happen in life are so significant they're etched with a permanent marker in the memory sections of our brain. The exact time and date of the experience can be easily remembered and can generate the emotions and details of that time in history. Instances such as what we were doing when man first landed on the moon, or on 9/11.

On the morning of Tuesday 13 February 1979, I was on planned leave from Hornsby Hospital, preparing for the birth of our first child due in just a few weeks' time. We were living at Baulkham Hills, and Carol was heavily pregnant when we received the phone call. My brother-in-law, Dr Graeme Lucas, rang with the message no-one ever wants to hear: 'I am sorry to be the one to tell you, Gary, but I am afraid your mother has died.'

There was disbelief since we'd only seen her two days beforehand. We prepared as quickly as possible to travel over to where my parents lived in Lugarno and the tears in the shower flowed more quickly than the water from the spout. On our long journey over to Lugarno, it was disturbing to witness that life was going on as normal for the rest of Sydney, while my life was on pause.

Mum had seemingly died as a result of cascading events: taking an excessive amount of medications causing drowsiness and a resultant fall and head injury, then with reduced level of consciousness aspiration of vomitus. Unbeknownst to the family and her treating doctors, Mum had been given potentially harmful medications by her father to help her sleep.

There was a lead-up to this overwhelming situation that needs explanation. First, to explain how it could have been prevented; second, what can be learnt from this tragedy; and third, to honour her life.

Mum had been experiencing months of depression, not helped by all of her children in recent years having left home to be married. She was facing an empty nest, and dealing with a number of other life stressors. Mum had been under the care of a competent psychiatrist who had prescribed her appropriate antidepressants for the time. However, these older style medicines were associated with more side effects and were not as efficacious or as safe as the ones available now. Unfortunately, Mum had also been turning to alcohol to try to relieve her emotional pain and lift her mood.

Mum had a role in our church teaching young teenagers about God and the Bible, but it came with an inherent responsibility. Drinking alcohol was not permitted as a member of The Salvation Army, especially in a leadership role. On the Sunday before her death, the pastor of our church removed Mum from her teaching role. Although this action was understood at the time by us as a family – we knew of this regulation and the responsibility of the pastor to enforce it – it was still a devastating and humiliating blow to Mum in her state of mind.

Having a supply of her father's medications (barbiturates), as well as her prescribed antidepressants, there existed a potentially lethal cocktail. The shame and grief of losing her leadership role a few days before seemed to me to be a possible precipitant to what happened next. Despair can often be associated with major depression. When there was an extra stressful incident involved, it was understandable that Mum took medication to help herself cope with increased anxiety and need for sleep.

The exact circumstances of what happened on that Monday evening no-one will ever know. All the family believed it was not intentional because she had much to live for and dearly loved her two young grandchildren and was excited about a third grandchild arriving within weeks. The coroner's report couldn't determine intent, only that medicines were involved. His certificate is a tragically sad document, stating Mum's age of 51 years and referring to my dad as a 'widower'.

The Five Stages of Grief is a theory developed by psychiatrist Elisabeth Kübler-Ross. It suggests that we go through five distinct stages after the loss of a loved one. These stages are denial, anger, bargaining, depression and acceptance. I certainly experienced some of these. I was in denial for a relatively short period of time but anger was certainly present. I was angry at my grandfather for wrongly sharing his personal medications; at my church for its rigid regulations without empathy for what an individual might be experiencing leading up to their predicament; and even at myself and other medical personnel involved for underestimating how devastated Mum would have been feeling.

I did not go through a depressive stage and I found the only way I could overcome the trauma of Mum's untimely death and evaluate if there was any purpose to it was to reclaim my trust in an all-knowing and caring God. To move towards acceptance of this tragedy there needed to be forgiveness. Forgiveness is always difficult and sometimes a slow process, as it was for me, but it's necessary if we're to move on and not let ourselves become victims of un-forgiveness.

Years later, I was to fully understand this intentional forgiveness, when being enmeshed in the lives of humble people from a small country in the middle of Africa.

In circumstances in life where there is doubt and lack of certainty, questions always arise, and the one that I experienced was this: 'Is taking your own life, be it intentional or not, an unforgivable sin?' This is a reasonable but sensitive question to ask as a Christian and I believe the answer is 'no'.

I believe it is not our prerogative to take our own life, not even in cases of euthanasia. God determines our life spans, not us. But it is not the unforgivable sin. Rather it is a sad act of despair showing a great need. As a Christian, I believe that God knows the whole story and not just part of it, and he is a loving God of grace and mercy.

The main question I needed to ask myself was this: did Mum as a Christian possess the promise of life after death because of her trust and relationship with the God she knew personally? The answer was a definitive 'yes'! God knows and understands every detail of people in this extreme situation, and He is the one who determines their eternal destiny – it's not up to us to judge.

My mother's funeral is rather a blur in my memory. I was in such a state of grief. I recall it being simultaneously a profoundly sad event and yet a celebration of a wonderful woman and mother. This has been my experience in Christian funeral services: a combination of earthly grief shown by loved ones and friends, and a joyous celebration of a life well lived with the eternal hope the person possessed.

The teenagers my mum taught and The Salvation Army band, formed a guard of honour on the main street outside the church and the band played quietly as the funeral procession slowly departed.

A tribute in the Salvation Army Australia-wide newspaper acknowledged Mum as a 'person of exceptional character, whose tenderness and caring nature reached out to innumerable lives'.

When I was a teenager, I used to think 51 years was old, but when I reached that age myself I soon changed my mind. Mum has been sadly missed since 1979, the same amount of time I've been practicing medicine. There are many times the nagging thoughts on 'what could have been' enter my mind, the many missed celebrations in life with her children, the absence of a grandmother for my children, the loss of the sweetheart partner for Dad. The deep wounds that have been open for a long time have undergone some healing, but the scar of grief is still obvious to those who were close to her. For myself, writing about her story has been therapeutic in my healing and the lyrics of Ed Sheeran in the song 'Supermarket Flowers', 'A heart that's broke is a heart that's been loved' has been of comfort.

Those who know my family, and who may be reading this story for the first time and wonder why it has not been fully explained previously, need to understand the depth of the trauma of this event.

Mental health problems were not openly discussed or accepted in that era in the way they fortunately are today. There was significant stigma attached to mental health problems, much of which brought guilt and shame. I do not desire to denigrate the life of a beautiful woman, nor to let this event define her life, as she lived a wonderful and dedicated life that blessed many. Our own personal stories are also larger than just a small part that may be told or written about us. Mistakes, accidents or poor outcomes do not necessarily define us either.

Mum also understood her eternal destiny, a question we will each need to consider at some point in our life, be it early on or when we're older – I think preferably the former since we don't know the number of our days.

## Sisters

I'm the brother of two sisters, Carolyn and Darryle. I'm the middle child, which has sometimes worked to my advantage! As siblings, we all got on well and holidays and travel as a family were definitely a time of fun together.

Understandably, as I grew up I tended to spend more time with the other boys in my street and at church and school. I never felt lonely or disappointed that I didn't have a brother. I appreciated my sisters, and we each seemed to just get along and get on with life. My sisters attended a different high school to me (Beverly Hills Girls). This meant that most times together were on the weekend and within youth groups. Carolyn, being three years older, belonged to a different group of friends. Darryle, however, tended to spend time with the friends I associated with. We both shared many wonderful adolescent experiences in a relatively safe community.

We are each so grateful for the upbringing we had. I was very thankful for the kind-hearted sisters I was fortunate to be close to. As we look back, we can see the love and care we had as children. My older sister remembers Dad fanning us with wet towels as we were trying to sleep when it was hot. Personally, I can also reflect that although we may not have verbalised it enough, we did love each other.

We all knew that Mum was a good listener, whereas Dad was more a disciplinarian and, if he became reactive, Mum would always talk him round. Dad would tell Mum to make sure I had my long hair cut to avoid a confrontation with me. Although not obvious at the time and common to most families with more than one child, Carolyn was subject to stricter parental discipline than myself, and it then seemed to soften with each progressive child. No family is perfect, but we were very blessed to have had such loving parents.

I was also close with the spouses of my two sisters. One became my friend and partner in a medical practice for many years (Graeme), and another became a lifelong friend (David).

When my sisters and I were older and had our own families, we lived in close proximity to each other, and so we were able to share in special family occasions such as Easter and Christmas time. We have witnessed and participated in the life stages of our children, and then grandchildren, and now in our later years, although separated geographically, we still enjoy getting together for birthday celebrations or keeping up-to-date with family news over a meal. I find myself, as time goes on, valuing our relationships much more and desiring to maximise our future times together.

I felt that Carolyn and Darryle clearly adopted the values and interests of our mother. They are both wonderful homemakers, something I feel modern society doesn't seem to appreciate much. My sisters also strongly value the importance of family, seeing the greater importance to society as a whole.

We still talk about the trauma of our mother's death, and the circumstances surrounding it, and we encourage our families to be open and honest about how they're feeling at any given time so we can support them.

## Honour your father and your mother

Not uncommonly in my professional and personal life, I've encountered people who did not have a healthy relationship with their parents, some even saying they held hatred towards them for the way they were raised.

To those whose experience was like this, it may not be very helpful to quote one of the Ten Commandments: 'Honour your father and your mother'. However, an interpretation that I believe may be helpful to anyone in this predicament is 'Be thankful for what they (hopefully) did well, and forgive them for what they didn't do well.' Personally, I'm fortunate that my experience has been overwhelmingly more on the being thankful side.

# CHAPTER FOUR

# SCHOOLING

'My children, listen to me. Listen to your father's instruction. Pay attention and grow wise, I am giving you good guidance. Don't turn away from my teaching... Learn to be wise, and develop good judgement.'

– **Proverbs 4:1–5**

# Schooling

Many teachers in the late 1950s and 1960s smoked heavily, as did most adults at the time, incredibly including a number of medical doctors, all believing this pastime was healthy and provided a relaxing experience. The teacher's kitchen and meal area in my primary school was a small room, thickly laden with cigarette smoke that had caused brown stained walls and ceilings (which were originally white). As students, we had the 'privilege' of being rostered on for washing the teachers' used crockery and cutlery. It seemed that the teachers had three or more teaspoons of sugar in their tea but didn't bother to stir any of it, so this one centimetre of thick sludge had to be scraped out of each cup when washing up, all the while simultaneously trying to breathe! There were occasional opportunities for revenge such as when one teacher requested that the student on duty duck down to the canteen to buy him something 'hot'. The two dollars supplied was used by the astute student to buy 200 1 cent hot Tarzan Jubes. Not surprisingly, the student did not appear again on the roster after that incident!

## Primary school

My first school was Peakhurst Public School, a stately if not daunting 'castle' situated on Bonds Road in Peakhurst. It was within a 15 minute walk from my home and, initially for the first few years because I was only five years of age, my mother walked me to kindergarten, but eventually when safe enough and old enough, I walked on my own.

In 1958 there was no easing into school life by attending pre-school. I recall it was a frightening experience moving from being constantly at home with mum to suddenly five days a week at kindergarten, not helped by an early experience of an accidental soiling of my pants whilst sitting on the classroom floor after my teacher made it forcefully clear that 'no-one else' could ask to go to the toilet. I think that instruction was regretted by the teacher that day when she had to assist in the clean-up. The outcome was having to wear 'special brown shorts' used by the school for such incidents – a clear statement to all of what had taken place. I anxiously waited for my mother to pick me up at the end of that long day. Some experiences and the associated feelings are never forgotten. Despite my main memory of kindergarten being wearing a pair of brown shorts, things improved when I graduated to primary classes.

Another memory of my primary school experience was the size and appearance of the main school building. It was an older two-storey grey cement-rendered construction, similar to school buildings in the United Kingdom built many decades ago. The school had resonant timber floors and enclosed rooms with only windows on one side so creating a somewhat dark atmosphere. The rooms had rows of old style double-seated timber desks, which were fixed to the floor and had sloping lift-up tops that stored writing materials and books underneath. They had inkwells that provided the ink for what they called 'fountain pens'. We all wrote with slope cards so that we could learn how to do running writing and we had blotting paper under the top sheets of our paper to absorb the penetrating ink.

Old school photos show a smart-looking small lad with blue eyes, freckles and a friendly smile. At least the blue eyes have remained, but the freckles have unfortunately been replaced by sunspots.

Friendships from kindergarten developed and continued into later primary school and some into high school. Some school friends even became patients to this present day. I had my first 'girlfriend', Alice. Or so I thought. The feelings were not really mutual, so it was more a crush. There was abundant fun to engage in during schoolyard games like bull rush, football and marbles.

Primary schooling in the 1950s–1960s was associated with a free daily supply of full cream milk, a one-third of a pint glass bottle with a silver cap – a worthy idea except the only problem was the milk was delivered daily in crates and left in the hot sun, even in summer! Delivered in the morning, the milk would not be consumed until recess and it often left us all with a milk moustache for hours later. The taste of warm and sometimes 'off' milk with its top layer of thick, clumpy cream ironically turned many students away from this healthy drink for the rest of their lives.

Decades later when discussing with post-menopausal female patients why they needed to consume dairy products for its calcium content and thus prevention of osteoporosis, I was repeatedly reminded of their lifetime distaste for milk from this unpleasant primary school experience. Some ideas that initially have good intentions don't necessarily have the desired outcome – a lesson applicable to many areas of our lives, including medicine.

Male teachers during this era were highly revered and feared, especially when they used 'the cane' (a one-metre long pole made of flexible, thin round timber called 'rattan'). This weapon of discipline was all too easily used for punishment for any unacceptable behaviour – be it talking instead of working or just being late for school. The cane was handed out by two, four or six lashes on an outstretched palm or fingers of the hand and given in front of the class. Sometimes one's pride was hurt more than one's hand. There were tricks that we would all try at various times to lessen the associated pain, such as wiping our hand through our hair full of 'Brylcreem' (a popular hair gel at that time), which caused the cane to slip off our hand on the downstroke. Another was to judge when the downstroke was coming and allow our hand to fall at the same time to try to cause a 'sliding' effect. Teachers, of course, knew about these attempts to deflect the cane and when recognised would immediately bring the cane up underneath the knuckles of the fingers, with the 'upstroke' often hurting a lot more than the original stroke.

My sixth class teacher particularly was an expert in giving the cane. Mr Carter was a competent teacher but did not take well to stupidity or any resemblance of misbehaviour. Unfortunately, I was sometimes a recipient of his caning skills. Fortuitously, he later became a patient of mine at Lugarno about 20 years later, and I recall being tempted to use blunt needles when giving him immunisations in some sort of sadistic retaliation endeavour (but fortunately I resisted).

When I revisited my primary school in recent years, everything seemed so different, so small and inconsequential. Back then when we performed on stage in the indoor auditorium of the main building it seemed so large and daunting.

# High school – the teenage years

Even though I didn't pay much attention to my grades during primary school years, when I graduated into high school, I ended up in the 'A' grade classes for all my subjects.

Peakhurst High School had only been opened for three years when I entered in 1966 – the year decimal currency was introduced. I would be educated at this secondary school until age 18. It was an exciting time that I generally enjoyed and it provided many wonderful learning and social experiences, especially in view of it being a young state school.

When I commenced Year 7 at the age of 12, it was the decade infamous for its association with social and sexual revolutions – the introduction of the contraceptive pill, illicit drug-taking, Beatlemania and long hair.

On hindsight, I was very privileged to have been protected by my parents' upbringing. My church involvement and my religious convictions allowed me to eschew experimental involvement with drugs, alcohol and smoking, which were virtually all the norm in this era. This is something I'm extremely grateful for now in later life, observing the devastation these behaviours have caused to many future generations. That is not to say that I didn't thoroughly enjoy rock-and-roll music in general (still evident these days on my Spotify playlists, decades after l lost contact with my EP and LP vinyl records). I enjoyed watching the infamous Woodstock concert at the movies and the musical talents this showcased: Janice Joplin; Jimi Hendrix; Santana and Crosby, Stills, Nash and Young.

I also grew my hair long with an attempted beard to match, much to the disgust of my dad. Despite not agreeing with such an appearance (especially in the clean-cut Salvation Army band to which I belonged), he somehow tolerated it with perhaps an awareness that this was an expression of teenage rebellion. On reflection, even more poignant is that my father at that age of 17 was enrolling to risk his life for his country during wartime. It was also gracious of a very strict Salvation Army bandmaster to allow young men with such scraggly appearance to be allowed to be part of a men's brass band. I appreciated that he made an allowance for my long hair at that age.

Most young people and teenagers grow up being different in some way to others around them and unfortunately attract the undesired attention of others who wrongly think they are the only 'normal' and 'cool' ones. This difference can be the colour of our skin, how tall we are, whether we're thin or overweight, our academic achievements or lack of such, whether we wear glasses or not, the colour of our hair, our speech (such as stuttering, or poor English) or many other variables.

For me it was my height, my freckles, my academic interests and, later, my religious beliefs. These attracted my share of bullying. Usually bullying was sorted out with a fistfight in the school playground or after school (which, having not learnt boxing, I tried to avoid). I remember in Year 7 being picked up by some larger boys in Year 9 and put head-first into a metal garbage bin in the school quadrangle much to my embarrassment. Fortunately for me, this improved with time and now I'm thankful there was no internet, no computers or smartphones so no cyberbullying, which currently seems to be a worse degree of bullying. There was no video of my garbage bin ordeal to be uploaded to TikTok, Facebook or Instagram to be seen on demand forever (a situation my grandchildren may have to unpleasantly face). Hopefully, my grandchildren can get through school and avoid such unacceptable and abusive behaviour by others.

My dad helped me balance the concern over the bullying regarding my height by reminding me that he was saved twice in the Second World War because he was short. The prominent story was when he was climbing a steep incline in Papua New Guinea called Shaggy Ridge. The soldier directly above his head was suddenly shot in the ankle, collapsing over Dad. Dad realised that the Japanese sniper had been aiming at his head but the recoil of the rifle meant the bullet lodged in the ankle of the person six inches above him. As was his custom, Dad 'counted his blessings' and was actually thankful for his short stature. These days the main opportunity for me to do the same is when I find myself sitting in economy class when flying!

Despite some earlier difficulties, I really enjoyed these six years at high school: playing rugby league as a half-back, changing musical instrument preferences from cornet (which I really did not enjoy and struggled trying to develop my 'embouchure') to drums, and thriving in an academic environment that encouraged good performance and embraced supportive teaching. Earlier years involved subjects including metalwork and woodwork (some of the projects that I have kept to this time).

I was fortunate and privileged to remain in the 'A' classes and by Years 9 and 10 was thoroughly enjoying mathematics and commerce as subjects. By Year 10 School Certificate, I had topped the year in both of these subjects. A major reason for the success was the dedication and quality of two particular teachers – Mrs

Jan Noonan for commerce (and later economics) and Mr Laurie Johnson for mathematics, for the School Certificate and the Higher School Certificate (HSC).

It has been said that teachers can have 'experience' or 'passion' or both. It takes both wings for a plane to fly and it takes both of these qualities to be a good teacher. This was as true for my generation as it is today. Teachers ideally try to develop relationships with their students as humans and not just as pupils. We all have an un-repayable debt to our educators. One of the 'silver linings' of the pandemic in 2020–2022 was appreciating teachers more after parents were required to undertake home-schooling with their children.

In later years at school, I was encouraged by my school academic advisers to apply for actuarial studies at university, as an outcome of my results in maths and economics. On hindsight, I clearly observed God's providential good plan for my life by not proceeding down this path. I'm so grateful that I've found fulfilment and enjoyment for nearly 50 years, initially studying medicine at uni, then working in hospitals and, finally, general practice. Ironically, I believe the two teachers who taught me in maths and commerce are also thankful I didn't undertake actuarial studies since I've been their general practitioner for over four decades. Not uncommonly, I will come out to the waiting room to call one of them into my consulting room to find them both talking to each other. This is one of those twists and turns of life that make it interesting to say the least and emphasises again the truth of Proverbs 11:25, this time for those two teachers: 'Those who refresh others will indeed be refreshed – those who help others will be helped.'

## Music and sport

Music was a major influence and enjoyment of mine and continues even now. As well, I was an avid fan of the Beatles and I also followed other bands such as Cream (with Eric Clapton), Tully, the Eagles, as well as soloists such as Carol King, James Taylor and Bob Dylan. All this music spans the decades and is still enjoyed in the present attracting new and young generations. The Beatles would release a new song or album weekly that I would hear on my 'tranny' or car radio and would inevitably make number one on the charts. The quality of the lyrics and tunes of Lennon and McCartney has never been repeated.

I must have been significantly influenced by the Beatles' legacy as I recall helping my eldest son in primary school on a project on beetles with details of information, facts and photos. We included a reference that these insects are so unique that there was a famous music group named after them, with pictures to support. It was a dead give-away that Justin had been helped by a parent in the project and the teacher made it clear to me at the next parent-teacher interview, along with the fact that it was different spelling!

In 2017, Carol and I finally made it to the hallowed ground of Liverpool where the Beatles originated, visiting the Cavern, the underground nightclub where they first became famous, as well as the Beatles museum. We visited Penny Lane and sat and reflected on the same location where Paul McCartney wrote the lyrics about the different shops in the famous street.

A local popular group at that time of my teenage years was the Delltones with the powerful bass voice of their tall lead singer Pee Wee Wilson. He lived in Lugarno, became a patient of mine for many years, and it was always an experience that caused me to reminisce whilst consulting him and to listen again to his deep voice (speaking that is, rather than singing).

I really enjoyed playing the drums, especially through my teenage years – whether it was in a casual ad-lib rock group at high school, regurgitating popular music at any place we were invited to play, or playing drums in Salvation Army musicals or the Dulwich Hill Salvation Army Band to which I belonged. I learnt that being a drummer was not necessarily an easy role to perform. There is a degree of pressure to keep an accurate tempo and rhythm, otherwise the whole band suffers, but at least you won't be noted out of tune as a singer or keyboard player might be. A drum kit was inconvenient to cart around and often required a station wagon to transport. Setting up and packing down is also more time-consuming compared to the other members of the band (who have already left to have a coffee). Lastly, trying to practice is not very conducive to those you live with, nor your neighbours. It's just repetitive thumping with no identifying melody to listen to. I well recall the unintentionally humorous signs on two neighbours' properties Carol and I witnessed when we repeatedly drove up to the central coast many years later. Being on a main road, the sign on the first property read 'Drumming lessons – apply within'. The sign on the next property was a large one that read 'For Sale'!

Playing the side drum in the band and belonging to a drum corps were wonderful experiences. The Salvation Army band marched regularly in the streets in those days, especially on Anzac Day in the city. It was a time of pride and fun, and sometimes humour.

On one such occasion, when marching at the rear of a large band and timbrel (tambourine) group at the front, I noticed the whole procession suddenly concertinaed to an abrupt halt. The reason being due to the front flag-bearer getting the flag pole stuck in a tree branch and being unable to proceed. The music and march recommenced to my drumbeat when everyone recomposed themselves from the laughter and the flag-bearer proceeded again with a somewhat flushed face!

High school was also a time where I developed my skills and enjoyment in sports that I enjoyed – surfing, football and waterskiing. Being a keen South Sydney follower, I wore their red and green football jersey when playing games with other teenagers in Webb Street. Being small and fairly quick, I gravitated to half-back position, but playing this position meant I was an obvious target for larger forwards of opposing teams. When playing for my school I found that the clever approach to playing around the scrum was to be an avid kicker of field goals in an attempt to avoid being crash tackled. On one occasion I was too late with this plan and was knocked unconscious and chipped a front tooth – the cost of dental work was not welcomed by my parents. I loved attending many games when South Sydney were playing, including one of their famous grand final wins and the glory of watching my heroes of Rugby League.

Surfing was a particular sport from my teenager years that I really enjoyed and still do. In earlier days it was small boards and in later years a nine-foot-long board that has given many hours of enjoyment with other surfing friends. Unfortunately, the outcome of this sport later in life saw me with many visits to my dermatologist with resultant skin cancers. Surfing for me these days is with a long-sleeve rash shirt, ear plugs for the exostoses (lumps in the ear canals from water exposure), a surfing hat and sun block lathered on before I head out. It's not really a good look, and causes other young surfers on their small boards to paddle away from the 'old fella' (fortunately leaving more waves for me ). These days I find great joy in watching two of my children, Justin and Racquel, and the grandchildren enjoying this sport and having fun on the waves. The surfing bug has now been caught by Jai, one of my grandchildren whose skills are far superior to mine as an adolescent, and whose surfing is enjoyably filmed by me on the beach, or by him with his GoPro, which was not even invented when I was his age.

Lastly, waterskiing. Wisely, my dad, who grew up loving boating thought that purchasing a runabout speedboat would be an interest that could hold the family together, especially during the teenage years and therefore a worthy investment for exercise and relationship purposes. The 13 foot yellow fibreglass boat with foam padded double-backed seats and a 65 horse power mercury outboard motor was launched with the predictable name of *Sally F* ('Sally' – Salvation Army, 'F' – Franks). This boat served our family and extended friends with years of enjoyment, teaching many to waterski and providing a common interest for the family. With lots of practise we improved our skills: starting with double skis and then one ski and ending up skiing barefoot.

We also used the boat for fishing at our holiday cottage at Pretty Beach. Skiing took place either in the Georges River, the Hawkesbury River or Gosford waterways. Dad trusted me to take it out with mates and friends – as long as it received a good wash on return, which it (mostly) did.

## The Austin

With high school and teenage years came the opportunity to obtain my driver's licence exactly on my 17th birthday – 15 May 1970. I had no intention of delaying getting onto the roads with my classy grey and white secondhand Austin A40, my first beast of a car that handled like a 'hippo', and had the speed of a 'sloth'. It had front and rear bench seats, installed seatbelts, a small milk bottle jammed on the end of the gearstick and four-inch re-treaded tyres. It provided transport to high school in my last 2 years there. As a novice mechanic, it was enjoyable and a challenge to work on and allowed me to learn how to change motors and brake linings. The car provided a workout when it had to be pushed down the street to clutch-start due to having the inevitable flat battery after leaving an inside light on.

The Austin and I were lucky to survive many misadventures including the Glebe runaway incident. Late one dark night, I dropped a friend home after a youth group event in the city. She lived at the top of a street in Glebe. I was unaware of the sudden steep hill at the end of the street, which tested the brakes of the old Austin when I came over the crest at what did not seem excessive speed. Heading downhill quickly I came to a noisy stop at the bottom. I realised that the radiator cooling fan was still spinning, but on the wrong side of the radiator. The engine had dislodged from the engine mounts and it, plus the gearbox (and everything else) had moved at least a foot forward. In the dark, I eventually found a phone box in Glebe and eventually returned home after being chauffeur-driven by an NRMA tow truck. The Austin lasted a number of years after that, until eventually being towed away as scrap metal and replaced by a bright blue secondhand four-door Ford Cortina – a vast improvement for that era.

High school in the later years, especially Years 11 and 12, were more enjoyable. I was driving, more independent, and was enjoying my drumming and sports. I had my first high school girlfriend and I was elected as a prefect and enjoyed the responsibility.

In 2016, a 50-year-reunion was arranged for the students of Class 66 of Peakhurst High School. It was an interesting evening. It was expected that we'd changed so much that we would require name tags – this proved to be accurate. We had to study the name tags before commencing conversation. Some of the stories that were shared that evening really impacted me. Amongst the positive stories were a number of sad stories of wasted lives, suicides, broken marriages and drug and alcohol addiction.

As a young person during high school, trying to lead a life with a Christian worldview, it was understandable to compare myself to what others were doing and enjoying and feel a sense of being deprived or missing out on freedoms others seem to have enjoyed. Later, I reflected that I'd been fortunate to avoid damaging life-changing outcomes as I steamrolled through adolescent years, not always thinking through the consequences or risks of certain behaviours, rather than just the instant gratification. The boundaries my parents had put in place for me, even though I did not appreciate them at the time, had protected me from harm and actually produced true freedom.

Later as a parent and GP, I learnt about the teenage brain, especially in boys whose brains prune right back by 40 percent, ready for extensive learning, and then is slow to rewire and to mature until their mid-20s, and during this time, can lead to risky behaviours due to poor insight. I now can use this knowledge on occasions with Carol when we mentor teenagers through the tumultuous years of adolescence.

It had been six valuable years of a vast array of experiences and opportunities while I was navigating the teenage 'white water rafting years' and trying to stay aboard the raft and not sink. On hindsight, I attribute the reasons why I survived this time was that I had supportive, prayerful and loving parents; encouraging and fun church friends and leaders; sincere and interested teachers; and a balance of healthy interests, hobbies and sports. Looking back, I'm, thankful to God that I came out of school and my teenage years relatively unscathed and was now ready with anticipation for the next chapter of my life that God was preparing for me.

# CHAPTER FIVE

# UNIVERSITY

*'Look straight ahead and fix your eyes on what lies before you. Mark out a straight path for your feet, then stick to the path and stay safe. Don't get sidetracked, keep your feet from doing evil.'*

**– Proverbs 4:25–26**

# Initiation

The first day at medical school at the University of NSW in March 1972 was a challenge to say the least and an initiation of unexpected proportions. Entering the doors of the Wallace Wurth building and the main auditorium were about 250 young fresh-faced medical students. Some had desired to undertake medical studies for many years. For others, like me, it was a more recent decision. The far majority were not used to the sight of blood or what their chosen profession might reveal to them.

Whether it was intentional to educate these 'fresh men and women', or to quickly condition them to future exposure, or to weed out those not suitable to continue studying medicine, the lecturers on that introduction day decided to show us all an explicit open heart operation video. It was a hot, stuffy, crowded and poorly ventilated auditorium. We were stuck, with the options of leaving, closing our eyes, persevering as if we were cool, or fainting! Understandably, there was a certain peer pressure not to leave even if we found it all too confronting – the blood, the noise of operative tools and the exposed organs. The trouble with anyone fainting was that there was only one way to go and that was straight down onto the desk with our heads. So began the sickening thud of one head at a time hitting the desk! I fortunately survived without being a victim of a head injury but witnessed many not so fortunate. I figured that because I managed to survive my first day without fainting I should keep persisting. And I'm glad I did.

## Undergraduate years

The first year of six years of medicine at university was a rehash of some high school subjects on biology, chemistry and physics. It was rather tedious and seemed an unnecessary repetition at the time.

Nineteen seventy-two was a year where I could have been conscripted into national service by ballot for training, and then deployed to the Vietnam War. I'd turned 18 years of age. This created in me mixed emotions. I did not agree with the rationale behind the Vietnam War. However, I was conscious of upholding the legacy of my father and volunteering to fight for my country as he had. I would have been willing to be conscripted if it came to that, but I did not need to make the decision, as compulsory national service was abolished in 1972 by the then Labor government due to the high casualties of the war sparking major Australian protests. It was also opportune that this same government led by Gough Whitlam introduced free tertiary education – this lasted through my university years. A generosity that has never been repeated.

The Vietnam War was correctly considered futile. It was a war that we should not have become involved in (a mistake that was to be repeated decades later in other conflicts). Unfortunately, the returned conscripted and regular soldiers came back to a country who had become ambivalent, and they did not receive the needed and appropriate recognition for their obedience to the call and sacrifice for their country.

I soon realised at uni there was no physical bullying, nor schoolyard fights, nor supportive interested teachers. We were on our own to ensure we learnt, took handwritten notes (computers hadn't been invented yet) and disciplined ourselves to study. It was soon apparent that students tended to segregate into certain groups – the intellectual self-confident ones, the cool group that thought uni was only about drinking, parties and concerts, and then there was the rest of us who were somewhere in-between.

Lectures at university were didactic with no ability to check notes online if missed or not understood, but tutorials were more hands-on and interesting. At the time I went to uni, the curriculum was three full-time years of study on campus and then three years shared between hospitals and campus, but mainly clinical work in the hospital. These days students are exposed to patients and hospitals in the first year. This is wise since it allows practical application of the theory taught in health to real patients.

Lecturers varied in their ability to bring to life the vastness of medical knowledge. Some were incredibly passionate, engaging and enthusiastic, some less so, and there were very occasionally non-engaging ones.

One such lecturer entered the auditorium, placed his notes on the lectern and set about reading them with his head down for 50 minutes or so, then left. It seemed he was not aware of whether there were students in attendance and whether they were asleep or awake. A few of the 'cool' students who were easily encouraged to perform activities that attracted attention or humour came to the conclusion that nothing would distract this particular lecturer. These were the years of the popular act of 'streaking' at cricket and football matches. So one particular day, whilst this lecturer was in the midst of his presentation, four of these bravado students entered stage right wearing only motorbike helmets to conceal their identity, running across in front of the stage from right to left in front of 300 or so students – causing many a gasp and much laughter. The lecturer did not budge and maintained his note reading in the same monotoned voice. I guess there was at least some anatomical education via this prank for the concentrating medicos in attendance.

I was living at home with my parents for my first four years of uni, initially in Riverwood, then from late 1974 at Lugarno in their new home. The latter was was close to some ex-schoolmates who were travelling to the same uni. We carpooled and shared the driving, a great help for all of us. The Austin with it's bench seats undertook its fair share of transport duties, albeit slowly when there was six uni students on board, listening to music from our favourite groups. The upside was I never had to be concerned about speeding fines.

One day we thought it would be a good idea to ride our bikes to uni for exercise and to save on petrol. We underestimated both the distance and the time to ride to Randwick from Lugarno, especially since one bike was a tandem. We rode twice that day – the first and the last time!

At the end of each year, having passed the necessary exams, I commenced my ritual of working casual jobs in the three months of uni holidays. Jobs such as rolling and cutting carpet in a carpet factory, working at a lawn bowling club doing all sorts of jobs including cleaning out the used cigarette butts from the empty battery cases at the end of each bowling green. Another job was washing up at night in the kitchen of a restaurant in the city. It wasn't just dishes I had to wash: it included the washing out of lobster carcasses so that they could be refilled with frozen lobster! It was not only lobster but pineapple 'carcasses' that would also be washed and refilled.

Another casual job was obtained for me by my friend Denis who was working then for the DMR (Department of Main Roads). This entailed holding a measuring pole for the surveyors involved in the building of the Kings Cross Tunnel. I was usually some distance from where the surveyors were peering through their theodolites, and I found it difficult to concentrate on keeping the pole perfectly vertical and straight. The tunnel when completed, had a large curve in its direction under Kings Cross. I often contemplate when driving through 'my tunnel' whether it was supposed to be straight – and whether I was to blame for the fact that it wasn't!

Second year of uni studies was much more interesting and relevant to a career in medicine with subjects of anatomy, physiology and biochemistry. Through witnessing cadavers dissected, comprehensive anatomy manuals and tutorials, I was exposed to the extremely intricate make-up of the human body. At the same time I was also learning about the function of these beautifully arranged organs and systems. These experiences and revelations strongly reinforced my belief in intelligent design.

In particular, three of the body's systems – the anatomy and physiology of the workings of the eye and our sight; the ear and our hearing; the brain and our ability to function, think and feel – were so complex that they seem to defy explanation just by evolution and natural selection.

Just take the example of the anatomy and function of the ear that we all take so much for granted. This most beautiful structure brings to us – the birds singing, the leaves rustling, rain on a tin roof and, of course, music. Sound is so important to life and it starts with sound waves from a source that have to reach our brain before we can hear and interpret what we're hearing. The ear is such a small and sophisticated organ that gives us our hearing and provides us with so much happiness. Rich auditory information allows us to engage with others in life. (Refer to Appendix A 'The anatomy and physiology of the ear'.)

The complexity of our DNA and how it functions in the cell with its exact sequencing of amino acids does not allow for mistakes and the mathematical odds that this was just by chance are extremely low. Even the coagulation system in our blood is so unique that any adaptation or change in its evolution would have led to excessive clotting or bleeding (being not conducive to life). Studying anatomy and physiology forced me to stop and consider how body systems and organs came into existence.

At the end of my second year, I quickly set off to travel overseas – my first time out of Australia. The itinerary was to take me on my maiden visit to Africa and then onto Europe.

After six weeks working alongside two excellent doctors in Zambia, I planned to meet my brother-in-law David in London and then to travel via train visiting as many places throughout Europe as we could within the timeframe we had. My first international flight was to Johannesburg. I was staggered to realise that smoking was allowed on board the plane, with a seat number separating smokers and non-smokers. Needless to say there was no control over where the cigarette smoke ended up.

My time of six weeks at Chikankata influenced me greatly. It gave me a love of the African continent and its beautiful people. It allowed me to understand in an uncomfortable way the disparity of health and wealth between developed Western countries and poor undeveloped countries like Zambia. It gave me an appreciation of my opportunities and privilege of being born into a country like Australia, to be given an education and not having to struggle daily to survive. It also reminded me of the responsibility I had as a medical student and later medical practitioner towards those less fortunate in the world. Along with the opportunity to learn about tropical medicine and infectious diseases not seen in Australia, this journey to Africa was also a life-changing experience spiritually, one that gave me clarity of the call and leading of God on my life.

## 'Almost Cut My Hair' – Crosby, Stills, Nash & Young

The second six weeks of the three-month uni vacation was to be spent exploring another continent: that of Europe, with its poignant history and culture –extreme opposite to remote Africa.

It commenced with some anxiety because the plan was that I was supposed to arrive at Heathrow Airport in London before David and his friend, and then meet them when their flight came in. Unfortunately, my flight from Zambia to Johannesburg was significantly delayed and so I was late for my next flight to London. I arrived in London after my friends and had no ability to communicate via mobile phone or email. I found myself in one of the largest and busiest cities in the world having no idea where my friends were staying since they'd arranged the accommodation. I found a hotel near the airport and tried to discover where they were but with no success. I recalled that David's uncle had been the training principle of the Salvation Army Officer College in London a few years prior and that perhaps his cousin was still living in London.

I was able to track down an address in outer London, by contacting the training college and made my way to this location via the underground rail with my suitcases, only to find that no-one was home. An elderly woman in the same street observed me standing on the kerb looking lost. Despite my scruffy appearance, and not knowing who I was, she invited me into her house and gave me a cup of tea. On reflection that was risky but nonetheless, a very kind gesture. The invitation was also extra special in that she had a real colour TV (with no coloured perspex), the first one I'd ever seen. I was mesmerised. After some time and explaining my position, she was kind enough to ring her next door neighbour. To everyone's surprise, I was being given hospitality next to my travelling companions. On coming out on the street, I met them in the middle of this metropolis! Another experience of God's providential care.

We travelled via Eurail through most of the well-known European countries, staying in 'pensione' – individual rooms rented out in homes. We had tried backpackers in Paris but were subjected to someone firing a gun so we quickly abandoned that style of accommodation. I also tried converse in Germany by using my recall of this language learnt in high school, with limited success. Languages other than English have not been a strength of mine over my lifetime.

It was winter and the weather in general was overcast and cold, but it was still an exciting adventure and an exposure to many cultures and languages that I greatly enjoyed. This European holiday, from the snow-capped alps of Switzerland, to the charm of Paris, gave me a love of travel and a desire to revisit in the future – in less inclement weather, which I was able to do later with Carol.

The return flight back to Australia by myself proved to be another experience I would not quickly forget. These were still the days of the influence of rock-and-roll and long hair – and mine was no exception at shoulder length. Some countries decided to take a tough stand and ban anything to do with Beatlemania and the general appearance of my generation, and one of those countries was Singapore. One of the appearances they would not tolerate was long hair, perhaps believing that it usually led to other unpleasant behaviours such as illicit drug-taking and antisocial behaviour. Fortunately, my long hair never led me into these vices, but it did result in my first and only arrest. I was flying back from London via Singapore with a transit within the airport to catch a Singapore Airlines flight back to Sydney. In preparation, I'd enquired with the Singapore consulate in Sydney before leaving whether my long hair would be an issue if I was just transiting. I was reassured there would not be an issue– which turned out to be incorrect.

On my arrival at Immigration, I observed a line-up of mainly young men desiring entry into Singapore and trying to hide their long hair tucked up under a beanie or hat. On one side of the immigration officer was a barber cutting men's hair short on the spot and on the other side was a police officer armed with a machine gun. When it was my turn I explained that I was only in transit and was informed that my long hair would not pose a problem since I would not be leaving the airport. That explanation unfortunately did not impress the immigration officer who in broken English made it clear – 'haircut or arrest?' Feeling a sense of injustice I said, 'no haircut' and immediately had my passport and airline ticket confiscated and then marched by police to an isolated room and held with a few other dissenters by the armed guard who stood just outside our small room. Hours later, just before my flight was due to leave,

I was marched out onto the tarmac and at the steps of the plane and in front of many peering eyes from the plane's small windows, I was handed back my documents and ordered to never return!

It would be some decades with a more conservative appearance and a post-Beatles hair cut that I returned to Singapore with Carol. On lining up at Immigration this time to gain entry, I had some reservations as to whether there would be a record of my arrest and whether that would result in me being left at the airport while my wife gained entry. Fortunately for me, the barber had retired and my misdemeanours had been overlooked or perhaps pardoned.

Arriving back on Aussie ground after a number of months away overseas, I commenced preparation for my third year of medicine in 1974. This was the year I also reached the milestone of turning 21, and I celebrated at home with friends and family. This study year turned out to be one of my favourites, especially studying pathology – anatomical pathology, histopathology and microbiology. I understood and enjoyed these subjects since they had application to understanding diseases that patients might be suffering from, and which I would soon observe in the hospital setting since pathology was the basis of medicine and surgery. I performed well in examinations with a distinction by the end of the two-year course. Other subjects studied included psychology and philosophy, the latter seemed to be more subjective and dependent on one's worldview and ability to think laterally than other more concrete and pragmatic subjects.

# Ambiguity

I generally flourished in my learning and study in medicine at uni in the years I was attending. But within the study of medical science there is an inherent tension and ambiguity for someone with a Christian worldview, and I did struggle with this over these years. I was encouraged by remembering past medical and scientific forebears who were famous and extremely clever scientists, but who humbly maintained their faith in God and a Christian worldview, and who also acknowledged the way science and religion intersected and could cohabit, rather than requiring a belief in science or religion. People such as Kepler, Pascale, Newton, Faraday, Decanta, Mendal and Boyle to mention just a few.

Despite a widespread lack of obvious Christian expression or acceptance of Christian worldview at university, I was able to befriend a few students who had similar worldviews to myself, and I enjoyed their friendship through the next six years. For a student with such a belief system, studying at uni is often a time of unprecedented crisis in one's faith, with the influence of a naturalistic, humanistic, atheistic environment – especially in the scientific and humanity subjects. Some students lost their faith in God altogether due to the intense peer pressure. Fortunately for me, despite the pressures, I was able to 'hang' onto mine and I'm very thankful to God for that.

Philosophy is defined as 'the pursuit of wisdom or the knowledge of things and their causes'. I personally found it more theoretical, speculative and moralistic. I held that wisdom was the actual application of knowledge, rather than just a pursuit for the sake of exploring various options. My knowledge was based on my own life experiences and also based on my understanding of

God and the biblical truths that I upheld. My worldview should be just as valid and respected as someone with completely the opposite beliefs – but this was not necessarily the case, especially at an establishment like university, where my worldview was clearly taught to be an inferior or an illogical line of thought and reasoning. It is still the same today, only more-so, where a Christian worldview discussion is not usually even considered or tolerated in schools or tertiary institutions.

## My 'Peter' experience

Michael was a wealthy medical student from Singapore and a likeable guy, and he had opposing beliefs to myself. I met and befriended him in my second year of university. He was a strong defender of his atheism. It was hard work to uphold and defend what I believed to him. There came a crisis of faith for me when one day we were discussing what we believed. Out of the blue he asked, 'You don't really believe all that do you?'

Being put on the spot, and for some inexplicable reason, I blurted back: 'No'. For those who understand the experience of the Apostle Peter in the Bible, this confrontation immediately brought him to my mind. He was one of the disciples who denied Jesus before his death on the cross.

This day has been firmly implanted in my mind as a day of regret and failure but also a day that I decided I needed to know and understand more of what I believed as a Christian to be able to defend my faith more vigorously but not aggressively. God allowed Peter, despite his failure, to become a 'rock of the Church' who influenced many to follow his God. I would never want a failure like this one to define me either.

Due to Michael and I being sent to different hospitals for our last three years of medical studies, and Michael having to repeat his sixth year, my friendship with him waned. We both ended up in general practice. I was saddened to hear a number of years after graduation that he became entangled with underground criminal influences and was murdered. It made me wonder if the outcome of his life could have been different if my response to his challenging question regarding my faith had been different. I will never know. But to all who call themselves Christians, we are all given opportunities, and as the Bible succinctly says 'Always be prepared to give an answer to everyone who asks you to give a reason for the hope that you have. But do this with gentleness and respect.' Shame can be a disincentive for sharing anything with another person, especially our faith, or it can be used to do better when another opportunity arises. With time and experience, I now feel more curious about others' differing beliefs – I'm more gracious and more respectful around this, but also more confident to give an answer as to what and why I believe.

# Marriage

Nineteen seventy-five was a year remembered in Australia for a few things: the dismissal of the Prime Minister Gough Whitlam; the Watergate Scandal; the first Apple-1 PC; the founding of Microsoft; and the fall of Saigon in the Vietnam War.

But for me it was the year I married Carol, in November after my fourth year of medicine. It was also the year I had been appointed to St George Public Hospital – a teaching hospital of the university to undertake clinical studies and experience in the wards with 'real patients' for the next three years. It was an exciting time whereby medical students could see the application of what they'd been learning the previous three years. Now was the time to understand history taking, examination of the patient, learning how to investigate appropriately, and then understanding the correct interpretation of the results. This applied to the subjects of medicine, surgery, paediatrics, psychiatry, obstetrics and gynaecology and emergency medicine. The practical skills were invaluable and essential. The involvement in assisting in surgery for as many operations as we could evoked the same 'head banging' faints experienced at our first day at uni – with some near misses for myself as well.

I first met Carol at the church we were both attending as teenagers, The Salvation Army at Dulwich Hill. Carols parents were Salvation Army officers who had been appointed to our church, so we did not know each other as children. Her father Albert and her mother Joy were certainly protective parents, as I observed in our courting years, but they were also wise, kind and generous to me and everyone they cared for in their pastoral roles. Dad Everitt was a dedicated, traditional pastor who took his work seriously and with diligence, being loved and admired by his wider congregation and those closer to him – such as a prospective son-in-law. Mum Everitt was one of the most humble people I have ever had a relationship with – her name Joy was a true reflection of her character. I never observed her being angry, disappointed or depressed in all the decades I knew her. I was soon to realise how fortunate I was to have such outstanding parents-in-law, and how much gratitude I had for what I learnt from them about living out the Christian faith in the world around us.

Carol had three siblings, Robyn, John and Janice. Our close relationships with each of them and their spouses has brought much enjoyment through our lives. Our families have grown and we love catching up when the opportunity arises.

Carol and I were married on 29 November 1975, at The Salvation Army church in Dulwich Hill by her father, Major Albert Everitt. We had time for a honeymoon and some settling down before the recommencement of my fifth year of studies. Our wedding day was a wonderful day of celebration with some close friends in our bridal party. These same people have continued to be lifelong friends. On my side were David (my brother-in-law), Denis and Brian (good friends). On Carol's side were Robyn and Janice (Carol's sisters) and Kathryn (Carol's best friend from work who ironically later married Brian). These relationships have been so important and valuable to all of us. It takes effort to keep any relationship alive and Carol and Kathy still 50 years later meet regularly in Bowral – halfway between Sydney (for Carol) and Canberra (for Kathy).

Sadly, Brian, one of my groomsmen, died in 2022, after years of illness related to a previous heart transplant. I was privileged to be asked by Kathy to give the eulogy at his funeral. I considered him a good friend who was always smiling and who didn't allow his illness to deplete him of his sense of humour. He is still sadly missed.

There were a few hiccups on the day of our wedding. Not the least being when the owner of the reception house became rather demanding – as well as intoxicated! As we drove away from the reception, I recall Carol's dad picking up all the confetti from the pebbled driveway after being told to clean up the mess, which he did without complaint so as not to spoil our day.

Our honeymoon was a planned drive to North Queensland. Knowing my old blue Cortina would probably not survive the trip, my dad came to the rescue and allowed us to take his brand new Ford station wagon – probably a decision he regretted when we broke a windscreen and a few other car parts. Although just like Carol's dad, he never voiced the inconvenience to him.

It rained most of the time on our honeymoon and although we look back and laugh at the photos of some of the mishaps and difficulties, we were both reminded that a marriage – its quality and longevity – is not dependent on the quality of the wedding day or the honeymoon, but rather the decades following. Working intentionally together, we have sought to make our marriage successful.

## Our first home

On our return from our budget honeymoon, Carol and I set about finding some accommodation for the next two years, realising that Carol would be supporting me with one income whilst I finished my studies. We found a flat in Kogarah under a real estate agent's office, and below street level, next to the Mecca movie theatre, and across the road from the Kogarah railway station. It was rather a dark, mouldy two-bedroom flat with an outside tin roofed toilet. It had a small kitchen that also included the laundry and bathroom and a shower over an old-fashioned bath. At $17 a week, it was a convenient and affordable place to call our first home. We set about renovating our new flat, including painting the roof black to hide the flaking ceiling as best as possible. We put a ply sheet of timber over the laundry tubs – that became our kitchen bench. Life was good and we were happy.

When the real estate agent inspected the flat he gave us a few weeks free rent, because he was so impressed with all the improvements. Carol and I nicknamed our flat 'The Cave' and enjoyed our time together establishing our marriage. In 1978, after finishing my degree and graduating, I was appointed to Hornsby Hospital as a resident and we moved to our own first home at Baulkham Hills, so that we were halfway between our family and my workplace. We were very blessed to be able to obtain a mortgage from the Commonwealth Bank and purchase a newly built house for $45,000, which seemed a huge amount then, but insignificant compared to the present day property values.

## St George Public Hospital

My fifth and sixth years in medicine seemed to go quickly and I had to prioritise my study and practical examinations above social invitations and, at the same time, try to spend time with Carol as best as possible. It was such a relief to finish my last examination in late 1977, after studying and being 'at school' for 19 years. Carol and I decided to have a holiday with friends and family as a way to wind down before me commencing work as an intern. We hadn't had a decent break since our honeymoon. Carol and I travelled on our first international holiday as a married couple to Fiji with our friends Denis and Bev and my sister Darryle and her husband David. It was a fun holiday. While we were away, my dad travelled out to the university medical school to look at my results being posted on the noticeboard since this was the antiquated way of communication for acquiring examination results. This phone call is one that's easy to remember for good reasons, as I learnt that I had passed my Medical Degree of MBBS with Honours – Class 2, Division 2.

The group celebrated that night over dinner in Fiji, and on return Mum and Dad arranged a night out at the Caprice restaurant in Rose Bay, a restaurant we only ever visited to celebrate important occasions. They were so proud, especially my dad as he had not been given the opportunity to study or obtain any degree due to the war. Mum and Dad had provided me with the means to do what they never had the opportunity to do themselves. They'd financially, physically, emotionally and spiritually supported me for those 19 years.

I was presented with a black leather doctor's bag by my parents that night and 45 years later it still travels with me every day to the surgery and on home visits – a bit tattered and worn, but symbolic of their support and love for me. This is irreplaceable because of its sentimentality.

# Graduation

My graduation ceremony was held at the UNSW on Wednesday 8 February 1978, after I had already commenced my internship at Hornsby Hospital, and it was a rewarding day of celebration. I was able to wear the symbolic black graduation cap and gown. My parents and Carol attended my graduation ceremony. Years later we both experienced the same feeling of parental pride that accompanies these occasions, when our youngest son Luke graduated from Macquarie University with a Masters of Psychology Degree, wearing his own black cap and gown.

In the UNSW Faculty of Medicine Graduation Year Book of 1977, each graduate had a photo and one paragraph written by our peers.

Mine read as follows:

'Five foot two, eyes of blue, bilateral tibial osteotomies too. Gary was the group's salvation, being a good organiser, dedicated, conscientious and thoughtful, putting up with the group's depravity but never lowering himself to the ultimate depths of others. He will be remembered for his prolific note-taking, for thwarting his surgical career after incising a professor's glove in the operating theatre and causing the arrest of many hearts by marrying the lovely Carol in fourth year. We wish Gary all the best in his pursuit of honesty and integrity in his medical career and in his future with the Sally Army.'

Many years later, I still ask lots of questions and take prolific notes, as I love to learn and I'm still occasionally clumsy. And I'm still happily married to Carol and still value honesty and integrity.

Our 1977 graduation year had a 40 year reunion in a Sydney hotel in the city in 2018, and Carol and I attended with an interest in meeting up with my old colleagues, and seeing what had eventuated in their lives. We reacquainted ourselves with the other doctors, and it was interesting to see the pathways they'd taken since so long ago. Some were professors of medicine, some were working in a specialist field and some were family physicians working in general practice. Our medical education at uni had given us the opportunity to follow our dreams and our own personal unique vocations.

# CHAPTER SIX

# HOSPITAL

*'A healthy spirit conquers adversity, but what can you do when the spirit is crushed? Wise men and women are always learning, always listening to fresh insights... The first speech in a court case is always convincing, until the cross examination starts.'*

**– Proverbs 18:14–17**

# Scramble!

'Scramble!' was the codeword broadcasted loudly throughout the Hornsby Hospital speaker system by receptionists when a patient had a suspected cardiac arrest anywhere on the grounds or wards of the hospital. At the announcement of this message and supporting warning horns, the plan was that any resident doctor working in the hospital at that time would run as fast as they could to the location and commence resuscitation on the victim. Most of the time the first responders were those who were nearest to the emergency (or those who were the fittest). The most senior registrar would take control of the situation, one doctor organising the defibrillator, another doctor the crash cart with equipment and drugs, another commencing CPR on the chest, and another giving mouth-to-mouth (if they had any breath left after their sprint) while waiting for the patient to be intubated. The outcomes of this intervention were variable. Fortunately, in many cases, the patient was successfully resuscitated.

There was never any room for humour. Except, that is, when doctors collided in narrow corridors or doorways and ended up on the floor, or the extremely rare scenario such as the mistaken identity of the victim. This latter situation occurred to me one day when I heard the message 'Scramble – Recovery.' Being close to the recovery room, which was just outside the surgery theatres, I powered down the corridor and burst through the doors amazed that I seemed to be the first one to arrive.

I was eyeballing the patient laying still on a trolley bed a few metres away with signs of pallor and appearing to be unconscious and not breathing. Running towards the motionless man, I was about to administer a cardiac thump in the middle of his sternum with a closed fist, when all of a sudden, he opened his eyes wide and sat up in horror as he realised he was about to be assaulted after just having had surgery! This was nearly enough to precipitate a cardiac arrest but, fortunately for us both, he survived his surgery and his recovery ward ordeal. That day I learned that there was more than one recovery room at Hornsby Hospital. I also learnt to decelerate my sprints to allow me to be the second to arrive and to be sure I had the correct location and patient.

## Hornsby Hospital

I was approaching the end of my six years training. All students were required to select a hospital they would prefer to be appointed to for their two to three years compulsory residency. Presently there's an additional three years of specific training for those desiring their medical career to be in general practice after the hospital residency. But in 1978, the only specific general practice training opportunity had recently been commenced within Hornsby District Hospital, and therefore had become a popular hospital to apply for. Knowing I desired to become a general practitioner, I was fortunate to be accepted into this smaller community-based hospital with its quaint buildings and excellent senior medical staff and administration.

There were only 11 new interns accepted and, after some basic introductory training, we were quickly commenced on a rotation of terms in emergency, medicine, general practice, orthopaedics, paediatrics, surgery and obstetrics. Expectations of work ethics, punctuality and avoidance of absenteeism, combined with high workloads led us each into the demands of hospital work under NSW Health. Within the first two months, I was summoned to the hospital respiratory clinic after my routine chest X-ray, which was to exclude tuberculosis. It showed that I had pneumonia, which although unwell I was unaware of. The pneumonia settled quickly with oral antibiotics and I was back in action after two days off work. On the positive side, it was a joy to receive my first regular wage after 13 years at school and six years at university. It was a change in roles for Carol and me, with me being the main wage earner.

For my first term, I was allocated the emergency department (ED). I was looking forward to these three months, but little did I know that Hornsby Hospital had just made arrangements with NSW Health to staff the ED every weekend of the recently completed Campbelltown Public Hospital in Western Sydney. So with a second year resident from Hornsby Hospital, I was seconded to this new hospital for weekend shifts – Friday evening 6 pm until 8 am Monday morning. Just the two of us had to run the department and attend to calls in the wards for the whole hospital on our weekend – a daunting task for someone fresh out of medical school. The first day I had a reasonable sized suitcase full of textbooks that I would refer to after interviewing a patient in the emergency room – excusing myself while I looked up rashes, children's illnesses I was uncertain about, and refreshed my management of not so common conditions with no Google or smartphones to rely on.

This was tiring and challenging work over a 62 hour shift, with only limited time for a brief sleep on a hard hospital bed in a dark room. However, my learning curve was exponential during this time. I was exposed to medical conditions I had to manage by myself or, if uncertain, with the help of a senior resident, a delightful woman who had an enormous amount of experience and patience.

Certainly there were some unique presentations, such as the young lady with an overdose of 'jimson weed', a plant that apparently grew wild in gardens and alongside the road, the leaves giving an emotional 'high' when smoked, and hallucinations when consumed in large amounts. Another presentation was of a male patient complaining of a bleeding haemorrhoid, or so he told me. I took this as a reasonable diagnosis until I examined him and found that he had been stabbed in the buttock with a knife. His management included a police interview. Such was the variety of patients in that hospital at that time.

Back at Hornsby ED, the head of the department always encouraged interns and residents to take photos with a supplied camera if there were any unusual presentations, or those that may have had some ongoing insurance or legal ramifications. My turn to photograph came one day when a young man presented with linear red and blue marks across his back, alleging that he had been assaulted by a policeman wielding a baton. Certainly the skin changes were consistent with the story so, remembering the policy, I took the appropriate photos.

Hoping there would not be any repercussions, and being encouraged by the head of emergency that I'd performed the correct action, I was surprised when I was summoned by both legal parties (the victim and the police) to the local court to be a prime witness. I've only had to give evidence once in 45 years of practice and this was that time. I've been thankful that it was the only occasion since it was an unnerving and intimidating experience. I had not been taught about court attendances as a medical witness at uni nor advised or prepared by the hospital medical administrator nor the director of the emergency department what would take place. It was thought that I would just need a straightforward proclamation of what I had found, the history given by the victim, and the supportive photographic evidence. The legal representation for the victim was a junior legal aid solicitor. The representation for the police was an experienced prosecutor/barrister who obviously had planned to undermine the quality of my evidence by undermining me as a naive, inexperienced doctor and as someone who for some unexplained reason had a 'gross dislike and distaste of police as a whole' (which was untrue).

The police barrister seemed to enjoy tearing apart my witness and evidence, and I felt like a lamb being led to the slaughter. Much to my disgust, besides the questions exploring my junior status, inexperience and character, I was appalled to observe the lack of any objection by both the victim's solicitor and the magistrate, both of whom allowed me to be denigrated for what appeared to be a lifetime in the witness stand. I felt as though I were the one on trial, and the main diversion for a likely overuse of force by a certain police officer who desired an innocent verdict.

I was not privy to (and never found out) the outcome of this case. To rub salt into the wound, I was called up to the medical administrator's office some weeks later asking why the local police had enquired as to why one of the doctors of the hospital was a 'police hater'. It took me many years to return to a comfortable acceptance of trust in police and the justice system as a whole. Trust was re-established slowly by treating many police officers as patients over the ensuring decades, becoming closely involved with the local area police command at Sutherland in later years, and mainly being invited to take part in the CAPP (Community Awareness of Policing Programme) by the then police commissioner.

During this first stressful year at Hornsby Hospital, Carol and I were involved with our not so local church at The Salvation Army in Dulwich Hill. With the difficulties of my long shifts, one small vehicle, and our distance from any public transport, we found ourselves physically separated from our church, family and friends.

When we moved into our Baulkham Hills home, I developed the backyard into a veggie garden that produced large zucchinis despite the fact that I did not realise if I picked them sooner and smaller, their taste would be much improved. I enjoy gardening and am looking forward to establishing and working in another vegetable patch in the future and furthering this interest.

We also re-established relationships with old friends from our youth group days, Geoff and Julie, who lived near Baulkham Hills. Geoff became my solicitor and later I became his GP. We have remained close friends and travel buddies to this present time and we look forward to spending time in retirement together as neighbours on the Sunshine Coast in Queensland.

The second year as a resident at Hornsby Hospital in 1979, would soon become some of the happiest and saddest times of my life. Carol was pregnant with our first child, a son to be named Justin, who was born on 8 March. But three weeks prior to his birth and the anticipated excitement of his arrival, we were faced with the emotional trauma of my mum's sudden death.

There were tears of joy with Justin's arrival and the amazing miracle of our first child, which brought great pleasure to us as his parents and our extended family, especially at a time of profoundly mixed emotions. Through this time, we had to recognise that God was with us in all of our life's circumstances, whether it be the ones we celebrated or the trials we had to accept.

Medical work in a hospital was both exhausting and exciting. There was the need to apply all that knowledge of six years study, yet there was still so much to learn, especially being a junior intern and then resident. Each rotating term was of three months duration. I belonged to a team consisting of myself, a senior registrar and a specialist. Despite the backup of others, I was still carrying a huge responsibility for the outcome of the patient. On one occasion, I remember speaking to an elderly patient I'd cared for during a lengthy period in the medical ward and as I was explaining to her that she could be discharged she suddenly died in front of me from an acute pulmonary embolism (lung clot), which was found at post-mortem. It's times like these that the satisfaction of helping to bring healing to an individual is suddenly lost by an unexpected and sad outcome. This experience is something I've had to learn to accept in my vocation.

Hornsby Hospital would be the first ED for urgent attention of patients involved in motor vehicle accidents on the Pacific Highway between Sydney and Newcastle. It was also the pioneering hospital for the trial of a planned paramedic program. This program commenced at our hospital, with the concept that if an ambulance was attending to calls for a potential heart attack or cardiac arrest victim, they would retrieve a doctor to attend with the ambulance officers and give urgent first aid in the home. This showed that the survival of the patient could be improved. This success led to the development of a life-changing paramedic ambulance service that we all now benefit from.

There was, as expected, significant advances in medicine even in the two and a half years I was working in hospitals. But some traditions still prevailed. We wore ties and white coats as compared to most hospital doctors who mainly now wear surgical scrubs. Nurses wore stiff starched white uniforms and round caps, while the senior nurses and the matron wore their unique triangular headpiece and red cape. Their appearance and the quality of their work demanded respect. Surgical and medical wards were separated by gender, with lengthy rows of beds facing the other patients across the other side of the room.

Unfortunately in public hospitals, it's now normal to have mixed gender wards, with four beds in a hospital room, and all patients having to embarrassingly share the one bathroom. I can't help but think that if politicians or health bureaucrats had to spend a night or two in these facilities they might change their views as to whether this is an acceptable situation.

## Sydney Children's Hospital

The frequency and severity of childhood infectious diseases was emphasised to me while undertaking paediatric terms at Hornsby Hospital and the Sydney Children's Hospital. Most evenings that I was on duty I would be involved in performing lumbar punctures on small children suffering from suspected bacterial meningitis, a condition if not swiftly managed, causes death or significant neurological consequences. This procedure is an unpleasant one for the child and a difficult one for the doctor, with a long needle placed into the spinal canal to obtain fluid to culture the bacteria. After this procedure, the child requires urgent IV cannulation so that antibiotics can be administered.

Invariably, the culprit was an aggressive bacteria called *Haemophilus influenza B* (HIB). This same contagion caused another life-threatening condition called epiglottitis, a severe swelling that blocks a child's airway, and without urgent treatment causes death. These two life-threatening conditions have virtually disappeared in most developed countries due to a safe and effective multivalent vaccine now available to all infants.

These two and a half years in various hospitals were stressful but simultaneously rewarding times, with growing confidence of making my own diagnoses, and planning investigations and treatments. The pressure of hospital work was later viewed to be a worthy training ground for general practice. Going through difficulties for any of us can be hard at times and wear us down, but the principle of persevering and then later hopefully observing the associated benefits builds character.

The strain of this sort of work is tiring, with its long hours and after-hours shifts and all the expectations within the hospital system. Combine this with the emotional demands of court attendances, the birth of a child and, in particular, the loss of my mum, this took its toll on me.

But it was not just about me and how I was coping. Carol was also being forced to deal with everything I was going through, also with the demands of caring for an unsettled newborn, and being often on her own. Fortunately, there was some light ahead. I was about to transition into general practice and a new future as well as about to improve my ability to support Carol.

# CHAPTER SEVEN

# GENERAL PRACTICE

*'Nobody cares how much you know,
until they know how much you care.'*
– **Teddy Roosevelt**


*'We make a living by what we get,
we make a life by what we give.'*
– **Winston Churchill**

# The green throne

Eight years after my mission experience in Zambia, and after two years at Hornsby Hospital and a three-month paediatric term at Sydney Children's Hospital in early 1980, I commenced general practice in Lugarno in Southern Sydney.

After accepting an invitation from Dr Richard Cumming and Dr Graeme Lucas to join their partnership – to be known for the next 20 years as 'Cumming, Lucas and Franks' – I attached my brass plate to the surgery front wall. The building at 16 Lime Kiln Road had been purpose-built and when I joined a new extension incorporating my consulting room was built at the rear. I was even able to choose my own furniture. On hindsight, the desk and bookcase were rather old fashioned in appearance and for some unknown reason I believed that a large bright green, high-backed cloth executive chair with gas struts suited the smallish room. Interior design has never been a creative gift of mine!

The magnitude of that chair seemed to swallow me up. One day 'the throne' was the source of an embarrassing experience. I was in the middle of a consultation, sitting comfortably and proudly on my large throne talking across my desk to patients I was consulting, when I was suddenly aware that I was sinking, moving in slow motion towards the floor as the gas strut of the chair began to fail. The proverb 'pride comes before a fall' flashed through my mind as I kept going south. My head had reached the level of the desk before the patients stood up to peer over the top of the desk at me and check that I was alright.

Beside the harm done to my pride, I was fine and quickly moved to a safer chair to finish the consult. The green throne was soon discarded and replaced by a more appropriate and smaller black office chair with improved gas struts. This experience taught me early in my career to always be prepared to laugh at myself and my experiences when appropriate, and also to get a second opinion when selecting furniture.

## Lugarno

The Lugarno years (1980–2009) working alongside two experienced and competent doctors were formative to my learning as a result of observing them and following their example. The other doctors at Lugarno were wonderful mentors, colleagues and friends. We had no written contracts of agreement. Our relationship was based on trust and a handshake. This worked for us, but I'm not suggesting that workplace agreements dealing with long-term relationships should usually be dealt this way.

The years from 1980 to the new millennium were years in medicine vastly different from now. There were no computers, internet, smartphones, online booking systems or temperature-controlled vaccine fridges. Even fax machines were a new invention that started to be used widely in general practice for improved communication. Scripts and medical notes were all handwritten, which led to inefficiency and therefore more errors than the present digital scripts, medical notes and databases on our computer systems. Fortunately, my handwriting, although messy and occasionally illegible (a common source of scorn for all doctors), was at least reasonably fast due to six years of copious note-taking at uni.

Medicine back then was as complex as it is now, with new life-saving developments occurring rapidly, such as coronary artery bypass surgery and laparoscopic surgery. New drugs were being developed such as statins for high cholesterol, and other heart medications, which have directly led to longevity of cardiac patients and control of heart failure, as well as advances in the management of asthma, diabetes, inflammatory arthritis and depression. Novel diagnostic imaging techniques such as CT and MRI scans were developed in these early years but now are considered standard. New and advanced pathology testing was available weekly. New antibiotics were being produced and new vaccines were significantly contributing to lessening the burden of commonly seen infections and infectious diseases, such as measles, mumps, chicken pox, rubella, hepatitis A and B, pertussis and meningitis. These were remarkable new discoveries that led to improved outcomes, especially in children.

In the 1980s–1990s, a bizarre new disease was emerging and causing anxiety and death in those affected. HIV/AIDS was the latest disease, terrifying at the time to those infected and to those caring for suffering patients. It was also causing stigma to arise in the community towards those most affected. Thirty years later, there are effective treatments for this disease, reducing mortality and morbidity and improving survival. However, there is still no vaccine against the complex virus HIV. Whereas HIV/AIDS was considered by the World Health Organization (WHO) to be an epidemic I did not expect I would be facing a pandemic 40 years later that would spread by a different means, but cause similar anxiety and indiscriminate death. On this later occasion, science had advanced and was able to quickly respond with new vaccines and targeted therapies.

During the years at Lugarno, it was expected (and normal) for general practitioners (GPs) to undertake house calls, especially for emergencies. This service we provided was tiring and arduous and it was not very conducive to planned social events or family times. It certainly led to increased skills of assessing patients in urgent situations in their homes or at the surgery, depending on the problem.

In 1997, Dr Lucas moved to Port Macquarie, and with less doctors available at the practice and a growing patient load, it was not feasible to continue offering house calls. I was saddened when Graeme died in 2022 after a prolonged illness. His funeral service was a celebration of a great doctor, a man of faith, a father and a friend, who for me personally had a profound influence on my life.

By the year 2000, Dr Cumming had retired and another Lugarno GP, Dr Berry – and his practice – amalgamated with us, providing a full house of doctors and staff. Within a few years, we came under the new ownership of Mayne Health, which resulted in less administration load and being able to concentrate on consulting patients.

## A changing landscape

In my early years of medicine, there was a different perception to now of the benefits of immunisation and the protection of vaccines against infectious diseases. The risk–benefit ratio was in favour of the benefits of vaccines. A complacency has crept in as the prevalence of the diseases concerned has decreased. Many younger patients have not known or witnessed victims who have suffered the effects from many of these diseases. The internet has become a source of misinformation about the safety and efficacy of immunisation, from unreliable internet sites and with poor quality research. The internet should be a source of facts and information about the deadly diseases we are trying to prevent and eliminate. When vaccination rates around the world decrease there is an increase in disease again.

HIV was not the only infectious disease GPs had to diagnose and manage in the last few decades of the 20th century. I had patients who had to contend with congenital complications such as deafness in their children from rubella caught during their pregnancy. Trying to explain male infertility to young men who had mumps as a child, damaging their testes, is an unpleasant task. More than one patient still limps into my room with deformity and weakness of their lower limbs due to polio. As a child, I still remember my mother lining up with her children in a long queue, with many other anxious parents at Hurstville Council, to obtain the newly invented oral Salk polio vaccine. Although there were some teething issues with the original live vaccine, which had to be modified, this vaccine saved the lives of countless children.

Pertussis, a severe respiratory disease in infancy, with significant mortality and potential permanent lung damage, is another disease preventable with vaccines. Some of my patients developed cerebral damage from childhood measles or chicken pox encephalitis, others lifelong nerve pain around their faces or elsewhere from severe shingles. Some lost their lives from pneumococcal pneumonia. Then there is the high annual hospitalisation rates and sometimes death of children, pregnant women and the elderly from seasonal influenza. There are many other vaccines available that save lives daily around the world and help keep a number of diseases from entering Australia or affecting Australians while travelling overseas.

It's evident that I'm passionate about this subject. Vaccinations save lives – especially young lives in Australia and around the world, as well as the lives of the frail and elderly. They are one of the reasons for improved childhood mortality over the last 100 years and one reason why we are all living longer by approximately 13 years (that is, due to the reduction in the death rate from infectious diseases).

Some countries of the world are considered to be a 'collective society', where citizens in general just don't behave in their own best interests, but more for the good of the majority. Australia is considered an 'individualistic society'. The same sentiments and attitudes towards vaccinations raise their ugly heads each time there are outbreaks of diseases and deaths, due to preventable infections, including when a new pandemic breaks out.

## Illawong

In 2008, the Lugarno practice was forced to close down due to Mayne Health being bought out by another corporation. Not wanting to work under this new company who insisted doctors and staff move to other locations they owned, the staff at Lugarno decided to split up and either join a practice at Oatley or Illawong Christian Medical Centre.

The Illawong practice was owned by Dr Anne Gilroy, a Christian GP who lived and worked in Bathurst. She had rescued this practice years before when it was under threat of closing. She'd built it up once more. Anne needed more doctors, and I needed a place to call home, so a number of us, including another doctor, Jackie (my nurse), Amy (my practice manager) and a few receptionists, moved over. We adjusted to the new practice quickly and I became the medical coordinator and worked there for the next six years until 2015.

At that time Carol and I were particularly interested and focused on the importance of strengthening marriages and building resilient parents. This was inspired by our work alongside Ian and Mary Grant from New Zealand, who we invited to run a number of seminars on the topics in our community. Anne Gilroy allowed us complete freedom to use the medical centre to meet community needs other than just medical. We set about building and maintaining a small library where patients could freely borrow resources on marriage and parenting, and we held a number of after-hours courses in the spacious waiting room.

These included courses on parenting, the addiction of pornography and another course called 'Laugh Your Way to a Better Marriage'. This DVD series attracted a large number of couples enjoying teaching with humour. Many of the men who didn't like reading books commented on how this had significantly changed their marriages. This was encouraging to us. Another series we ran was aimed at young people called 'The Truth Project'. This was an excellent course over many weeks outlining the many areas in life where the truths of the Christian faith stacked up against prevailing worldviews of materialism, humanism and naturalism.

## A little about a lot

It has been said that a GP knows 'a little about a lot, whereas a specialist knows a lot about a little'. The complexity and varied range of conditions that we GPs face and deal with on a daily basis would terrify a specialist, but it is actually one of the enjoyable and challenging aspects about being a GP. My specialist colleagues that I refer to are, however, highly respected doctors with vast experience. I need their expertise to assist me and my patients in their specialised areas of medicine. I cherish the relationships I've made with many consultant specialists over four decades of medicine.

What makes a good GP?

A century ago I may not have even been considered a GP since I don't deliver babies or undertake appendectomies. I now do the occasional home visit but not regularly before or after surgery like GPs used to. GPs are problem-solvers, with about 15 minutes in a consultation to do this and come up with a diagnosis and a solution, or at least a rational plan to attempt to manage the complaint. Not unlike a detective, our diagnostic skills must be honed as best we can based on experience, actively listening to patient history, performing a thorough examination, arranging and ordering appropriate investigations and prescribing safely and effectively, with simultaneous consideration of the costs and explaining the risks versus the benefits of any medicine suggested. A good GP will try to balance the need to refer to a specialist if they're uncertain, versus the cost and inconvenience to the patient.

Variety is the essence of general practice, which is a double-edged sword, bringing both major challenges and rewards every day. There's no room for boredom with the range of possibilities of presentations. Every day is different, and this paradoxically makes the job stressful but also interesting and rewarding at the same time. We do not always know what we'll be presented with but we have to be committed to manage it. The types of presentations are virtually limitless. One patient may present for a routine health or skin check, a prescription repeat and BP check, the next could be a suicidal patient to be fitted in urgently, or it could be a person with a laceration requiring suturing.

In the years of COVID-19, we have had the extra concern that any of our patients could be also an asymptomatic carrier of the virus, and we had to be aware of how close or how long we had contact with them, even with both parties wearing masks.

Recent research shows depression, anxiety, relationship breakdowns, and sleep disturbance were still the most commonly seen presentations in general practice. Although we are definitely seeing more cases of mental health problems, we are also helped by more access to clinical psychologists and other mental health professionals, largely due to increased government funding.

It is my belief that we are all broken in some way – psychologically, spiritually and physically. Some more in one area than the others. We all carry baggage from our past, our upbringing, our life experiences, exposure to traumatic events and broken relationships. We all tend to take on some of our wrong perceptions from our early years through life as 'lies and assumptions' in our life that need to be traced, faced and replaced by new truths about ourselves. (A helpful book to read on this is *Telling Yourself the Truth* – by psychologist William Bacchus.)

Perceptions and assumptions are not always aligned with reality. We each could do with 'a check-up from the neck up' at different times of our lives and be challenged on how we think, and clean up some of our faulty thinking. These experiences often require trauma counselling and psychological interventions to attempt to give insights and methods to cope with the issues, and new ways of thinking.

Realising my need to improve my counselling skills many years ago, along with my wife, I attended two counselling courses. The first course run by a psychologist at the Institute of Pastoral Counselling was more academic and had an emphasis on theories of counselling. We also learnt to always be aware of hearing both sides of a story. This was supported by another helpful Bible proverb 'Every story sounds true until someone tells the other side and sets the record straight.'

Another course Carol and I undertook that proved to be helpful in our daily lives, relationships, and in dealing with patients, taught more pragmatic content that gave insights to people. An insight for anxiety could be, for example: 'Is this experience you are describing unbearable, or just unpleasant?' Another insight for someone with addictive behaviour might be: 'If you choose this behaviour – you choose the outcomes', or 'If you always do what you have always done – you will always get what you have always got.'

# Wholistic care and continuity of care

Patients deserve more than just knowledge. They need personal care. Continuity of care has and must always remain a hallmark of general practice. Care for others is for the whole of their life: from the management of health in children to palliative end-of-life care. This leads to confidence and trust, earned over decades of simply just being there and being consistent. Research of many professions shows that society in general rates the medical profession near the top of the list when it comes to trust, but trust needs always to be earned, especially in our vocation with so much at stake.

Sadly, there are exceptions with doctors undermining this trust and being involved in inappropriate behaviour. This tarnishes the whole profession. We can rightly address this by removing offenders from being able to practice medicine. When that trust is broken it can be devastating, just as in any other life relationship. To try to prevent a fracture in relationships of trust by being accused of wrong behaviour, I've tried to protect my integrity and character by having photos of my wife and family in my room, which is a daily reminder of the people whose integrity I am also upholding. Having a chaperone present when undertaking sensitive examinations, especially with younger females, has been another way to protect myself and my patients. It also shows that I take these matters seriously.

General practice is about having conversations with people. It's about building relationships that can last a lifetime and be generational. I have a number of families that I care for, care that has now extended to four generations. General practice for me has been an exciting place to be. It has been a wonderful career where I've had the opportunity to make a difference in individual lives, but also a wider influence into families, society and population health.

The rewards of general practice come with a long list of responsibilities that can at times be overwhelming.

There is a need to respect all people irrespective of their background, colour, race, sexuality, age, behaviour and emotional health. Another obligation is to maintain integrity in my behaviour and words, and being thorough and spending the same amount of time and effort with each patient as if they were someone in my own family.

Trying to stay on time for appointments is another responsibility, and in general a reasonable expectation of patients. It's an ambitious aim for the GP that is not always achieved due to a combination of multiple unexpected interruptions: from emergencies, to phone calls from other health workers, as well as patient factors, when they overlook the time I need to deal with their presenting problems.

Fortunately for both general practice and patients, we have a health system that other countries envy and that allows the continuity of care mentioned above. Despite some frustrations with the system, recent global health research of 27 countries shows the majority of Australians rated the quality of healthcare to which they have access the highest of any other country. Although at times we tend to take it for granted, we are so fortunate to have such a comprehensive health system. Medicare, as a government-funded insurance scheme, allows all Australian citizens to access quality healthcare, which many countries of the world do not provide.

## Art and science

The Hippocratic Oath to which we abide as doctors of medicine states, 'Into whatsoever houses I enter, I will do so to help the sick, keeping myself free from all intentional wrongdoing and harm…'

In the practice of medicine there is no room for intentional wrongdoing and harm. To protect the patient and ourselves, there are now evidence-based guidelines in most areas of medicine, produced by various reliable resources that we can refer to, which were not freely available when I started practising as a GP. Although these guidelines are helpful and reassuring to lessen possible unintentional harm, they do have the potential to lead to over-investigating and treatment to be sure we have not missed anything. They don't cover every situation or predicament we come across. There are always exceptions that guidelines may not cover, be it diagnoses or management, and that's where the art of medicine from one's experience is helpful.

It is in the area of knowledge that the science of medicine is materialised. It's in the working out of this knowledge with real patients, on a long-term basis, and with experience that produces 'the art'. Wisdom (the correct application of knowledge) plus sincere caring are fundamental to our profession.

Medicine is an art and a science working alongside each other simultaneously. I well remember one of my best diagnoses that was life-saving that exemplifies this concept. An older, well-known patient had just returned from an overseas trip and he had developed watery diarrhoea. The logic and science of this presentation would have been that this was most likely traveller's diarrhoea, so the guidelines would have suggested to investigate and treat with various antibiotics or anti-parasite medicines, and to follow up if there was no improvement.

Experience (the 'art') made me stop and explore further in light of his age, combined with additional information that the diarrhoea had been there just before he left, which made me suspicious that something else was going on. A rectal examination is disliked by patients (as well as the one doing the examination), but it is at times an essential means to a diagnosis, as it was in this case. I found a 'hard rectal mass with velvety prongs', a classical textbook description of a malignant villous adenoma, which was soon surgically removed, curing this problem and saving the patient's life.

Striving for the balance of 'art versus science' does not equate to being perfect or faultless. I've made some mistakes in my career that I regret and have learnt from. But there is a big difference between neglect and accident, the latter occurring due to the fact that we are human, and humans make mistakes. The quote, 'Mistakes are not fatal, they are just an opportunity to learn' may be true with situations in life that have less serious consequences, but in dealing with people's health a mistake can be fatal. Fortunately, this has not been my experience.

Evidence and common sense suggests if one makes a mistake in medicine, the only way to deal with it is to be honest, admit it and apologise. It is essential that the person responsible for the mistake attempts to correct it if possible, and attend to any consequences or costs associated. Depending on the seriousness of the mistake, patients in general can accept this and offer forgiveness and allow the built trust and care to continue.

Some mistakes in my medical career have been relatively minor and embarrassing. Sometimes they are not through actions or behaviour, but rather through words.

One of these occasions occurred late on a Friday afternoon when consulting a new male patient with an ingrown toenail. Feeling tired at the end of a long week, but at the same time trying to appear interested and competent in his foot problem, I meant to ask what I thought was a relevant question: 'Do you pick your toes?' but unfortunately the words came out quite different: 'Do you pick your nose?' It only takes a microsecond to realise a mistake in word selection, and wait for the response back from the patient, which was on this occasion: 'No, do you?'

'No, not usually,' I sheepishly replied, trying to turn the embarrassing situation into a humorous one. I went on to discuss his management if he desired. I'm not quite sure why, but I never saw him again for follow-up on his nail problem or any other complaint for that matter!

I can relate to the words of the late Prince Philip, Duke of Edinburgh, who stated, 'After fifty-nine years of experience I feel it is tempting to give advice.' After 45 years of medical experience it is also 'tempting' to give advice to both patients and other doctors with less experience. The problem is knowing when to be confident to give that advice and to remain humble that sometimes one does not know and will never know everything about medicine and the body and how it works and fails. Medicine continues to advance: with increased awareness of how various organs function; with increased knowledge about the complexity of the physiology and biochemistry of the body at a microscopic level; with rapid advancements of treatment modalities from medicines to interventional procedures. The longer I work in this field, the more I realise how much more there is to learn.

# Teaching

When I entered general practice, I didn't expect to be involved in teaching, nor the various opportunities that would arise. As a medical student, part of my training was a number of weeks sitting under the supervision of a GP to experience what general practice was all about. This exposure was so appreciated that when I became a GP it was a pleasure to also supervise a number of final year medical students and give them the same encouragement and practical insights that I had been given as a student. It has been rewarding and satisfying when one of these students has returned years later and accepted a position working within my practice as a fully qualified doctor, as James did in 2022.

Other teaching opportunities involved high school students undertaking work experience in my medical practice and more recently when supervising GP registrars for 6–12 months at a time. These young doctors are in their final years of GP training and their learning needs, such as skin cancer identification and minor surgery, are focused on. After the training term and their attainment of Fellowship of the College of General Practice, they can be offered positions in a practice if the doctors desire to join. I've been fortunate that three so far have stayed and have added considerable value to my practice.

Teaching can take many different forms. It can be presentations to men's groups or conferences, teaching about preventative health, or it can include visiting preschools to talk to young children about what happens when they visit a doctor. Using props such as gloves blown up like a 'cow's udder', or arms bandaged and in slings, as well as role-playing, it has been a joy seeing children gain some understanding and confidence in the topic of medicine. My children thought it was special when I visited their preschool. I had a sense of deja vu when I repeated this with some of my grandchildren.

When it comes to teaching, patients are not exempt to being educated and informed about their conditions. Knowing that my elderly patients sometimes forget what I've discussed with them after leaving, I learned to write lists and notes for them. This required particular attention to producing a legible note as neatly as possible (an impossibility, some would argue) and then getting the patient to read through the list to make sure they not only could read it but understood the instruction.

Unfortunately, I sometimes forgot this last step and it has had some interesting consequences. On one particular occasion an elderly man had a low iron level and on enquiring how often he ate red meat, it was apparent that he needed to increase his intake to prevent anaemia. I emphasised that he should try to eat lean red meat three times per week and I wrote that down on his list – or so I thought. He returned six weeks later having put on weight, and his upset wife could no longer cope with or afford cooking red meat for him three times per day! Shocked with what they were doing, I emphasised that I had said three times per week, and she then produced the evidence: my legible note saying, 'three serves per day'. No projection of blame was appropriate since it was all mine, but some justification was reasonable. Needless to say, his iron levels returned to normal!

# QUM

Working in general practice for so long and with an interest in medication management and what is referred to as the 'quality use of medicines' (QUM) led me into some unexpected opportunities. I felt strongly about the need to use medicines carefully and wisely, especially antibiotics, with an emphasis of 'maximising benefit and minimising harm', and endeavouring to balance risk of side effects against benefits of a particular medicine.

I was aware of the threat of growing antibiotic resistance and the need for antibiotic stewardship. I accepted a GP representative position on the St George Hospital Pharmacy Committee, as well on the local public health unit QUM group. QUM means choosing a medicine that is appropriate for the reason of the prescribing and to make sure it is safe, efficacious (that it actually works) as well as considering its cost to the patient and the government.

As a result of my involvement on these committees, I was asked to be the Australian GP consultant to the newly established NPS (National Prescribing Service), a federal-government-funded initiative and organisation that had a proficient reputation for its unbiased advice and being independent of pharmaceutical companies on all details of medicines to consumers, doctors and pharmacists. It provided evidence-based information for these three groups to encourage safe use of medicines throughout Australia, with the aim of helping produce rational prescribers, competent dispensers and well-informed patients and, as a result, minimise harm to patients. This 20 year relationship from 1998–2018 was an enjoyable and challenging time for me, involved in preparing NPS facilitators who visited GPs throughout Australia to educate them on various medication-related topics. This gave me the ability to contribute to the big picture of improved population health as well as the individual health of my own patients. When I consider the past subtle influences of pharmaceutical companies over decades on the prescribing patterns of doctors, using lunch visits and conferences, the NPS changed the landscape of this behaviour by encouraging regulations and restrictions that are still fortunately in operation.

Unexpectedly, I was honoured to be chosen as the sole GP representative on the writing group for Therapeutic Guidelines of Australia on the subject of antibiotics. This group consisted of 15 infectious disease specialists and one lonely GP (feeling way out of his depth) who met monthly in Melbourne over two years. The group was chosen every three to four years to rewrite the guidelines for all doctors and pharmacists in Australia, as to which antibiotics should be prescribed and dispensed for any infections encountered in the community or in hospitals. This humbling opportunity allowed me to work alongside some of the best and brightest doctors in Australia who meticulously study all the research and evidence on infectious diseases. Recommendations from this group on safe antibiotic prescribing have the sole purpose of protecting all Australians from the threat of rapidly increasing antibiotic resistance of organisms and a potential future return to a pre-antibiotic era.

I was privileged to be a GP representative for three editions of the well-known reference book *Antibiotic* that most Australian doctors and pharmacists refer to on a daily basis in general practice and hospitals in Australia and overseas (especially developing countries). This again gave me a great sense of achievement through being able to contribute to improved health for all Aussies.

I believe God has given me these unexpected opportunities in medicine in a much larger and influential context than just general practice, with the purpose of helping others.

## Sutherland

In 2015, I was offered an opportunity to establish a new medical practice at Sutherland, in a purpose-designed and renovated premises, that is now called 'Shire Family Medical'. I commenced as the only GP and had the support of my nurse, my previous practice manager and a number of new receptionists.

I've always been an admirer of the concept of the 'Three Cs' for team members. It was always emphasised in job interviews that the values of 'competence, chemistry and most importantly character' were paramount in anyone joining our team. These values have allowed me to build a team that I can work with in trust and confidence, along with the comfortable assurance that conflict should be minimal, work ethics strong and the work environment enjoyable for all involved.

Jackie, my nurse, has been an incredibly loyal and faithful employee, who has worked with me in all three medical practice locations since 2000 (Lugarno, Illawong, Sutherland). Not only is she a competent nurse, she's a dependable work colleague and trusted friend. Such is our mutual involvement over 23 years that she can literally 'read my mind' as to what I need, whether that be preparing my next patient for minor surgery, giving a needed immunisation or other type of injection, or even making me a barista style coffee! She has a fine balance of compassion and assertiveness when appropriate... as a young man she found looking for drugs in her room found out!

Her competency with infection control, with double sterilising of all surgical instruments, would repeatably lead to praise at our three yearly inspections by auditors, for our compulsory practice accreditation. Jackie's dedication was highlighted one evening years ago when our vaccine fridge had a fault and our cold chain logger showed we had limited time to remove all vaccines to another location. Unbeknownst to myself, Jackie had already left and arrived home to prepare her family's meal. When she became aware of the problem, she immediately turned around and brought her large esky back and rescued our stock.

Jackie also volunteers as an RFS firefighter and spent a horrifying summer at the end of 2019 fighting bushfires in many locations (and thus started 2020 exhausted). She did not predict having to face a pandemic with her role as lead nurse in infection control, vaccine ordering, preparation and administration for the years that followed. Wanting to value her contributions to the community for wearing 'both hats', I nominated her for a Sutherland Shire Council community award at the end of 2021 with a successful and well-deserved outcome.

For 20 years I worked in general practice without a nurse, and looking back I wonder how I coped without this support. Nurses are an essential part of a practice. They are an extension of the GP with many extra skills that we GPs don't possess.

When you work with staff, other GPs and specialist colleagues for so long, you experience the good and the hard times of each other's lives. In general practice, you also get to experience similar times in most of your patient's lives as well and together Jackie and I have witnessed: the birth of children; the passing of loved ones; the struggles and disappointments with illness and age; and the suffering of others.

From 2015 to the present day at Sutherland, I've been fortunate to build a team that comprises six GPs, two nurses, a practice manager, a dietitian, a pathology collector and four gracious receptionists. I'm privileged at the time of writing to still be leading such an effective group of healthcare workers, who daily serve our local community and beyond, in all that general practice offers, as well as specialising in services such as disabled care, drug and alcohol care, Long Covid, aged-care, skin cancer and minor surgery.

Former New Zealand Prime Minister Jacinda Ardern said about leadership, 'In leadership you can be kind but strong, empathetic but decisive, optimistic yet focused.' What an excellent list of attributes to strive for in any organisation, including general practice.

## Sacrifice

Although many associate practising medicine as a sacrifice, this was not a suitable description of my experience, rather it should be considered apportioned to my wife and children. There is a significant unseen and unspoken burden and sacrifice made by others, which is inevitable if a physician is to do their job efficiently. For 45 years (less years for my children), my family has had to tolerate interruptions and delays to our usual weekly family schedule. It was Carol who had to work and support me when doing my uni degree. She spent the first few months with our first newborn baby on her own, as we had just moved into a new home and a new suburb. My mum's death a few weeks prior to Justin being born was such a difficult time for us both, with me also undertaking the compulsory long hours working in the Hornsby and Campbelltown hospitals.

It was Carol who was also woken in the middle of the night for the after-hours urgent calls, and then remaining awake waiting for me to arrive safely back home, sometimes being the one to listen to me debrief about what I'd just had to deal with. Carol and the kids spent many hours waiting outside the surgery for me to finish work since we only had one car. She read many books to Justin while waiting, and there was one occasion when Carol witnessed an armed robbery at the pharmacy next to the surgery, which was quite a traumatic experience for her.

Then there was the sacrifice of nights alone while I had to attend intermittent evenings after work at obligatory medical education meetings and for the years with the pandemic in the headlines. I had stayed up at night to concentrate on upskilling and seeking information from a number of medical sources on COVID-19. Understandably, the sacrifices of being the wife to a doctor are significant, but on the upside Carol says she has always loved having a doctor in the home. She sees that the years of interruptions in her life have been somewhat compensated for by having someone to attend to the injuries and illnesses as they occurred in our direct and extended family.

So frequent and unavoidable were these interruptions over the decades that I thought Carol would become resentful of them but, in fact, her beautiful heart for others has given her the grace and patience needed to not let these interfere with our marriage, something I'm extremely thankful for.

I'm grateful that she really meant it when she stated publicly on 29 November 1975 'for better, or for worse'.

## Endless empathy

In 1995, just a few days before Christmas, I had to undertake the most difficult home visit I have ever done. It was for my patient, Mary Cusumano, whose husband had been killed the night before in their shop – the Gamesmen. Ange Senior was a wonderful family man, a gentle giant, a person who had a warm smile and friendly persona. He had been working during the evening with other staff and his young son Ange Junior when an armed robbery took place. Ange tried to protect his son and the other staff and lost his life doing so.

As I was walking to the front door I was thinking where I would start to find the words to bring comfort to Mary. In certain life situations, there is inadequacy of words to express our emotions, and this was one of them. I even wondered why I was carrying my medical bag with me, as it contained no instruments or medicines that would make any difference.

Usually, hugging patients is kept to a minimum for concern of misinterpretation, but on this occasion there was no other management for the tangible grief other than to embrace in tears and utter the words, 'Oh Mary, I am so sorry.'

In the ensuing 28 years, I have been supporting Mary and the ever-expanding Cusamano families of her four children. Some consultations involved listening to how she was going and assisting her in the grieving. I've only had one other patient become a victim of homicide, an older man in Lugarno and a case of mistaken identity when he answered his front door.

Understandably, some individuals or families can become bitter victims of their experience, which leads to a deterioration in their physical and mental health. Mary and her family continued to operate and build Ange Senior's business, which now employs many of the family full time, and they've diverted their grief into action for others by being part of a multimillion dollar development of a large accommodation and counselling complex called Grace's Place. (Grace was the mother of Anita Cobby, who was a young victim of a shocking homicide.) It is inspiring to all when an individual like Mary and her family can turn a tragedy into triumph and provide healing to future generations of children, who will sadly go through the same ordeal. At the opening of Grace's Place in February 2023, there was much emotion expressed, but this time they were tears of joy and relief mixed with sadness.

I reflected as to why I was so emotional on this latter occasion, and understood that I was vicariously feeling the trauma of one of my patients again. I was reminded of the grief and loss of Mary's husband, Ange.

Not many in their working life have the opportunities afforded to them as a family doctor, being an intimate and trusted part of people's lives. I continue to count this work, not just as a responsibility but as an enormous privilege. Dr Albert Schweitzer, a German medical missionary who was inspired by the concept of service and love, said, 'Success is not the key to happiness. Happiness is the key to success. If you love what you are doing, you will be successful.'

For 45 years, the enjoyment and satisfaction of what I do on a daily basis, and its accompanying challenges and rewards, is what makes it easy to get out of bed every morning and go to work. There is a limited list of vocations where the opportunity to holistically help others brings such blessing and 'refreshment' in doing so.

# CHAPTER EIGHT

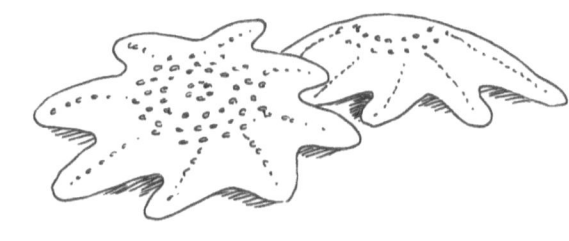

# MEDICINE AND MISSION

'We share the same world, but we do not share the same opportunities.'
– Queen Elizabeth II

'Do not withhold good from those who deserve it, when it is in your power to help them.'
– Proverbs 3:27

# Medicine and mission

Mixing medicine and mission work may at first glance sound rather adventurous and even glamorous saving less fortunate lives in difficult circumstances. The reality is, even although very rewarding for the participant, the work and outcomes can be arduous, stressful, frustrating and even dangerous (including loss of life).

In August 1973, my sister Carolyn and her husband Dr Graeme Lucas and their young son Andrew set off on a mission experience to Zambia, South-Central Africa for a number of years. They decided to transit via North India to visit Graeme's brother, Dr Walter Lucas, who was working as a missionary doctor for The Salvation Army in remote Dharawal with his wife and three small children. On the day they arrived, Walter unfortunately developed acute appendicitis, requiring urgent surgery at the small hospital he was working at. With only one other doctor available to do the appendicectomy, his brother Graeme had to give the general anaesthetic. Sadly Walter, aged 33, died of a cardiac arrest during surgery, leaving both families devastated.

I recall how I felt when I heard the news of this traumatic event and the loss of a highly regarded and admired Christian mission doctor when I was a second year medical student. I'd been encouraged by his example to study medicine.

The impact of Walter's death while on mission, and how he died, produced some subconscious concerns about the risks on the mission field. It prompted me years later to have a prophylactic appendicectomy simultaneously with a colonoscopy before one of my Rwandan mission trips in 2018.

# Africa

Africa has always held a special place in my life – a continent famous for its sense of adventure, wild animals, widespread poverty, numerous countries with dictators and corruption, apartheid and a complex and fascinating history. There is the association with childhood adventure heroes from *Tarzan* and *Jungle Jim* on TV shows to the real life adventure stories into deepest darkest Africa of physicians and explorers such as Dr David Livingstone and Dr Albert Schweitzer.

Most of us can relate to being told as young children by our parents that we should appreciate our food and not waste any since there were millions of starving children in Africa that would love to have as much to eat as we did. When hearing this hyperbole, I encouraged my parents to send them my brussel sprouts and other disliked vegetables.

More importantly, Africa is a continent with warm, friendly and humble people and the cutest children whose contentment and happiness does not depend on material possessions.

These days, missions to Africa mostly comprises of short-term mission (STM) groups from around the world, visiting for limited periods, which understandably produces questions and criticism of their limited effectiveness. It is healthy to reflect on this, so that our mission work does not become a hindrance, rather a benefit. Some would argue that if the finance spent by individual STM volunteers was collectively sent directly to the recipients of our ventures, it could be more effective.

The value of my repeated visits to Africa was clarified by the comments of just one man – Ben Kayumba, a Rwandan, and one of the most humble men I have ever met. He said in a public meeting to us, 'The most precious gift you can give us is your presence.' Effectively meaning that as you care enough to travel halfway around the world to serve them, is the greatest gift you can give. That one sentence made my repeated mission trips to Africa all worthwhile and inspired me to continue as long as I am able.

## Zambia

My first sojourn to this mysterious continent and my first overseas travel occurred in 1973 aged 20 at the end of my second year in medicine.

I had the great privilege and opportunity to work alongside my brother-in law, Dr Graeme Lucas, at Chikankata, a renowned two doctor Salvation Army hospital and secondary school in rural central Africa. Graeme was there on a full-time mission with his wife Carolyn (my sister) and their first son, Andrew. Having recently experienced the trauma of Walter's death in India, they arrived in Zambia, and they had only been there a month when I arrived to spend time on mission.

This tragic experience was the background on which this Australian family had to commence their mission work and at the same time adjust to the culture shock of village life in isolated rural Africa. In those years, not much was known about the importance of trauma counselling and, unfortunately, they did not have access to this, or the ability to have a period of grieving for a major loss before commencing their work on the field.

On the way to Zambia, I travelled through Johannesburg, South Africa and was escorted by a Salvation Army officer to Soweto where I observed firsthand the ugliness of apartheid and the inequality of life for black Africans living in abject poverty. I observed how distant this was to the living standards of the 'whites' in the same country. It was disconcerting to even observe in a Salvation Army church meeting the forced (by government) segregation based on the colour of one's skin.

Chikankata was a few hours' drive on rough dirt roads from Lusaka, the capital of Zambia. My first night's attempt to sleep is still a vivid memory, feeling quite fearful of the unfamiliar sounds and smells emanating from the villages surrounding the hospital and school complex. There was shouting of villagers, barking dogs, the smell of open cooking fires in typical Africa village huts and, of course, the sounds of wild animals that may have been lurking – even though the latter were more imagined than real!

The six week experience working in and observing the diseases and conditions seen in a remote African hospital was not only eye-opening but life-changing. I was mentored by the two high-quality doctors working there. One was Graeme and the other was Dr Paul du Plessis, a very experienced and skilled man who, with his wife, had lost a child themselves on the mission field. The two doctors would work together in the hospital and outpatients during the day, and take it in turns to be on call after-hours. They undertook many procedures in difficult circumstances and tackled most surgical cases.

Having studied and enjoyed anatomy in the uni year just completed, I was fascinated by the relevance of this discipline when observing the effects of the disease of leprosy in the dedicated clinic attached to the hospital, where the identification of nerves and muscles affected by this microorganism was essential. Leprosy has biblical connotations and it gave me new perspectives on the importance of pain awareness that we are born with – our inherent warning system.

Bono from U2 is a famous Christian singer whose lyrics in one of his songs says: 'The only pain is to feel nothing at all'. The lack of pain perception in those suffering from leprosy challenges the common criticism and confronting question of why God allows us to experience pain.

Victims of leprosy develop this disease (an infection with the leprosy bacterium) as a result of living in dirty and dusty surroundings. Once leprosy develops, it affects the peripheral nerves so the victim can't feel pain in their extremities. Because the damaged peripheral nerves innervate muscles, they can't withdraw their limbs from painful stimuli. The result was suffering terrible injuries such as burns to fingers and hands because they could not feel the heat from the cooking fires in their huts, nor could they feel the rats nibbling at their toes at night, which then became infected and required amputating, along with the fingers and toes from the burns.

This gave me a new appreciation of not only the need to understand the anatomy and physiology of the body, but the relevance to disease pathologies that I would have to treat in my career in medicine. It also reinforced my understanding of what I had read in the Bible that 'we are fearfully and wonderfully made'. Karl Faase (a well known Australian Christian commentator) correctly suggests, 'Both physical and emotional pain let us know when we are in danger. God created us with emotional and physical systems that tell us when we are in danger. Thank God for the challenge and the gift that pain is for you'.

I quickly learnt the benefits of immunisation to the children of the world, when I saw firsthand the many devastating illnesses and infectious diseases that vaccinations can prevent. These diseases cause significant morbidity and mortality, especially in the developing world. There is high infant mortality in most African countries because of the prevalence of infectious diseases that affect children. This explains why any travel to Africa necessitates the largest number of immunisations for the traveller compared with anywhere else in the world.

I soon learnt to love the African people with their warm humility, beaming white smiles, their resilience, simple happiness and contentment despite circumstances of poverty, and the lack of basic privileges such as nutritious food, clean running water, sanitation, basic healthcare and even justice and security.

During this time in Zambia, I clearly witnessed the dedication and competency of Christian doctors, nurses and teachers, who had forgone a more affluent lifestyle and position of influence in the West to serve those less fortunate just because they were born in a different latitude and were victims of an unjust distribution of the world's wealth.

It is a common criticism of God that he cannot be 'loving', otherwise He would not allow poverty and starvation. The response to this criticism is that poverty and starvation has come about in the world largely to man's greed – and there are few places on Earth that reveal this more than Africa.

These experiences and observations cemented in me a desire to try to be obedient to God's calling in my life, and I believe this desire has led to wonderful opportunities over four decades and has allowed me to feel truly 'refreshed' during my career.

# Uganda

It was not until 2017 that I was able to return to Africa, this time with Carol. We went with a small group from our church to work at Watoto village in Kampala, Uganda (Watoto means 'children' in Swahili).

The Watoto project saved thousands of orphans from living on the streets by placing them in groups of six other orphans and with an adopted mother who had been widowed. A house was built for each family of seven, who were each provided with food and free education at purpose-built primary and secondary schools. Our team of six mission workers had the task of helping build a new home for a family and provide the funds for all the materials involved over the two weeks. It was very satisfying to know what help had been provided for a family in need – to be given a hope of a better life, and children who had been given the gift of a loving mother. The house we had made of bricks became a home of love.

The visit also gave me the opportunity to work in the medical clinic of the school and in the infant clinic, assisting with rescued abandoned and malnourished babies. We even met 'Ronald–Reagan'. Two of the abandoned boys aged about two years were found wandering the wards of Kampala Hospital. They were unrelated but found friendship and security together in the wards. They were brought to the nursery with unknown identities, so one was nicknamed 'Ronald' and the other 'Reagan', due to their inseparability. Their destiny was to grow up as brothers in one of the homes with a new mother and family. Some readers may remember the Watoto Children's Choirs that toured Australia annually in the pre-COVID-19 years. This experience in Uganda also assisted me when it came time to visit another African nation.

## Rwanda – 'A country of a thousand hills'

To understand the profound effect on someone visiting Rwanda and working alongside its people, one has to understand some of its history and, in particular, its infamous genocide and how that eventuated. Between April and June 1994, and largely unknown to the world, an estimated one million Rwandans were killed in the space of 100 days of terror. Most of the dead were from the Tutsi tribe – and most of those who perpetrated the violence were from the Hutu tribe.

This was not just a short history of unrest that precipitated the genocide, rather decades of unrest since colonial days and inflammatory infiltration of French influence in the Hutu population in the years preceding 1994.

After the shooting down of the president's plane in Kigali, the presidential guard immediately initiated a campaign of retribution. Within hours, recruits were dispatched all over the country to carry out a wave of slaughter. The early organisers included military officials, politicians and businessmen, but soon others joined the mayhem. Organised gangs of government soldiers and militias hacked their way through the Tutsi population with machetes. The gangs even killed Tutsi in churches that they thought were safe.

Rwandans were largely abandoned by the international community, in particular the five member security council of the UN, which included France, who had vested interests (including their language) in Rwanda and who were the main suppliers of weapons used by the Hutus. Decades later, President Clinton apologised for not taking strong action early in the genocide and allowing a million people to die, thousands to become orphaned and millions more to suffer. Most of the UN troops withdrew after the murder of 10 Belgian soldiers who had tried to protect the prime minister. Their sacrifice is still honoured by monuments in Kigali that have been put in place next to bullet-ridden shelters they defended.

Tutsi refugees in Uganda formed the Rwandan Patriotic Front (RPF), led by Paul Kagame. The day after the president's death, the RPF renewed their assault from surrounding countries and, in July, captured Kigali. Soon after, the government collapsed and the RPF declared a ceasefire.

Paul Kagame became president in 1994. He has been unanimously elected as president ever since. Irrespective of various opinions about him, there appears to be overwhelming support by the population for his leadership, which has brought stability, peace, security and economic prosperity for the last 26 years.

The titles Hutu and Tutsi were replaced by everyone being referred to equally as Rwandans. Justice courts were set up from 1994 to 2014 in Arusha, Tanzania to trial, judge and punish known perpetrators. Reconciliation and forgiveness community courts in local neighbourhoods across the country were established, allowing victims and perpetrators to meet, justice to be given, with offenders encouraged to repent their wrongdoing and ask for forgiveness from those they had harmed. This powerful practice is based on Christian ethics and has allowed this nation and its people to move forward and become an example to the world.

What I have observed over many years brings reality to the wise statement: 'Peace is not the absence of conflict but the presence of a reconciling spirit.' The pain, loss and grief are still felt, and still very real, but acts of repentance and forgiveness are occurring and were witnessed each visit I made, both in public meetings and individual interactions and relationships.

Another change in Rwanda was the commencement of compulsory monthly Saturdays called 'Umuganda' whereby everyone in the nation ceases any form of work and comes together to work towards improving their local community, producing social cohesion and support of each other. Rwanda has become a collective society, working together for the sake of the country – unlike most Western countries being individualistic societies.

I first visited Rwanda in 2012 with feelings of uncertainty and knowing the unstable history. This beautiful country is the size of Tasmania with a population of about 11 million people.

This first mission trip was part of a comprehensive team from Caringbah Baptist Church (CBC) led by an early childhood teacher with experience in Rwanda – Michele Black, who was ironically nicknamed 'Blackie'. My role was to lead a medical team including two nurses and two doctors with the desired goal of undertaking health assessments on 350 children – nursery and primary in the Fruits of Hope Academy School in Kigali. These children generally had not had any medical checks in the past and possibly not even at birth.

The overall team consisted of a teaching team, administration staff, a building team and sewing team, each with skills ready to be put to use in the school and surrounding community.

Because of our cultural awareness training, we could not just assume we knew all that our hosts needed and that we had all the solutions and answers. It has been our desire and intention to ask our hosts what the community's needs were and how we could meet those needs, especially if they were not able to be met from local people and resources.

Although each team member was responsible for their own travel and accommodation expenses, as a team we raised funds for months prior to leaving that would be used for expenses in the field to help with the material needs of the school and the church. I was particularly moved when some of my patients became aware of some of those needs and donated significant finance to be used in Rwanda.

I personally met for the first time a visionary and humble Christian man – Fred Buyinza. He was the headmaster of the school who dreamt of building a school. I was also introduced to the charismatic and jovial Bishop James – the brother of Fred and the senior pastor of affiliated church Revival Palace, positioned next to the school.

Fred and James are both warm, loveable characters with wide, beaming African smiles. It was evident over the eight years of visiting that James loved the congregation he'd been given to pastor. Fred was devoted to his teachers and students that he'd been given the privilege to teach, mentor and educate in a Christian environment. James has always cherished his herd of cows which, when we first visited, were housed in an adjoining paddock next to the church. Apparently on more than one occasion, cows would put their heads through the windows of the church, to the familiarity of the usual congregation, but to the astonishment of the visitors.

Over the years, as we grew to know Fred and James in much deeper relationships – they became like extended family, not just friends. We also grew in admiration of their resilience and love of God and His people. We were often moved to hear their own personal stories and sacrifice in life – both pre- and post-genocide.

Fred understood the importance of education to guide children into a meaningful and self-sufficient adulthood. Born in 1971, he later became a refugee from his own country, fleeing to Uganda, missing out on an education in refugee camps. On returning to his homeland, Fred was determined to catch up on his education and so enrolled in Grade 3 in primary school at the age of 12. He was much older and taller than all the other students. That experience and determination were to become the springboards to the Fruits of Hope Academy. Fred's achievements are many, and it has always been encouraging to observe what he has achieved – not the least him being fluent in four languages: English, French, Kinyarwanda and Swahili.

We set about check-ups for every child in the school and then to attempt to resource local medical and dental help for children where problems were found. The children ranged from three-year-olds, whose cuteness with their curly hair, large white eyes and shorts that touched the ground endeared the attention of the whole team, and the other end of the spectrum with the 6th grade primary students, who at 12 years of age often towered over me.

The only way to achieve a thorough assessment of every child over two weeks was the well-planned organisation and administration of a production line in the small school library with open metal windows and concrete floors.

Fortunately, one of the team members had the administrative skills and biomedical qualifications to organise a personal record for each child, with their name, class and age. I observed Lyndal Salter step into this organising in such a proficient and loving way, that later on with our return to Australia and with my commencement of a new medical practice at Sutherland in 2015, she became an obvious choice to be given an invitation to become one of our medical receptionists. If she could make a health system work from basics to what we achieved in Rwanda that first year, and the many years following, I was confident of her abilities in the Australian general practice health system. She provided the same high-quality work in my practice, especially during COVID-19 times (whilst missing the African missions she co-led with me for nearly a decade).

The first station in our production line was for one team member to record a child's weight, height and head circumference and to plot these on WHO percentile graphs. This was recorded so as to observe for outliers that might suggest malnutrition, short statue, and poor brain growth. Over the years these measurements were added to records and students progressive growth checked. The next port of call in our system was a team member checking eyesight on an iPad app to look for visual defects. This procedure was not short of difficulties due to understanding of language and shyness of most children, especially the younger ones who spoke with the softest voice. At station three, each child's hearing was tested using a crude 'whisper test'. In later years, we upgraded by using an app on our iPads.

After this preliminary screening, one of the doctors assessed the information obtained and undertook a thorough examination of each child, allowing for as much privacy as possible by setting up some makeshift screens. The examination needed to be thorough and complete and cover all body systems. Eye checks included testing for squints; ears for thick obstructing wax, hearing loss and middle ear infections and perforations; listening to the heart for murmurs and to lungs checking for asthma; the abdomen for malabsorption, organ enlargement, hernias (which were common); and testes being fully descended. Needless to say, this part of the examination had to be done discretely and sensitively with parent permission, but also where one other adult was present in the room.

It was necessary to have these examinations despite the difficulties. I found a number of previously undiagnosed cases of bilateral undescended testes. If these are not surgically brought down into the scrotum by the age of eight, the child may be infertile in later years. I still recall the tears of joy from a mother after her son had surgery that we had arranged and paid for because she realised the importance of her child's fertility, especially as a male. This straightforward surgery changed the trajectory of her son's life.

There is a well-known story of a boy who made a life-giving difference to a starfish he found stranded on a beach, which to me was an analogy of this experience. (Refer to Appendix B 'The Boy and the Starfish' for the full starfish story.)

In the context of overseas missions, some might wonder whether there's any impact on the overall situation of helping the masses. There is still an importance in helping just one person, as this can have an indirect impact on the whole population, or make a generational change for that particular individual.

After this 'round robin' of examination stations, children were classified into either 'no problems identified' or 'needing further attention'. This could be a further check of the following: their vision by an optometrist or an ophthalmologist; referral to one of only 11 dentists in Rwanda for dental caries; referral to a surgeon for surgery indicated for a range of conditions (in particular, large umbilical hernias) or referral to a reliable paediatrician for malabsorption, heart murmurs and other general medical complaints requiring the back up of this speciality. Because there was so much dental disease and severe caries, we educated every child in the school to avoid sugar in their diet (difficult when their drink brought to school was usually soft drink, and most brought unhealthy snacks and lollipops) and each year we reminded them to clean their teeth daily. My dentist Dr Brett Taylor generously supplied us with 300 hundred toothbrushes and toothpaste tubes before each visit so that each child received new supplies along with reminder instructions on how to use them. Over the years we noted a decline in the severity and the degree of dental disease requiring further treatment.

Lyndal would coordinate the files into appropriate bundles for follow-up, and together we would organise any referral letters. It really was an efficient team effort. There was much room for laughter, fun with the kids and reassuring cuddles by the women in the team for the apprehensive little ones when needed. After each tiring day, we would long for a coffee. We would reflect on our day and feel fulfilled and satisfied. We believed we were making a difference in these children's lives.

As much as possible, we would try to deal with the more acute problems identified with the medical equipment we took with us. This included treating asthma with puffers, dressings for wounds, lancing of abscesses, treating fungal infections and impetigo, and treating bacterial infections with antibiotics.

For our young asthma patients needing Ventolin or other puffers, Lyndal cleverly devised a 'spacer' device from one of our plastic water bottles, by cutting a hole in the base for the device to be attached to.

In our work, we often softened the hard wax that was reducing hearing which had built up in many children's ear canals because of the dusty environment in which they lived. We tried syringing the wax initially with a small plastic syringe and, in later years, took over an ear syringing machine, which was much more successful. The treatment produced grimaces from the children but the outcome brought huge smiles as they could suddenly hear again. Over the years, we tipped the dirty water and wax from the collecting container straight out of the nearest window into the garden and we were amused to observe each year the extra growth of nearby plants that I thought seemed to have more 'waxy' leaves!

## 'Albertine'

On return from my first mission trip to Rwanda and its people, I realised that I had been deeply affected by what I'd witnessed. I was challenged further when listening to a song written by Brooke Fraser after she had also visited Rwanda and evidenced the horror of the genocide and its effects on individuals, one of whom was a young orphaned girl called Albertine. The lyrics of this powerful song 'Albertine' are haunting. The most impacting words for me were 'Now that I have seen, I am responsible. Faith without deeds is dead.' It was obvious I needed to return, which I did with various teams each year up until COVID-19 interrupted our ongoing relationships with Rwanda and our friends there.

I love Proverbs 3:27: 'Do not withhold good from those who deserve it, when it is in your power to help them.' This is a challenge for everyone – to care for all mankind in all countries of the world. As a Christian, the awareness of the love of God in our lives has to be followed through with action to love others. It is easy to develop 'hard hearts and soft feet' when it comes to serving those less fortunate, whereas we should be developing 'soft hearts and hard feet'.

Over the ensuing six years, with fewer team members available to the mission team, our medical examinations had to be restricted to new pupils at the school. In particular, students with pre-identified problems found by teachers or teachers themselves with a health concern – as well any urgent cases, injuries or medical complaints that took place whilst we were at the school. As time went on, our medical outreach extended to health checks at another school at Bugasera, about a two-hour drive south of Kigali. Bugasera was the location of a disturbing memorial of people who lost their lives in the genocide, where there had been deliberate 'rounding up' of Tutsis displaced due to malaria-infested mosquito grounds. One memorial in particular that adversely impacted every member of our team was the Catholic memorial at Nyamata that had been left untouched since 1994, with the blood-stained clothes of people killed still on the church pews, and bullet-holed and bloodied walls.

The particularly horrid element of this church's history was that many thousands of scared Tutsis came to the church assuming they would be safe, only to discover that the priests had informed the police and militia of their presence. The militia systematically went about murdering men, women and children. Post-genocide, there is still resentment aimed at the Catholic Church for such betrayal and this anger led to an official apology by the pope decades later and excommunication of the offending priests.

Besides the health assessments of students and teachers at the schools, there were other opportunities to be involved in using my medical background. One of these was to hold information nights for Rwandan dentists and doctors on antibiotic stewardship. This was challenging since I had to be sensitive in my suggestions of the need of changed use of antibiotics to lessen the risk of antibiotic resistance.

Another opportunity given to us each year during the Rwanda missions was weeknight talks to parents of the school children. These talks were held in the main church building. Surprisingly, this was well attended with up to 200 parents to whom we presented basic health education and prevention strategies to assist them and their families. These talks were always challenging in that Headmaster Fred had to interpret everything I said medically from English to Kinyarwanda. Sometimes I had to hope my messages came across accurately. There were many times where Fred and I would break out in laughter when what I was trying to emphasise was lost in the translation.

In one particular talk, I was embarrassingly the cause of an outbreak of uncontrolled laughter. As was often the case, it was around my feeble attempts to speak the native Kinyarwanda language with any clarity. I was well-known for significant blunders, such as on my first visit out with the team on an early morning walk, instead of greeting local people with the Kinyarwanda term for hello of 'Muraho', I somehow repeatedly confused that with the Hawaiian greeting of the same meaning 'Aloha'! Little wonder no-one repeated the greeting back to me, instead giving stares of confusion.

On one particular parent information evening, I desired to impress the gathered audience at the end of the one-hour presentation with some native language. I wanted to end my talk by saying 'thank you very much' (for their attendance), which in Kinyarwanda is 'murakoze chani'. The dark faces of the parents were difficult to see in the church due to poor lighting. All week I had been examining children and in my attempts at communicating with them, I'd been trying to get them to understand my simple instructions to look inside their mouth by saying 'acima chani' (open wide please). So instead of ending my talk to my local audience with 'murakoze chani', I unintentionally said 'acima chani' and immediately 200 dark faces opened their mouths spontaneously. All I could see in the darkening room was numerous sets of pearly white teeth, and all I could hear was loud laughter including that of my interpreter, now bent over in hysterics. No need for interpretation – rather just bi-culturally understood simple embarrassment!

To my and Carol's pleasure, we had many opportunities to enjoy the country and the people when we were not working. These included early morning walks around our guesthouse, visits to Rwandan coffee plantations (growing some of the best coffee in the world), the Kigali markets and the Rwandan wild animal park (Akagera).

In 2019, our last trip before COVID-19, I had the thrill of a mountain trek in northern Rwanda to visit one of the gorilla families high in the rainforests. It was a tiring, difficult and long uphill trek with armed guards. Being close to these large animals in the wild was a uniquely profound experience, observing their strength yet their care for each other, especially the elderly of the family. I had a close encounter with a large silverback who was uphill from where we were standing. He decided to stand up and walk down the hill but we were in his way. Our guides yelled out for us to stand still and try to get down low. In my attempt to do this, I slipped on the wet ferns and found myself lying on my back looking up at the clear African sky just as the silverback simply stepped over me in slow motion like a gentle giant.

## Holistic healing

Another profound experience in Rwanda for Carol and myself occurred on our first visit in 2012 to Mesanzi, in the northern district of Rwanda. We were asked to go to a remote clinic to offer a few days of medical care to an isolated community. Unfortunately for us, there was a message announced to the village that 'Australian eye specialists' were visiting, and so on our arrival the first morning, we were met with a large crowd spilling out of the small clinic, some who had been waiting for three days. The building had no electricity, no running water and was dark and dusty. A few local nurses were doing their best to cope with the number of patients in attendance and the severity of conditions. We only had one interpreter for three Aussie doctors who were all working in one small room. We had one of our nurses attempting to triage patients so we could cope, but we were feeling overwhelmed.

I had previously taught at medical seminars back in Australia about the different types of stress we can experience – 'under' stress, 'hypo' stress, 'hyper' stress, and 'distress'. Distress occurs at one end of the spectrum, where we do not cope well due to the overwhelming nature of the stressors that we're facing. This is exactly how I felt on that first day. I was way out of my comfort zone, seeing some of the worst medical conditions I had ever seen and being able to do very little other than write a letter to the only doctor at a hospital miles away, and send these poor patients via a makeshift ambulance – our small transit van.

There were cases of fungating cancers, young people with racing heart palpitations and noisy heart murmurs, and discharging open colostomy wounds as well other severe medical conditions. Due to the dusty conditions of the geography and cooking fires within houses there were many cases of inflamed, red painful eyes. I recall feeling emotionally and physically exhausted, and defeated, and I wondered if it was worthwhile attending the next day due to the little we could achieve.

That night, Carol woke up after having had a dream where she felt compelled to tell the people waiting at the clinic for healing that God loved them and forgiveness was part of that love.

The next day we headed back to the clinic. We commenced consulting, while other helpers on our team handed out water, bananas and biscuits to those waiting in the heat. I noted in the late morning there seemed to be less people than usual waiting in the corridors. When I went to investigate, I could see a group of people outside circling Carol, who was talking to the crowd through the help of an interpreter and the local Anglican pastor. I could see many bowing their heads and praying, as a simple message of God's love for them was explained.

A profound message of hope and grace that has transformed millions of lives for over 2000 years was given that day and at least 30 people accepted Jesus' forgiveness. There was a round of cheering and clapping, and the weeping was tangible. The tears were not just confined to those who were responding, but to those ministering and to those like me looking on. The realisation clearly hit me, that in reality what God had foreseen and wanted us to witness was not just the temporal healing of their physical lives, but the healing of people's souls – which has eternal consequences.

That experience reminded us all that our ministry had to be led by God and driven by the need of those we went to serve, not necessarily what we thought was the need – which to us as medicos, was physical healing: a lesson of obedience that impacted the direction, thinking, attitude and preparation for all future mission trips.

## The Ministry of Presence – Ben's story

The 'Ministry of Presence' was a term I first heard from Ben Kayumba, the owner of the Good News Guest House where we boarded when on mission in Rwanda. He is the director of Good News International (GNI), which is funded by those who rent the guesthouse. This guesthouse is a comfortable retreat with beautiful gardens, nutritious local food and mostly hot showers that overlooked Kigali. It is within a 20 minute drive of the school and church where we volunteered. As well as being a business that supports a greater ministry, it was an obvious choice of accommodation due to its location.

GNI had a number of organised groups that have been working to support and practically help people for 26 years. It includes assistance for orphans and widows of the genocide with housing, a youth and women's vocational training school and, most importantly, provides a monthly service of reconciliation for survivors and perpetrators of the Rwandan genocide, which is held in the grounds of the guesthouse.

We had the privilege of participating in these services – services that demonstrated that the healing in people's lives is still taking place. When an individual shares their story for the first time in 26 years of what they experienced during the genocide, it has a cathartic effect on them – and to those listening to the story as well.

The stories of victims ranged from an ageing woman who revealed that she was raped in the genocide and now has HIV/AIDS, to a man in his 30s explaining how he lost his whole family and witnessed their deaths. In some cases, the storyteller could be a perpetrator who has never sought forgiveness until this particular time. The impact of these stories was powerful. It was obvious to us that the only way forward for both the victim and the offender alike was confession and then forgiveness, to produce reconciliation. On an individual, community or country scale, this is the successful method that Rwanda has demonstrated to the world how it has rebuilt 'beauty from ashes'. Rwanda has been a shining example in this.

The demonstration of man's forgiveness of one another through God's love is the only way forward, especially after tragic events such as the Rwandan genocide. This has allowed Rwandans to rebuild relationships. Even with forgiveness sought by perpetrators, and then given by victims, traumatic memories last a lifetime. What happened in the genocide is never forgotten, and the whole country remembers the events annually, with large billboards erected all over the country reminding the people, with just one compelling word – KWIBUKA ('remember'). All school students must visit the Genocide Museum in Kigali during their high school years, another way of them never forgetting the past.

In 2018, as part of our Rwandan mission team, we had the opportunity of inviting three girls from the local high school, who belonged to our church's mentoring group. The aim was to allow them to work alongside the team in the Kigali school, and experience the history of Rwanda they'd learnt about in their school studies. This was a life-changing experience for them all and they learnt so much about Rwanda and about themselves.

Ben Kayumba is a humble and friendly Christian gentleman with his own powerful story of survival. Through his courage and forgiveness he has rebuilt his own life and contributed to that of his nation. He was a young man in 1994 and had been working with Compassion International years before the genocide, helping to build orphanages for the many displaced children in Rwanda. Being a Tutsi he was already aware of the victimisation against his tribe. When the genocide started, Ben found himself in his family home surrounded by Hutus yelling for him to come out. He thought it was probable he would die that night. All that everyone in the home could do was phone loved ones to say goodbye, pray and wait in fear. At the last minute, he was miraculously rescued by one of the Belgian UN soldiers who sadly died protecting the prime minister a few weeks later.

Ben was forced to leave his country, later discovering that his family and fiancée were all murdered. He had no desire to ever enter his home country again. Being expatriated to Canada, he soon felt compelled to return to his country where he worked alongside two Australian volunteers from Compassion International and commenced the building of many needed orphanages. After that work he found his calling to the ministry of 'GNI'.

Some of the most rewarding and refreshing experiences of my career in medicine has been the medical work undertaken on mission. Be that in Africa or India, the feeling and sense of purpose that you are making a difference in the lives of needy people is extremely rewarding and refreshing.

As many who experience short- or long-term mission trips know, one returns much more blessed than the people you sought to be a blessing to. Returning from mission gives one a reality check and an acute appreciation of how blessed we are in Australia, both in our ability to enjoy a quality and efficient health system, accommodation that is comfortable, a justice system that offers security, and expected resources such as food, clean water and clothing that we often take for granted.

Regardless of where people are born or the communities they belong to, equal access to healthcare should be a fundamental human right. I remember returning after one trip to Rwanda, having dealt with many eyesight problems in children and adults, and having insufficient resources to make major improvements. I found myself in the waiting room of a retinal specialist after I was found to have retinal tears in one of my eyes, which could have resulted in retinal detachment and blindness. As I was waiting for my turn for laser treatment, I recall being at peace and being thankful to God for his goodness to me by having access to such life altering medical care. I was also feeling sadness after what I had recently experienced where I was limited to what I could do for children and adults whose eyesight was just as important as mine. It was only a few weeks later that this same condition unexpectedly occurred in my other eye. The pervasive thought that I could have been left totally blind within a month has persisted as a stimulus for ongoing thankfulness.

Sharing these stories and experiences with other doctors and medical students that I've been involved with in mentoring over my life has also been a wonderful blessing, especially when some changed the course of their lives to be full-time medical missionaries. One such medical student was a clever and dedicated Christian young man – Samuel McDowell, who is presently working with his wife Kate (also a medical doctor) and their four children, in Paraguay, offering medical and spiritual care to remote communities and continuing to demonstrate to them – 'The Ministry of Presence'.

# CHAPTER NINE

# COVID-19

*'The prudent person foresees the danger ahead and takes precautions. The simpleton goes blindly on and suffers the consequences.'*
**– Proverbs 27:12**

*'It's not the existence of danger that is of utmost importance, but rather the understanding of the danger.'*
**– Unknown**

# The day the world stood still

I arrived at work on a Monday morning in late March 2020 as usual around 8 am. The contrast between the scene that day compared to a typical Monday morning could not have been sharper. The day was austere, surreal and it made me quickly realise that the world as I had known it had just been turned upside down for an undetermined time. The world around me had literally changed overnight.

There was a cognitive dissonance that I desired to somehow reconcile in my mind.

The streets surrounding our surgery at Sutherland are usually busy and noisy, being a main thoroughfare with long lines of banked up traffic. There was usually an absence of parking spots. People would normally be busily heading to the railway station at the end of our street. Hundreds of school children carrying their backpacks would be making their way to their nearby primary and high schools.

That morning, things were very different. The streets were devoid of cars. It was eerily quiet. There was no traffic and no school children. The only line-up was that of adults, stretching along the street in front of my surgery from the Centrelink office on the next corner (which hadn't yet even opened). I had never seen this before. The line was one of men and women with masks on, not conversing, standing a few metres apart, and ranged from tradesmen, office workers, to Qantas pilots in uniform, and a wide variety of ages. I realised that this was just a small representation of Australians – the tip of a growing iceberg.

I stood quietly and respectfully, staring at the long line of despondent looking people finding themselves in a desperate situation, facing uncertainty due to no fault of their own. Like their moods, my mood was one of melancholy. I was thinking about what I could do to ease their plight. Could I take them a coffee or a drink? Since no shops were open, and as I had to remain socially distanced, there was little I could do immediately.

I simultaneously reflected on what my role could be or would look like facing the cause of the scene before me, both personally and medically. I felt some justified concerns of the personal risk, risks to family and friends, as well as the burden of responsibility I had for my patients and staff, to protect them in my decision-making and preparations. I was thankful and privileged to be amongst the few who still had employment and for our business to remain open due to our position as an essential service.

Despite the feelings of anxiety surrounding this scene before me, I simultaneously felt a peace within. I believe this was as a result of my faith in an all-knowing God and past experiences in my life. I was still able to sense that He was still in control – even within the ambiguity of what I was observing.

The reason for this scene before me was obvious: the arrival on our shores of SARS-Cov-2, a novel virus that would cause the new COVID-19 disease. The impact and outcome of this unseen enemy, which had commenced a 'war' against all of humanity, was at that time unpredictable and concerning. The hope I had was that the world could come together at this unprecedented time in all our lives to overcome this foe.

With time, I was to realise that this was an unrealistic expectation.

## Uncertainty

At this time the COVID-19 virus was being spread into our country via arriving passengers on international flights and cruise ships, and it threatened to overwhelm our health system and cause countless deaths, as it had already done in other countries. A common cold variety of coronavirus had mutated into a much more virulent strain, most likely as a result of an animal intermediary, initially through bats and racoon dogs in a crowded Chinese wet market, where live animals were sold for human consumption. These infected animals were implicated in the spread to humans, the virus then mutating to allow for human-to-human spread. It was a matter of rapid transmission of this highly infectious, potentially deadly and invisible contagion that no human immune system had previously been exposed to. This novel virus threatened the whole of humanity.

The origin of this virus has been established as Wuhan in China, but the reasons for its spread are less certain, ironically due to the same reason, namely its origin in China. This precluded accuracy on its exact origin – and still does.

With increasing case numbers across the world, and realising that this was a public health emergency extending beyond the border of every country, the federal government needed to act strongly and swiftly, taking the advice of leading health officials and epidemiologists. The government enacted constitutional powers and closed our international borders, cutting off our country to the rest of the world and allowing our unique island geography to protect us.

Because they knew that human contact was spreading infection, and to limit viral spread, the government enforced a sudden countrywide lockdown and the isolation and quarantining of positive cases and all arriving international travellers. There was also cancellation of public gatherings including sporting events, school education and church services.

Irrespective of individual opinion of Prime Minister Scott Morrison, his following of public health advice at that time gave Australia a head start against the virus. Despite the virus sporadically entering the country, the radical and costly decision kept the pandemic at bay for more than a year, buying time until vaccines became available, time to develop testing and contact and tracing facilities, and time to build up medical supplies and capability. This action was considered appropriate by the experts, to hopefully alter the progression of the virus and to 'flatten the curve', while protecting the vulnerable and also preventing our health system from collapsing.

Leaders of many other countries did not follow similar advice from health officials and decided to try to achieve herd immunity by exposure of their population to natural infection for the sake of the economy. This assumption unfortunately led to thousands of unnecessary deaths, and worsened the recovery of the respective country's economy. I personally found it was encouraging to observe an assertive decision to label what we were all facing as a pandemic well before this was announced by the WHO. 'Lives before livelihoods' became a mantra that was acceptable to most, despite its difficulties in real life.

New Zealand, fortunately, had a leader who acted courageously, early and prudently. Our youngest son, Luke, his partner Travis and their greyhound Barkly had just arrived in Christchurch, New Zealand from Melbourne to permanently take up residence in early 2020. Despite finding themselves in Stage 4 lockdown for many months, aiming for effective elimination, New Zealand also felt safe with low risk while health services prepared themselves. Taiwan and New Zealand were the most successful countries in minimising the impact for both health and the economy against COVID-19.

Initially, the Wuhan strain of the virus was causing a mortality of 5% of all those infected and 20% in anyone over 70 years of age. The virus seemed to have no regard to the age of its victims, and it was not, as some wrongly suggested, just the 'flu'. It was unlike influenza, because it did not generally affect children as seriously, fatalities were much higher, and the nature of the disease often included a delayed (one week) inflammatory response called a 'cytokine storm'. The virus's behaviour was similar to influenza, however, in the way it could cause serious disease in the elderly, those who were immunocompromised and pregnant women.

As the virus spread across the world, news of high mortality figures of victims in the early affected countries like China, Italy and the USA was shared with medical authorities and healthcare workers on the frontline, including GPs. Reading in medical journals, and authoritative online sources what was heading our way, and our likely inability to 'dodge the bullet', was the cause of significant concern among all health professionals. The news of 100 doctors dying in Italy alone was enough to cause sleepless nights for most medical personnel, myself included. By 2021, the WHO estimated that at least 180,000 previously well health workers had died from COVID-19 in the line of duty.

As predicted, hospitals around the world could not cope with the influx of COVID-19 cases. Case numbers exceeded ICU beds and ventilators. Makeshift hospitals and morgues had to be built quickly. Doctors, nurses and all other healthcare workers became overwhelmed, with many becoming victims to the virus themselves. Some healthcare workers even took their own lives when they could no longer cope. These same carers had to daily and repeatedly make the difficult decision as to who to offer an ICU bed and ventilator. This was based on the age of the patient and their comorbidities. In Italy, at their height of infection, the cut-off for a ventilator was 40 years of age. In London, paramedics were instructed early in the outbreak to avoid bringing anyone over 65 years of age with COVID-19 to hospital.

Early in the pandemic, Italian newspapers published statements such as: 'Everything has changed', 'intensivists have never felt so stressed', 'most of the newspaper is an obituary', 'a viral storm has spread through', 'everyone is scared and trying not to panic', 'so many doctors are broken inside' 'there is a changed DNA of what makes community tick', 'the elderly have gone.'

Other local media reports, specialist interviews and government announcements elevated the concerns of the vast majority of the Australian population. Deputy chief medical officer Dr Paul Kelly warned of a possible worst case scenario for Australia of 150,000 deaths unless public health measures were followed. Rather than thinking about the latest surf report when we heard the word 'waves', it now referred to the coming 'wave' of infection, be it the second or third and so on.

'Uncertainty' became a commonly used word in the public arena and in personal conversations. We all heard not-so-reassuring quotes such as 'The most challenging thing was the anxiety about the uncertainty.' Predictability is the modus operandi of most people, rather than uncertainty. We had to adapt, and COVID-19 forced that to occur - and quickly.

These quotes augmented the anxiety being experienced by most, myself included. I needed to reconcile this again and again with my faith, as I had in what I first observed in late March of the first year of the pandemic.

The description of the undesired predicament as being a 'war' was an appropriate one and applicable for the whole world, with similar consequences to that of war, with physical death and disability, mental health decline, economic loss, and isolation, all as a result of COVID-19. Decisions by leaders and countries during the threat of war are never perfect, just as the Australian response was not perfect during the pandemic, but it was a response based on the best evidence at the time, with best intentions and in the needed timeframe.

What I did not anticipate was the huge disinformation war. Although most felt that WHO was too slow to declare COVID-19 a pandemic, it was quicker to cast judgement on another problem: the mass spread of information (either wrong or incomplete) about SARS-Cov-2, which it labelled an 'infodemic'. This was defined as 'an abundance of information… that makes it hard for people to find trustworthy sources and reliable guidance when they need it'.

The highly respected epidemiologist Professor Raina McIntyre stated: 'The COVID-19 pandemic has brought with it disinformation, political meddling, counternarratives and a flood of pseudo-experts, willing to sell themselves for power and favour. Information warfare has become more insidious and powerful with the widespread use of social media.' It soon became apparent that GPs and other healthcare workers would not only be managing the disease but also human reaction to the disease.

## Avoid it like the plague

During my lifetime there has been a frequently used cliche: 'avoid it like the plague'. A statement that required little explanation, as it was self-explanatory, and could relate to many areas of our lives.

In the years 2020–2023, it has become apparent to me that this platitude was not followed by everyone, especially when it came to an obvious issue they really should have avoided, namely the viral pandemic. Just like viruses, this statement's meaning mutated to suggest to 'avoid it like the plague, as long as it suits your viewpoint, and you think it's real in the first place, even if this viewpoint conflicts with reason and evidence and is repeatedly reinforced by social media algorithms'.

The inflexibility to change or alter one's opinion when an opposite viewpoint is based on good scientific evidence and authoritative commentary from reputable authorities seems to be a change in social attitude. This attitude of rigidity in thinking and beliefs, with regards to the nuances of the pandemic led to a growing polarity and division in relationships between individuals, families, communities and countries. Freedom of expression in the mass media and on social media without responsibility also inflamed the problem. The change also coincided with other divisive issues such as Black Lives Matter and climate change created along with the pandemic and COVID-19-defiance, a perfect storm of issues causing potential conflict.

When Dr Anthony Fauci retired in the later part of 2022, after 50 years as a leader in infection control and public health in the USA – in particular, the HIV epidemic, and more recently COVID-19 pandemic – he was asked what was the greatest disappointment he experienced during the last three years of COVID-19. He responded, 'That despite working only for the good of individuals and the population as a whole, to achieve best outcomes for their health and safety, by providing factual advice on various infections and proven public health measures, that many chose to ignore such advice and recommendations such as vaccinations.' The result for the USA was one of the highest death rates of any country in the world. By 2022, life expectancy in that country had dropped by an incredible two years due to the overwhelming numbers of those who had succumbed to COVID-19.

My approach with regards to COVID-19 was gleaned from significant time invested in researching, and being informed from reliable sources that I have trusted throughout my entire career. Independent groups such as the TGA, ATAGI, NCIRS (see Appendix B 'COVID-19 facts') sought favourable outcomes for the health of our nation by providing the best and latest researched evidence and advice. These groups were genuinely concerned about the wellbeing of the population as a whole with the public health advice they gave government, the medical profession and individuals in the community.

Were they always 100% correct? Of course not. The reasons included the nature of the pandemic and its uniqueness, as well as the evolving scientific research data as the pandemic progressed, and unexpected changes in the behaviour of the virus. As the authorities and we as medical carers at the coalface learned more about this viral infection, appropriate changes in advice and recommendations were developed and communicated to patients and the population as a whole.

For example, advice regarding the mode of transmission had to be altered when it was discovered that viral transmission was mostly via small aerosolised particles rather than larger droplets. This led to the increased emphasis on quality masks and good ventilation and less on cleaning surfaces and the 'deep clean' of buildings.

It was difficult for me to understand people refusing protective vaccines that were overall safe and effective – especially early in the pandemic – with higher death rates in all age ranges because of the more virulent strains circulating at that time. It was another level of surprise and disappointment to try to understand COVID-19 defiance by those who refused to abide by public health measures such as social distancing, hand disinfection and mask wearing in public places and health facilities. The importance of these were explained numerous times by authorities, as was the need to protect our health system, especially frontline workers. I was not asked very often for a mask exemption certificate, but I did make rare exceptions, such as one elderly lady with dementia. I did not write any certificates of medical exemption for vaccination since the criteria was very tight, requiring evidence of allergic or adverse reactions to two of the available vaccines.

# Checkpoint Charlie

A universal challenge and source of grief and frustration during the pandemic was the separation from family and friends that most Australians experienced. We all tried to stay in contact via the efficient but impersonal Zoom or FaceTime sessions. It was wonderful to observe the faces of family and especially grandchildren, even though young children quickly lost attention staring at a computer screen to converse. The reality was that we were all missing important celebrations and family events that had special meaning to us: Christmas, Easter, birthdays, holidays, Father's Day and Mother's Day and, for some of us, remembering our loved ones who contributed to the importance of Anzac Day. For too many, it was even more emotionally distressing to realise that they missed once-in-a-lifetime events such as graduations, weddings and loved one's funerals.

It seemed logical that with most of my family living in Queensland, and others in Christchurch, and with strict and enforced state and international border closures, that one had to be ready to act quickly when these were eased at certain times.

In the first year of the pandemic during July 2020, Carol and I had planned a flight to the Sunshine Coast to visit family. The day before leaving to fly up, we discovered the Queensland border was closing in 48 hours due to an outbreak of COVID-19 cases in NSW. Having travelled to the airport by train, we discovered that our flight had also been cancelled, and soon after learnt we had a similar fate with our accommodation. We were offered to be rescheduled on a flight the next morning, but we felt that was too close and risky, in case it also was cancelled since the border was closing for an indeterminate time. It was fortunate we did not take up that offer, as it turned out there was an infected diplomat on that flight and passengers had to self-isolate for 14 days. Collecting our bags again after just checking them in, we headed back home on the train, transferred our bags into our car and headed off on the journey to Queensland overnight, a task at our age we somewhat regretted over the next 24 hours.

We decided to travel via the New England Highway, thinking it would be less crowded at that border checkpoint than the Pacific Highway checkpoint, which turned out to be the case. At midnight, we approached the border crossing which seemed to be 'out the back of nowhere'. How we were greeted turned out to be another surreal experience. In the dark and cold of winter, and with low fog around, we found we were the only car on the highway approaching the conspicuously fortified barrier, where we were met by a number of police officers. Some of them were closely surrounding a large 44 gallon drum full of burning timber, with their outstretched hands to keep warm. They were dressed in dark overcoats with hoods, which covered their uniforms. One of them made their way to our car window with a flashlight, suggesting we were about to be interrogated. Having shown our pre-completed border passes, our driver's licences for ID, and having answered a number of questions on our origin and purpose for visiting, we were allowed to cross over. We felt somewhat intimidated having not previously experienced a border closure of this nature.

Carol and I had visited Checkpoint Charlie in Berlin a few years previous when we travelled to Europe. This original bastion between East and West Berlin has been preserved after the Berlin Wall came down. It was the main border crossing between the divided Germany for many decades after WWII, and was renowned for its tight and robust security and its threat of consequences to citizens trying to pass through if they did not have the correct paperwork. I recalled seeing photos of the original checkpoint and its ominous armed guards huddled around an open fire emanating from a large metal drum, dressed in winter overcoats while they interrogated subjects desiring to cross over. It seemed that we'd just had a deja vu experience, despite the fact we were only crossing a state border in our own country and not in the middle of the Cold War! In reality, there were no German soldiers or tanks and the police were only doing their allocated duty, and Queensland was only doing what the whole country had been undertaking – trying to protect its own people.

Throughout these years, most of the world's population were exposed to varying surreal experiences, inconveniences, disappointments and interruptions to their normal lives. Even before COVID-19 arrived, a quarter of Australians were suffering from loneliness. The above circumstances understandably aggravated this ordeal. Sadly, millions had to contend with considerably much more pain and suffering than others, with severe and ongoing illness from COVID-19, loneliness and isolation, economic hardship and the grief of loss of family and friends (exponentially compounded by the fact that loved ones sometimes died alone in crowded hospital wards).

## Vaccines: The good, bad, ugly and humorous

*The Good:* Although there was some initial teething issues with the choice and arrival of COVID-19 vaccines in Australia, they were a pleasing sight to see when they finally arrived at our practice. Needless to say, uptake and interest was high amongst patients, especially the elderly when the AstraZenica vaccines first arrived. Our surgery abided by government recommendations for delivery, but when our supplies of Pfizer mRNA vaccines were delivered, I felt we needed a different approach. Frontline workers and emergency services, as well as GPs, had generally been vaccinated in hospital clinics and although we were advised which age groups to do in order, we intentionally contacted those we thought were at greater risk to attend prior to general patients. These included pregnant women, school teachers, pharmacy workers, receptionists of specialist and radiology practices, and police from our nearby police station who'd missed the hospital clinics.

Over the course of 2021–2023 (and still ongoing), our surgery had provided over 8000 vaccinations of various types. All vaccines and services given were at no cost to the patient. Rather, the cost was covered by Medicare. To date, over 13 billion doses of vaccines have been given around the world, and these recorded doses and the subsequent follow-up provided a massive and unprecedented database of information to observe possible emerging side effects of these vaccines. Fortunately, the overall safety of these vaccines has been proven, despite the contrary suggestions by some antagonists.

Our practice has not seen any severe complications from any of the COVID-19 vaccines, for which we are thankful. In general, despite some fears and anxiety about their safety, the benefits of vaccines have far outweighed any side effects seen (which have mainly been local reactions). The vaccines have been shown to partially reduce the risk of becoming infected in the first place, diminish the severity of COVID-19, and to reduce the risk of severe complications, hospitalisation and death. There is also clear evidence supporting that vaccination reduced the risk of Long Covid. (Refer to Appendix C 'COVID-19 facts'.)

*The Bad:* It was disappointing as the pandemic progressed to discover that although the available vaccines had significant benefits, they were not absolute in their protection and so breakthrough infection still occurred despite vaccination. Protection against infection after vaccination wanes with time, due to variants mutating and leading to what is called 'vaccine escape'.

In July 2021, the director of the US Centers of Disease Control and Prevention during the deadly Delta outbreak warned 'that this pandemic was becoming a pandemic of the unvaccinated', a statement that at the time may have seemed to be correct, but on hindsight was premature, incorrect and actually harmful to societal relationships. This predated the Omicron variant outbreak, a variant that was much more infectious. There was growing evidence that vaccines against Omicron did not fully prevent transmission. It took the accumulation of data over time to show this. At the beginning, the world did not have the luxury of time since large numbers of people were rapidly dying.

Any medical intervention, medication or vaccine should have a risk–benefit analysis by the doctor and patient, the patient then making a decision after being informed. It has become evident from statistics about COVID-19, corroborated with my anecdotal experience, that the disease itself carries a vastly increased risk of death and complications compared to the vaccines themselves. Earlier in the pandemic, the benefits when we were facing more virulent strains of the virus, definitely outweighed risks, even in children. The data and advice changed as the pandemic progressed, so the risk versus benefit analysis understandably also changed. By the fourth year of COVID-19, with less virulent strains circulating around the world, the analysis favoured vaccine-use in those of greater risk (aged over 65) and with other health issues, rather than people who were well and in lower age groups.

Unfortunately in Australia, there have been 14 deaths associated with both COVID-19 vaccines, 13 of these from the AZ vaccine due to thromboses. As sad as this figure is, and the personal lives it represents, the estimated loss of lives from COVID-19 infections worldwide was far higher, and many more deaths were prevented by these vaccines. Some authorities quoted tens of thousands of deaths, but the exact figure will never be known. The figures for Australia regarding deaths from COVID-19 at the time of writing is approximately 20,000 mostly in 2022 after restrictions were removed in 2021. This is a significant increase above usual annual mortality figures.

The COVID-19 vaccines were shown to be safe overall, with significant side effects presently being in approximately 1 in 100,000 people immunised in Australia. One side effect was myocarditis in males less than 30 years after the second dose, which was usually mild and resolved over ensuing weeks. Fortunately we only had one such mild case in our clinic. Emerging evidence has also shown that concerns such as myocarditis, pericarditis, clots and any other side effects occurred much more frequently in patients who had suffered COVID-19 infection as compared to any vaccine reaction.

It is evident that there has been some rare injuries from the actual vaccine, and I believe that it is fair and appropriate that compensation for injuries was offered by our federal government to cover costs associated with these injuries. This would not appear to be the case in most countries around the world.

When it came to equality of vaccine access, it was disappointing despite recurrent comments by the WHO that 'we are not safe until everyone is safe', that more wealthy countries focused mainly on their needs and overlooked less fortunate ones. Countries such as those in Africa had limited access to vaccines, yet these countries had same desire to protect their peoples as that in the West. This was a reminder to me of the ongoing gross inequality of the resources and wealth in the world and that suffering by many is determined solely by their birthplace. The hope I wished for on 27 March 2020 (the day the world stood still), that a pandemic might bring unity, care and compassion for the whole world, has not eventuated as it should have and this has been disappointing.

*The Ugly:* It was my observation that most GPs were frustrated and disappointed in the attitude of some who had sourced their advice on COVID-19, and in particular the vaccines from various sources. Most of these sources were not medically reliable and certainly not evidence-based or from our own health authorities and experts.

According to counsellor David Riddell from New Zealand, one of the fundamentals of emotional and mental health is 'the ability to submit to correction from those who know better than me'. I found it a shame that this basic principle was overlooked by many during the pandemic.

There was no shortage of conspiracy theories and mistruths we had to contend with, ranging from the common statement that the vaccines were produced too quickly without the proper trials (which was incorrect) to the bizarre rumour that anyone who received a vaccination would be dead in four years! (fortunately also untrue). Additionally, there was the incorrect theory that somehow mRNA vaccines changed the DNA structure of cells when, in fact, all they did was produce proteins in the cytoplasm of the cell to stimulate the immune system and did not affect the nucleus of a cell where DNA resides and functions. The mRNA from the vaccines is also unstable and is quickly broken down by the body.

Another incorrect claim was that natural infection would produce herd immunity. The countries that followed this belief lost many more lives than those that did not. Only through vaccinating enough of the world's population is herd immunity usually achieved, but this did not happen and COVID-19 variants have mutated and escaped the protection of current vaccines. At present, hybrid immunity (both natural infection and vaccination) has been shown to be the most effective type of immunity, in keeping antibody levels high and offering maximum protection.

Initially, I genuinely tried to understand most people's misgivings about the COVID-19 vaccinations and their speedy development, especially given our relatively low case numbers in 2021. I became fatigued with the discussions due to the evidence being made fully public, and the anecdotal evidence increasingly evident. I could not tolerate some of the behaviour experienced, such as people verbally abusing parents who were lining up outside our surgery for their children to be vaccinated. This was but one example of the 'ugly' we experienced.

Despite earlier optimistic hopes, the vaccines have shown so far that they are only part of the control of the pandemic. What was also needed to help stop the spread of the virus was improved ventilation and mask wearing in crowded situations, social distancing and hand sanitising (which a minority intentionally ignored).

*The Humorous:* Initially, my practice commenced our vaccination procedures indoors, with strict infection control protocols. As numbers of patients increased, we re-located to the rear of the property, into our car park. We required a production line, similar to what we did in our Rwandan clinics with check-in: giving of the vaccination, seated under the shade of a tent, and then observation for 15 minutes for any immediate adverse or allergic effects. There was a range of responses from recipients receiving their first COVID-19 shot: from thankfulness and relief, abruptness, calmness and acceptance, and at the other end of the spectrum – anxiety and panic. Many of these people were not known to us since we had opened up our clinic to anyone who wanted a vaccination, or required it for their work. We had a mobile foldable bed ready for anyone who felt faint. On some hot days when we were in full PPE (personal protective equipment) and with little time to eat or drink we ourselves felt at times that we might require the 'sick bed'!

I thought it would be prudent to provide background music for the patients sitting after their vaccination, for a number of reasons. Firstly, if it was quiet instrumental music, it would help them to relax. Secondly, it gave more privacy to our conversation with people in the 'tent' while taking their histories or allaying any anxiety. Lastly, if some of the younger generation were engrossed on their phones and their 15 minute mandatory observation time had expired, as indicated on a red card given to them, I could switch to different music on my Spotify playlists, such as genres from my era of the 60s–70s, and that would see them leave quickly and make way for others!

On one occasion, when I ducked inside to obtain more vaccines from our vaccine fridge, I returned to hear the significant concern from one of my nurses who stated that the music now playing to the 20 or so people waiting post-vaccination was 'The Last Post'! Embarrassingly, I'd forgotten that I had downloaded a beautiful trumpet and piano version by Alexis French of this tune associated with sacrificial death, and it was on the end of the playlist I was using. I quickly corrected the mistake, but a tad late for those in the 'observation ward' whose anxiety had just multiplied, but who graciously did not complain, rather they just smiled! Fortunately also was the fact that this blooper did not precipitate a chain reaction of people fainting like my first day at medical school.

## The pandemic's progress

It was a few years before the long-term effects on the health of those who developed COVID-19 and survived the illness was clearly seen. Morbidity from COVID-19 included virtually any organ system – cardiovascular, neurological, haematological, immunological, respiratory. At the time of writing, disturbing statistics showed that approximately 800 million cases of COVID-19 recorded worldwide, with close to 7 million direct deaths (much higher figures expressed as excessive deaths), including the death of over 700 children, and with 200,000 children orphaned in the US alone, and an estimated seven million children orphaned worldwide. Worldwide excess (higher than expected) deaths and are expected to approach four million per year ongoing for the foreseeable future. Since the start of the pandemic life expectancy globally has reduced substantially for the first time in 70 years.

Despite these appalling figures, the number of deaths was significantly less than the influenza pandemic of

1917–1918 where there was an estimated 40–50 million deaths worldwide. This was particularly surprising considering an increased world population and the spread of infection by international travel in our time. Although there are multiple explanations for the difference in figures between the two pandemics, the triad of border closures, public health measures, testing and tracing, and the vaccines seem to me to be the most obvious explanations. In 2021, weekly deaths peaked worldwide, but by 2023 that number had reduced due to vaccines, antiviral medications and milder variants of COVID-19. Due to the strategic interventions, and being an island, Australia did much better early on compared to the rest of the world. That is until 2022, when COVID-19 became the third leading cause of death in the country, the first time an infectious disease was in the top five in five decades. As of 2023 there have been approximately 11 million cases of COVID-19 in Australia and 22,000 deaths directly due to COVID-19.

As the world progressed through the pandemic, and had the availability and option of vaccinations and boosters, and later antiviral medications, combined with the evolving less serious strains of Omicron, it became apparent that harsh lockdowns and border closures were not as essential. The death rate in Australia had dropped to approximately 0.2% of cases due to lessened severity of the Omicron variant and the high rate of vaccinations, especially in the elderly. The relaxing of the severe restrictions and mandates seemed appropriate and greatly appreciated by all, even though that meant there would be increased cases occurring.

Unfortunately, the public health measures that had been both effective and essential were discarded by government and society as a whole in October 2021. By throwing 'the baby out with the bathwater' meant that

Australia ironically had now become one of the hotspots of the world for COVID-19. For myself, after the intense work and effort to minimise the harm of this virus, it seemed a shame that proven public health measures suddenly became obsolete. It became evident that as a society we had not even learnt to copy the respectable behaviour of our south-east Asian neighbours by wearing a well-fitted face mask when unwell with any infectious illness, with the intent that this simple behaviour protected and honoured others.

The Australian outcomes compared to the rest of the world reveals some interesting ironies. We had one of the highest vaccination rates per capita in the world which, along with other measures previously mentioned, resulted in one of the lowest mortality rates of any country. We then became complacent and abolished all our protective strategies over a short period of time, which then resulted in us achieving the unenviable record of having the highest transmission rates in the world by 2023. Fortunately by then, the later variants (including Omicron) had begun attenuating, and although more infectious they were less virulent. With the initial severity of the earlier COVID-19 viral strains, we had gone through what has now been labelled by some as a 'panic cycle' between 2019–2022, now replaced by a 'cycle of neglect', where many wouldn't even bother testing for infection, had vaccine fatigue, didn't wear masks even when unwell and with some not isolating when infected with COVID-19 and therefore remaining infectious to others.

We are now facing the possible burden of Long Covid cases, estimated to be around 5% of COVID-19 cases and it is likely we will continue to face a substantial burden of COVID-19-related chronic disease disability. What this will cause in the future to adults and children is still unknown. In anticipation of this Long Covid burden and the 12 month waiting time at clinics set up at some hospitals to deal with this, our surgery has commenced a weekly specialty clinic for both our patients and other victims of Long Covid. Patients were offered a wholistic assessment and multi-disciplinary management program, after exclusion of other causes for their various symptoms.

Needless to say, what I have written is my personal perspective and personal medical experience of the pandemic but I can appreciate that not everyone will share this view based on a number of factors.

For instance, what might have differed throughout COVID-19 is political viewpoint, age and risk of infection, access and accuracy of sources of information and each person's personal experiences over those years.

I have tried to remain transparent and provide objective truth and rational argument. Like any disagreement, there may be a clash of opinions, but what is important to remember is that debate and discussion needs to not be personal. Ultimately, as fellow Australians, we need to remain friends and neighbours rather than enemies when discussing the factors pertinent to COVID-19, especially with those we love the most.

## Silver linings

The law of unintended consequences is a frequently observed phenomenon that applies when the actions of people and governments have effects that have not been anticipated. The superfluous consequences may or may not be foreseeable or even immediately observable, and they may be beneficial, harmful or neutral in their impact. Despite the tragedy of the COVID-19 pandemic with its negative outcomes on health and the economy, as well as the havoc caused globally to individual lives by the virus, there were some positives that arose. These occurred in society as a whole, in medical practice, and to me personally.

Sometimes something disastrous can be a catalyst for change. As Karl Faase correctly stated: 'Tough and challenging times can actually be a blessing. You just need the eyes to see, and the courage to follow some new opportunities that God is opening up to you.' Sometimes we only learn from challenging times. The pandemic led to restrictions and limitations on what we all could do and achieve and there's nothing like limitations to exercise and stimulate the mind.

In society, lockdowns, isolation and quarantine were claimed to be harmful to emotional and mental health, which was particularly true for those who were alone. There was unfortunately in some households increased alcohol consumption and cases of domestic violence. On the contrary, many reported improved relationships between couples and in families. This was thought to have been due to increased periods of quality time spent with each other, and ironically this reduced levels of stress by being able to work from home, and benefiting from government financial incentives like JobKeeper.

The new revolution of working from home also led to reduced travel, allowing more time for exercise and relaxation and this has become the new normal for many. There was worldwide reduction in pollution and emissions due to less cars being on the road and because of some industries closing down temporarily. Less cars on the road was also associated with fewer Australian road deaths due to car accidents.

Anzac Day services during the COVID-19 years were held on driveways at dawn, there was positive feedback that not only were they personally meaningful but produced a great sense of community spirit and neighbourhood fellowship.

With further evaluation of Australia's overall performance in the pandemic, it is likely to be recommended that we have our own Centre for Disease Control, to prevent the difference of opinions and interpretations and resultant conflicts between Australian state governments and the federal government and their respective health ministers. Hopefully, this new authoritative medical body may prevent state border closures and provide a more coordinated and universal approach to managing future pandemics and is well overdue and desired by a majority of medical authorities and healthcare workers such as GPs.

Former Victorian Chief Health Officer Professor Brett Sutton suggested the establishment of a national health misinformation strategy in light of the misinformation that was peddled on social media during the COVID-19 pandemic and the scarier prospect for the next pandemic: created content using artificial intelligence. He states: 'During the 2009 (H1N1pandemic), traditional media was really key. Through the one we've just gone through, social media was pre-eminent, and the next one will be the AI chatbot fake video'.

In medical practice, patients and doctors have benefitted from the wise introduction of universal telehealth, allowing Medicare rebatable consultations to take place between doctors and allied healthcare workers and their patients by phone or live video. This resulted in less COVID-19 spread and deaths, especially in the elderly, due to patients being able to access adequate care, counselling and medicines for most conditions without them having to leave the relative safety of their homes. Although its scope has been narrowed since its inception, telehealth would appear to be here to stay and will benefit most patients, especially those in rural areas.

Another 'positive' witnessed in the medical field was the absence for at least three years of a number of other infectious diseases such as pertussis (whooping cough), influenza, norovirus (gastroenteritis virus) and RSV (respiratory syncytial virus) in children. The obvious reasons were the closure of international borders, isolation and quarantine, and public health measures such as mask wearing. When viral infections such as these (spread by close contact) are reduced, we also see reductions in secondary bacterial infections such as streptococcal infections and meningococcal meningitis, and this is what occurred.

Ongoing medical benefits during the COVID-19 years have included the further development of mRNA vaccines to prevent potentially fatal RSV infections in young children, and also in the treatment of late stage melanoma patients. These will be game changing in medicine: mRNA vaccines will eventually expand to cover other infectious diseases and common cancers and hopefully lessen the side effects of chemotherapy treatments and be advantageous to all. The head of mRNA research at Monash University stated: 'The technology is amazing and the promise enormous.'

The personal 'silver linings' of the pandemic were numerous, from the mundane task of mask wearing meaning not having to shave daily, to the challenge of being forced to think quickly and laterally due to the continuously changing circumstances the world found itself in. Ageing not uncommonly is associated with inflexibility in thinking and reliance on what is known and tested. The challenges in medicine that this virus caused required this inflexibility to be confronted, with 'curveballs' being thrown daily, and with rapidly emerging changes and adjustments in approach requiring us to be malleable to prevent poor outcomes.

Leading my staff and doctors at the surgery required a collaborative approach in decision-making and strategic planning. It was ultimately my responsibility to ensure protection of all staff and at the same time provide usual and extra care required for patients.

It would be foolish to not admit it was stressful during these times, but it was not unbearable due to the support I had both practically and prayerfully from numerous avenues. It is times like these, that one's work community shines and combines to help and support each other. Our surgery, unlike many others, stayed open most days to serve our community, sometimes seven days a week. I was encouraged by all that our team achieved in a constant shifting predicament that was often frustrating, exhausting and, at times, confusing.

Another positive was that my dress code radically changed, as it did for all our doctors and nurses at my clinic. For over 40 years, I would always prefer to dress professionally in trousers, long business shirt and tie, and jacket when cooler. At the beginning of the pandemic, it was encouraged that all medical health workers wore clothes that could be washed each night in case of contamination, so we all purchased 'surgical scrubs'. They were so practical and comfortable that all our GPs still wear them and we won't be returning to the 'old ways' of dress code. This alteration in apparel led to some light-hearted in-house 'competition' to be brave enough to wear the brightest colour scrubs.

Initially I thought I would most likely be consulting large numbers of very unwell patients with COVID-19, but due to our generally efficient public health measures and large scale vaccination program this did not turn out to be the case. I considered this a blessing. Certainly, there has been the caring for the innumerable patients with COVID-19 for over two years, and now some with Long Covid.

In early 2022, I experienced the paradoxical situation where there were large case numbers of COVID-19 and staff shortages in all businesses and writing 'Not Sick Certificates'. These certificates indicated that patients had recovered from COVID-19 and were actually fit to return to work, or had symptoms that were not COVID-19 related and did not have to isolate. The usual for the prior 40 years was writing medical certificates when patients were unwell and could not work!

## The three Cs

The 'Three Cs' of teamwork previously mentioned really came to the fore during the years of the pandemic.

*Chemistry:* this takes place when people work together as a team, not only thinking about themselves but more importantly about each other, and thereby actually showing altruistic attitude in their behaviour and actions. This chemistry is normally tangible for me with my staff, but I was able to see it raised to another level in the years of the pandemic.

It was evident in the help the team at my practice offered to each other and in the concern they showed for their teammates, particularly in the willingness to cover each other's shifts and workloads, watching out for one another for fatigue and burnout. When the inevitable first of our team and her family succumbed in late 2021, 'pastoral care' sprung into overdrive. Food supplies were quickly dropped off at their doorstep to help get them through the 14 day isolation period. These food hamper drop-offs continued over the ensuing three years when any of our team members needed to isolate.

In December 2020, we had planned an end of year Christmas dinner for all staff, but there was a Sydney outbreak and lockdown announced, so we quickly readjusted and made meals for every staff member and their families and home delivered them just before Christmas Eve. By 2022, our Christmas was a much more relaxed and an equally memorable event, with a meal out together and a test of our *chemistry* when we were all literally locked up in two fun 'escape rooms' (for team challenges ) in the city for our special team Christmas break-up. Metaphorically it also seemed to represent our escape from COVID-19 at least for a while!

We work on our chemistry at our surgery and it's not hard. For instance, when we celebrate someone's birthday, a cake is made or bought and everyone signs a card to take part in the special occasion. Singing 'Happy Birthday' took a humorous turn during the pandemic when we all had to socially distance, wear tight masks and avoid blowing out the candles. However, there was an upside in that the quality of the singing seemed to markedly improve since it was muffled by the N95s! From my observation, it was apparent our friendships have deepened and strengthened as a result of what we went through together over the three years of COVID-19.

*Competency:* this was advanced for all of us in the numerous hours of extra study from multiple sources focused on COVID-19 management, and training for the new vaccines we were now dealing with. We shared information multiple ways via internal messages at work, and regular GP meetings where everyone's ideas were expressed and valued, including all staff. Then there were the Zoom conferences on some weekends and frequent discussion on WhatsApp where we shared relevant advice with each other.

GPs intentionally try to listen to their patients, as no-one knows the patient better than themselves (or their parents). In times of conflict or change, there is a particular need to listen to colleagues and staff with the intent to understand, rather than just leading with your own agenda. Listening and sharing builds mutual trust, allows a different point of view, encourages collaborative ideas and solutions, and helps to address individual concerns and fears – especially in the middle of a pandemic. I think as a team we did this well.

On a normal working day over the last three years, I attentively tuned into up-to-date COVID-19 podcasts on the drive to and from work. Then, after dinner, I listened to webinars from different reputable medical organisations and experts, or read relevant emails and GP chat room comments, and spent time searching health websites from the College of GPs (RACGP), NSW Health and the federal government. Other GPs did the same, and we shared changing information at the practice on a daily basis. Our competency with accessing information and knowledge on COVID-19 and vaccines not only grew exponentially but also had to be kept current to keep us and our patients safe.

At our surgery we quickly introduced a common sense initiative that has proven to be effective and will stay for the foreseeable future. We commenced 'well' and 'unwell' clinics during morning and afternoon sessions each day of the week. This meant that 'well' patients were effectively kept separated from 'unwell' patients with symptoms and sicknesses that suggested a viral respiratory infection and potential cases of COVID-19. After the 'unwell' patients were triaged on the phone, we would consult the 'well' patients coming for the usual needs for the first few hours of the morning and afternoon sessions, with us wearing masks and scrubs, and patients wearing masks. Then one or more of the GPs, depending on demand, would wear full PPE consisting of apron, N95 mask, goggles or a face shield and gloves. 'Unwell' patients were asked to stay in their cars after arriving and phone reception. When the doctor was ready, the patients were taken straight into the consulting room to avoid the waiting room. The consult would be succinct. While a GP was consulting in the 'unwell' clinic, other GPs would conduct their telehealth consults and then the consulting clinic, the room would be cleaned thoroughly.

Unlike many other GP practices, this system allowed us to remain open throughout the pandemic years, seeing well patients, and dealing with their issues and performing regular check-ups (such as skin cancer screening). The unwell were consulted separately. These patients were appreciative that they did not have to attend hospital emergency departments, especially with their children, and with possible COVID-19 cases in the hospital. At the same time, the doctors and other staff from the clinic were able to stay safe, even though we found we'd seen many patients in the unwell clinics who later turned out to be positive COVID-19 cases. The exercise came with a cost – financially for the practice, and for the doctors wearing claustrophobic and hot PPE apparel, especially in summer. Our team of doctors just kept downplaying the inconvenience as 'unpleasant' as compared to our colleagues working in ED and ICU who had to wear PPE for long work shifts. That would have been unbearable.

*Character:* all my staff and doctors worked the hardest they had ever worked, and without complaining during the pandemic. Reception staff stayed back into the evening, working long hours to register the thousands of new patients who urgently requested the scarce vaccines that they could not access. The staff then sent out and coordinated consent forms and appointment times. For three years plus, they have worked tirelessly behind glass screens wearing masks every day, triaging many thousands of patients but simultaneously caring for every individual. They showed endless empathy, especially for the worried elderly, who at times were overwhelmed and anxious with what was happening and needed reassurance, patience and calm from the very people they knew and trusted.

All staff and most GPs took turns in the vaccine clinics that were running nearly daily, with 150 patients per day, including every Saturday and occasional Sundays throughout late 2021 and 2022. The vaccine clinics mainly took place in our carpark at the rear of the surgery, which required cleaning before every clinic began for the day and turned into an outside makeshift mini-mobile-hospital site. This was hard and tiring work requiring incredible logistics that I could not have achieved alone. I was fortunate to have extra help from some men from church and friends of the practice and this eased the burden of the set up.

For the outdoor mass vaccination clinic to operate successfully there was much preparation and organisation required to allow it to run smoothly and cope with the multitude of recipients on most days of the week and weekend. This work included preparing check-in and consent forms; setting up tents, tables, chairs and a bed; and nurses led by Jackie spending hours on the tedious and accurate work of vaccine preparation with the ultra-strict cold chain storage. Before immunisation, each patient had to be counselled before immunisation and then observed afterwards for any allergic vaccine reactions, which were thankfully non-existent in our experience.

Carol often helped out, checking patient details for those lining up for the carpark vaccine clinics, making people feel comfortable and allaying as many fears as she could.

On Father's Day 2021, the practice held a Sunday vaccine clinic just for dads. As well as a jab in one arm, the attendees received a card of encouragement in one hand and a handmade treat in the other. Channel 9 news found out about this opportunity to support dads during the pandemic and created a story for the news that night. This was my practice's one and only claim to fame.

I've never been so proud of every staff member of the practice team, and I became much closer to them and their families throughout this period. Respect, admiration and gratitude were also shared from patients in letters, emails and, most importantly, chocolate!

There is something valuable in belonging to a team, especially one that is functional and productive. You realise that you are involved in something that is far greater than yourself. The friendships and memories of such times remain and you receive a sense of satisfaction in the contribution of helping others.

Despite the physical fatigue and personal angst this pandemic has caused, I believe that each of our team was personally 'refreshed' in their spirit as a result of what they achieved together. I was reminded that leading by serving fulfils a deep-seated need in all of us to do good to others.

It has been shown through history that we tend to remember the things we should forget, and forget the things we should remember. The 'lens' of history should help us to avoid repeating the mistakes of the past. Hopefully, we will have learnt from this COVID-19 pandemic and be able to apply that learning to any other future pandemics. And there will be another pandemic – with a prediction from experts of one every 25 years.

Society needs to be prepared for future pandemics. We need to be proactive in being alert for coordinated worldwide surveillance of any impending contagion, and to have the resources to respond early to outbreaks. In the meantime, we should not let our guard down. The threat of SARS-Cov-2 will be with us for the long haul. On the 5th of May 2023, the public health emergency of international concern for COVID-19 was deemed officially over. This statement did not mean that COVID-19 had gone ,rather that it was ongoing and established. Even though it is now with us to a lesser degree, it is still a global problem.

Karl Faase puts a Christian perspective on the pandemic when he stated, 'This disaster should remind us that we will face other dangers in the future. Our grip on life is very tenuous, and our mortality can't be ignored… God has our eternal existence in his hands.'

# CHAPTER TEN

# MEDICINE AND FAITH

'I believe in Christianity as I believe that the sun has risen: not only because I see it but because by it I see everything else.'
– CS Lewis

'I know just how much I rely on my faith to guide me through the good times and the bad.'
– Queen Elizabeth II

# The foundations of my faith

Faith and religion are often used as interchangeable terms. To have faith is to personally trust in someone or something. Everyone exercises some sort of faith daily in their lives. The religion of Christianity is a personal belief that God is explained in the person of Jesus as revealed in the Bible. Religion is more the way this belief is expressed in thought and action. Its definition can also allude to a persuasion, worldview or denomination.

By now, readers may have observed the thread of faith interwoven throughout my life. My experience of faith and religion was largely shaped by being raised from a very young age in a family deeply rooted in The Salvation Army, a Christian denomination that had a clear understanding that 'we are saved to serve'. During my life, I have been encouraged to use my Christian understanding as a springboard to serving others in the world, especially those with a need – be it physical, psychological or spiritual – demonstrating God's love as our motivation.

This reflects the biblical teaching of Jesus, who stated that the two main commandments were: 'Love God and love others'. Growing up with this belief was an aspiration and one that I've never regretted.

William Booth was a Methodist with a charismatic personality who established The Salvation Army as a religion in 1865, initially naming it the 'East London Christian Mission'. The structured, military style framework of The Salvation Army had its benefits and disadvantages. Because of war around the turn of the century, the idea of regimentation, an 'army', was very popular at that point in history. The population in the United Kingdom was familiar with uniforms being worn, which had the advantage of allowing uniformity: with everyone dressed the same, there was no distinction based on wealth or position.

William Booth had seen firsthand the injustices and poverty around him in London, such as the use of child labour in factories and chimney cleaning, and the tragic effects of alcohol abuse. He understood the need for men and women to have radically transformed lives, with new purpose, meaning and an abstinence for past destructive behaviours. This transformation came from the power of God through a supportive community of believers, who together served others and changed the fabric of society. The history of this, The Salvation Army, and the understanding of potential harm were the reasons why Salvation Army guidelines were set down to encourage the abstinence of smoking and alcoholic beverages.

As a result of individuals following these pragmatic guidelines, I have personally witnessed numerous lives having been radically changed, such as alcoholics who never drank again, and drug addicts who slowly overcame their addictions in specialised programs and centres.

My parents were both soldiers (members) of The Salvation Army and fully involved in church life. As children we followed their path of faith and involvement with The Salvation Army – like osmosis. We thoroughly enjoyed this involvement, being exposed to music, moral teaching, spiritual principles and a great number of friendships made in youth groups.

We were exposed to brass band music, with my sisters playing the tambourine, and myself learning a brass instrument and, later, drums. I belonged to the youth band and later the senior band as an older teenager. We also had unique opportunities of being involved in Salvation Army musical productions, which had catchy lyrics and tunes. Despite never making Broadway, the music was popular in its appeal.

We progressed through different groups, such as Junior Soldiers and Corps Cadets, which each had opportunities to learn about belief in God, Christianity and The Salvation Army, and what was required of us to eventually become a Senior Soldier through ceremonies in the church service. Carol and I still possess some of our certificates, decades old now. The guidelines presented to us as teenagers within these groups helped establish our character at a crucial time in our lives and had the potential of protecting us because of moral teaching.

After we were married, Carol and I were bemused to be asked to represent the Salvos on their annual calendar published and distributed throughout their Australian churches and in hotels. Our photos in Salvation Army uniform were blown up onto an A3 poster with calendar details at the bottom. We thought it was hilarious to discover that many people who had kept the calendar for the year, mentioned that they looked at us every day on the back of their toilet door!

There is a realisation that this may all sound rather strange to the reader and that we belonged to a 'cult'. But there was no coercion. For us growing up in the Salvos, it was an important time of Christian development and commitment. The world might sometimes suggest that Christianity is too restrictive and leads to a lack of freedom. My experience has been that it is actually the opposite. When I played rugby league, boundaries and rules were essential, and within those restrictions came the freedom to enjoy our game but also be kept safe. By allowing boundaries and guidelines in my life, Christianity gave a sense of safety, freedom and enjoyment for all that life offers us.

I've always enjoyed the subject of 'Christian apologetics' (those who defend the faith). The reasoned defence of Christianity is intended to help 'thinkers believe and believers to think!' There is much to investigate and understand in the Christian faith, and it is not an easy subject to be thoroughly competent in without dedicated theological study. When it comes to matters of spirituality and faith, I still struggle with wanting to know everything. But this ideal is unrealistic. For example, I'll never fully understand the body's functioning completely, especially the largely untapped knowledge of the mind. However, this doesn't stop me from learning more each day and applying what I already do know to do my best in medicine. Even then, I still have to utilise a degree of faith that a particular treatment should work based on past experience.

## The Bible

The Bible is the most popular book ever written and it is still the bestseller with 100 million copies sold each year. Its authenticity compared to other historical books has been shown by 'textural criticism'. (Refer to Appendix D 'Textural criticism'.) Its 40 authors are believed to have been inspired by God. The Bible speaks to both non-Christians and Christians. To a Christian, it is authoritative, in that it shows what we believe and how we should live. Having a belief in God and being guided by biblical examples and truths gave me a standard to live by, as well as direction in life. One of the reasons the Bible is filled with stories is so that we can identify with the humanity of people whom God either used for good, or whom He wanted us to view as cautionary examples for what behaviours we should avoid.

The Bible is not just a book of stories, nor just a rulebook for an ancient Jewish culture, it is also a historically accurate record. There are contradictions that I struggle with, and that I do not fully understand. Yet I trust it represents truth. It is a guidebook to understand God, seen through the lens of His son Jesus – this helps in the overall interpretation of its contents and the ultimate revelation of God.

'Christianity is first and foremost about relationships rather than rules. Relationship with the God who made us and our relationships with others. It is about a person (Jesus Christ) more than a philosophy. We can test the claims of Christianity because it is a historical faith, based on historical evidence. Some people think that Jesus was just a "good religious teacher"; however, that does not fit with the facts – His claims, His character and His conquest of death. The teaching of the life, death and resurrection of Jesus Christ, as revealed in the Bible is persuasive, and the evidence strong – showing that it is not an irrational act to have faith.' – Nicky Gumbel

Former Lord Chief Justice of England Lord Darling said of the resurrection, 'In its favour as living truth, there exists such overwhelming evidence, positive and negative, factual and circumstantial, that no intelligent jury in the world could fail to bring in a verdict that the resurrection story is true.'

Why is the God of the Bible different from any other form of God? Why can't we believe in any god? Do all roads of faith lead to the same destination? American pastor Erwin McManus says of his experience. 'Every religion was me chasing after God, but the message of Jesus was God chasing after me.'

'Here is the unique feature of Christian belief. It is not so much us striving to find God, but rather God reaching into history, humanity and our lives, and drawing us to Himself. This combined with grace freely given to all who respond, are Christianity's unique features.' – Karl Faase

# Church

There are a number of popular conceptions as to what the 'church' is. These include the building, the services, the clergy or a given denomination. The church has been described as a 'hospital' where people can be healed, and a 'school' where people can be taught. The 'real' church, however, is made up of individual Christians, who each have a passion and responsibility to represent it well, based on the premise of all that they believe. We go to 'church' but we are also 'the church'. Church is about relationships in what has been called the family of God. It is a place where everyone should feel welcome, irrespective of age, race, colour, status in society or sexual orientation.

There is the 'universal church' consisting of two billion people and who each belong to 'local churches'. There are different denominations, with the common goal of realising that 'What unites us is infinitely greater than what divides us.' – Nicky Gumbel

The church is important to me. It is much more than a club I belong to. It is an extension of my own family and my medical work, as well as providing mission opportunities overseas.

In different countries of the world, the church has its own uniqueness, fashioned on each culture but, in essence, still in unity with the global church. For instance in Rwanda, church can be vibrant, with long services and energetic worshipping in typical African rhythm. I'm thankful that in Australia I can freely attend my church, but this is not a universal practice. Approximately 60 countries persecute Christians for their faith and ban their church attendance, and even destroy their buildings.

The church, however, has been its own worst enemy in turning people away from religion and Christianity, especially in my lifetime. Its reputation has largely been tarnished by the poor behaviour of a Christian minority, which is sad. Issues that have led to this situation include the treatment of same-sex attracted people; child abuse by some of its members and, even worse, authority figures such as pastors and priests; financial misappropriation; and emphasis on wealth. These issues have not endowed the church well to individuals or society as a whole, and they have robbed the church of its true, godly identity.

Billy Graham is considered the most successful evangelist and preacher in recent history. One of the reasons for his success was his desire to have three mentors who helped him be accountable for lust and sexual compromise; combating power and prestige; and wealth and greed.

This accountability enabled him to protect his integrity, which was essential to validate what he was preaching about and enabled him to safeguard his reputation his whole life. This example has been foolishly overlooked by many superstar pastors since that time, leading to their downfall and the disappointment and demise of their churches.

Early in my life, I particularly witnessed the church doing good and making a difference in society. Due to societal changes of self-sufficiency and materialism, and the harm caused by some individuals within the church, it is understandable that theologian RC Sproul stated, 'I doubt if there has been a period in all of Christian history, when so many Christians are so ineffectual in shaping their culture.'

This can, and will only change when Christian lives are based on the truths they believe, and move outside the walls of church buildings to love others. Church was never meant to be a 'holy huddle'. It has been suggested that the best thing the church can do in present times is to be seen to be 'doing good' in their community. The church should be known for its love, and only then can its reputation return to being the 'hope of the world'.

# Hypocrisy

Although the term 'hypocritical' is often used to describe or criticise Christians, who don't appear to have behaviours that authenticate what they say or believe, anyone can be a hypocrite due to their blind spots. Christians especially have to be constantly aware of being hypocritical, because we should desire to be an example of godliness.

Hypocrisy is a behaviour that contradicts what one claims to believe. It can be evident in many areas of life, and it is a behaviour where mentors can be so beneficial.

Hypocrisy can incorporate insincerity, dishonesty, pretence, phoniness and deceit. It can be intentional and deliberate or unintentional, habitual and unconscious. The latter is perhaps the more common type, where it is not even realised by the individual.

Unfortunately, it is a fact that 'good people can have bad behaviour'. Although I've tried to be aware of any hypocrisy in my own life, especially in light of my Christian beliefs, there are times of unintentional failure. Sometimes ironically, these failures although mortifying at the time, turn out to be humorous on hindsight.

Late one Friday evening some years ago, when feeling tired at the end of a busy week at my practice in Lugarno, I consulted a regular patient for a check-up and to discuss his recent pathology results. Our team at this practice had a ritual of sharing a cake for anyone having a birthday. It was usually a tall double sponge cake, with layers of cream and jam and thick icing on top. I used to try to avoid the calories and so on this occasion when a large piece of cake was brought to me for afternoon tea I placed it under my desk on top of my medical bag.

I spent some time with my patient giving him an explanation of his overweight status and possible consequences of such. With his high cholesterol and borderline, elevated blood sugar reading, I emphasised how he needed take his diet more seriously, reduce calories (including cakes and biscuits), lose weight and exercise more. After 30 minutes or so, he left my room with the intent of following up in a few months to look at improvement.

Feeling absolutely famished, I noticed the delivered birthday cake was still sitting there. Being alone, I gave into the temptation, lifted my cake onto the table and started to demolish the large slice. Unbeknownst to me, the patient who was now walking down the corridor to reception decided to return to my room since he'd forgotten to ask me a question. Walking into my room unannounced, he found me with a mouthful of cake, cream all over my lips and unable to talk. He stared at me, shook his head and left without asking his question!

Hypocrisy can appear easily and subtly, and I learnt that day that I needed to be more careful in 'practising what I preach' (and eat). Asking myself the difficult question such as, 'Is my speech, actions and life showing hypocrisy?' can be a protective barometer for my life.

## Science and Christianity

The theory portrayed by mass media, that science and Christian beliefs are in direct conflict, is more an issue of recent times since most of the famous scientists of the last five centuries have believed in God. For much of history, Christianity and scientific study have been allies, rather than opponents. One of the most famous of these scientists, Sir Isaac Newton, in the late 17th century, believed that no sciences were better attested than the religion of the Bible. 'Science cannot begin its work except by acts of faith – neither can Christianity.' – *Searching Issues* – Nicky Gumbel.

Having worked in medicine all my life, I believe that both science and religion are needed. Science gives me the 'what' of information and facts, and Christianity supplies the 'why'. Although I strongly adhere to the science of medicine, there have been many times where I have found that it was just not enough to explain the formation of our wonderfully complex bodies. Also, my personal experience of faith and my observations in the lives of others suggest there is more to life than just 'matter'. For me, faith in God is based on truth and reason, historical fact, and experiences that support these. It is not a 'psychological crutch' as some would suggest, rather it is science and faith acting together.

The two main sources of apparent conflict and contradiction between science and Christianity come in the discussions on the topics of 'miracles' and the 'theory of evolution'. These have always been challenging to me as a Christian doctor, to try to clarify, rationalise and reconcile with my belief system and worldview. The consternation of what is stated in Genesis about creation, and the obvious evidence of ongoing discoveries of age old fossil records, still remains. The reality is I will probably never fully understand them, as there is still more in the overarching story to be revealed in both science and theology. These topics and theories are also explained in *Searching Issues* chapter 'Is There a Conflict Between Science and Christianity?' by Nicky Gumbel, which has helped me come to an understanding of what I believe.

Dr Reverend John Polkinghorne, UK professor of mathematical physics wrote, 'Men of religion can learn from science what the physical world is really like in its structure and long evolving history. This constrains what religion can say where it speaks of that world as God's creation. Men of science can receive from religion a deeper understanding than could be obtained from science alone. The physical world's deep mathematical intelligibility (signs of the mind behind it) and finely tuned fruitfulness (expressive of divine purpose) are reflections of the fact that it is a creation.' I agree with his balanced viewpoint.

To me, science and scripture complement each other. God has revealed Himself in creation and supremely in the person of Jesus Christ. Science is the study of God's general revelation in creation. Biblical theology is the study of God's special revelation in Jesus and the scriptures. The Psalmist in Psalm 19:1–4a, and the apostle Paul in Romans 1:20 (refer to Appendix E 'Bible verses') both speak of the evidence we see in the world around us, of God's creation and His character. This is one of the joys I obtain by observing creation when I travel and by involving myself in landscape photography. It brings what Ken Duncan (Australia landscape photographer) describes as the 'fourth dimension' to this art – the spiritual awareness of the world around us.

What I witness around me, plus the obvious evidence of design, suggests our world is a good 'home' for life in general and especially for human beings. The physical constraints of nature are so finely tuned that if they were slightly different we would not exist – the so called 'anthropic principle'. Although Stephen Hawking did not believe in a creator God, his theory would seem to point in that direction. He asked the question: 'How was it that the initial density of the universe was chosen so carefully? Maybe there is some reason why the universe should have precisely the critical density.'

'It is not just life that has to be explained, but particularly intelligent life, the human mind, the rational structure of the world, human love, music, friendship, beauty and justice. These are all dimensions of reality that point beyond chemical and biological laws. Could all this simply be the result of blind chance and natural selection, with no intelligent mind behind the process? The evidence of science may point to the existence of God. General revelation suggests the tremendous power, intelligence and imagination of a personal creator. But without the special revelation of Jesus (Christ) we would have known little about Him.' – Nicky Gumbel

Albert Einstein said, 'A legitimate conflict between science and religion cannot exist. Science without religion is lame, religion without science is blind. God is not discoverable by purely scientific means. But this really proves nothing: it simply means the wrong instruments are being used for the job.'

The deepest needs of human experience, such as meaning and purpose, and whether there is an afterlife, are not met by science. It is also not able to solve the moral dilemmas of human existence such as wrongdoing and guilt. I uphold we need science and the theology – these confirm the truth revealed in the life, death and resurrection of Jesus. I believe it is true, that we will all worship something. For some, they will only worship science. This stance seems to avoid the personal implications for their own lives (and afterlife) if God truly exists. For others (including myself), it will be worshipping God as the source of truth and reality that brings them purpose and meaning in life, and the hope of life after death.

## Supernatural healing

Not surprisingly, the subject of supernatural healing did not appear in my medical university curriculum. Either that or I must have been absent on the day it was mentioned! It is a peculiar topic for someone working daily in the realm of objective medicine, and yet this subject is well known in the Christian community, and it is one I have had some anecdotal experience with, albeit limited experience.

The Bible teaches about the supernatural healing of God in the Old Testament, and much of the ministry of Jesus on Earth was about his teaching and his healing. The Greek word for saviour is 'sosto', which means 'I heal' and 'I save', both of which Jesus did.

I have observed that supernatural healing can come about by a Christian praying for someone else with a health need, or even for themselves for that matter. Healing does not occur every time someone is prayed for, but if we pray for no-one, then no-one will be healed, but if we pray for some, then some may be healed. As medical professionals, we are discouraged by medical authorities to offer prayer for patients, unless they ask for it. There are times when I consider prayer is appropriate, and in those circumstances I will always ask permission from a patient beforehand. When people are prayed for and the result is healing, it is not the person that prays who provides the healing – rather it is God.

My understanding on this subject is that God can heal 'explicably' through the medical profession and at other times 'inexplicably' – without their intervention. Having worked in Africa and Australia, it seems the former (explicably) takes place more often in countries where there are strong health systems for the majority of the population, and the latter (inexplicably) can be seen to take place more often in those without adequate health services. It is beyond the scope of human intelligence when miraculous healing takes place since it involves God's supernatural power.

Years ago, I had arranged for Carol to have shoulder surgery from an orthopaedic surgeon for rotator cuff tears and impingement that had not improved with standard management over many months including physiotherapy, medication, cortisone injections and rest.

A week before her surgery a visiting minister at our church offered prayer for healing during a service and Carol did not hesitate to accept this option. Her pain went quickly and has never returned, which left us both elated, and me with an unusual conversation to have with the specialist when I rang to cancel her surgery.

A particularly relevant example took place in recent years that highlighted the often simultaneous occurrence of both 'explicable' and 'inexplicable' healing of God - on this occasion of profound importance to my family. Wayne, (the father of my son-in-law Joel), is a pastor, close friend and has been a patient of mine for years. One morning, he along with his wife Robyn, ran for the 'tube' (train) only to discover that by the time he reached his office (The Salvation Army International Headquarters London) he was feeling unwell with chest pain.

Robyn astutely called an ambulance and waited in the foyer of the building. In front of the arriving paramedics, Wayne had a cardiac arrest which immediately led to them performing CPR and use of a defibrillator on numerous occasions over the ensuing hour. Amazingly he was successfully resuscitated by a number of support paramedic teams and transported unconscious to a nearby cardiac hospital and proceeded to angioplasty and stent insertion into his obstructed coronary artery. Being in a coma in ICU, Robyn was told by a specialist that Wayne may not survive the night and if he did, would most likely be disabled due to brain damage from anoxia.

Believing in the power of prayer, Robyn quickly set into motion a world-wide request for prayer for healing which we gladly participated in along with hundreds of other shocked family, friends and acquaintances globally. Miraculously, and to the absolute surprise of the treating physicians, Wayne regained consciousness the following morning without severe medical consequences and was cognitively intact!. This story was yet another reminder to myself that God still works in mysterious ways and can allow supernatural and unexplained healing to occur conjointly with medical science and the care of health care professionals. Now fully recovered, Wayne and Robyn continue their work for The Salvation Army as leaders over South East Asia - and no doubt retelling their extraordinary story.

One delightful elderly patient had recurrent skin cancers, which I would arrange to remove surgically after an initial consult. On a number of occasions, these skin cancers would disappear by the time I met with her on the surgery date. She told me that she would pray for healing of her skin cancers when I diagnosed them. I suggested with 'tongue in cheek' that perhaps she might avoid praying about just some of these lesions, so I wouldn't lose my surgery skills!

Often healing takes place when both natural means through available healthcare and supernatural healing combine. In fact, this takes place on a daily basis when someone, for instance, has surgery that is successful, but their wounds and scars still have to heal. Or when a serious infection is appropriately treated with antibiotics, but the body still has to recover. We may just dismiss this as natural and expected – our own body just doing its job, but it is worth thinking deeper as to what allows this to occur. This suggests to me that there is a Creator behind the natural healing processes that happens within all of us on a daily basis and that we take for granted.

## Abortion and euthanasia

Today, abortion is so readily available to patients who seek it, that GPs rarely have consults to discuss the topic with a pregnant woman considering a termination. There is no referral required, so women simply look up online the nearest centre to them and attend once they've made their decision. Either that, or they can attend a GP and simply be prescribed a combination of abortion inducing medicines, rather than arranging a surgical termination. In the past, I would usually consult and discuss a female patient's options, the risks of abortion, but also the risks and possible outcomes of proceeding with a pregnancy. Depending on the result of this discussion, I would either refer to a gynaecologist for the procedure, if the woman was still intent on her decision, or refer to a maternity hospital for antenatal care.

I am obliged to care primarily for the patient, and not force my own attitude on abortion or the right to life of an unborn foetus. It has been difficult to have these conversations because I do not agree with abortion. My belief is that life is sacred, even for an unborn foetus, and that it is not up to me as a doctor to decide whether a life can be taken. The year I graduated medical school, doctors had to recite the Hippocratic Oath at their graduation ceremony, which states 'to refrain from causing harm or hurt' and which also related to my attitude.

I remember two young unmarried women who I consulted on different occasions in the 1980s, who came to request a referral for an abortion. Rather than just immediately supplying a referral, I discussed the pros and cons of the decision they were trying to work through (i.e. the physical and emotional consequences of having an abortion versus the other options of either keeping their baby or adoption). I encouraged a few days of thinking through their choices before making up their minds, and both came back and decided to proceed with the pregnancy and keep the baby. I continued to support them in their choice for the following years, as single mothers. Thirty years later, it is heartening to still be consulting and offering medical care to one of the mothers and as well now to her adult son.

Despite recent laws introduced in various states of Australia legalising euthanasia, I've never been involved in providing or referring for this type of management of a terminal illness or other condition. My beliefs are similar to abortion, that life, however difficult, is still precious, and it is not my prerogative to influence when a person dies. With regards to terminal cancers and other conditions, there is already excellent palliative care services that invariably ensure patients do not suffer. The effects of increasing doses of morphine not only effectively control pain in the majority of patients, but actually accelerate a peaceful passing as a consequence. Consideration of the need of relatives to be involved in the care of the patient is important in the grieving process for the patient and the relatives as well.

A concern I have about euthanasia is the risk of the 'slippery slope' effect, whereby, tightly controlled legislation can be watered down over time, allowing the intentional taking of life by doctors, for less serious conditions, or earlier in a disease process than is needed. I do accept that it is a sensitive and difficult issue when it comes to terminal and progressive neurological diseases, and my right as a family doctor to not be involved in euthanasia needs to also be balanced with the right of a patient and family to have a different value system and worldview when helping a patient in this predicament.

Because I believe in and am strongly committed to the notion of the 'sanctity of life', I align with the comment of past Prime Minister of Australia, Tony Abbott when he stated: 'There is a critical difference between declining to keep someone alive and who would otherwise be dead, and deliberately killing someone who would otherwise be alive.'

## The anatomy of faith

The Bible and the church teach about the 'heart, the mind and the soul'. These concepts have always made me reflect on how they relate to what I've learnt and understood about the anatomy and biology of the body. We doctors were not taught that the heart as an organ has emotions, rather it is a muscle that pumps blood, needs blood and oxygen, and its rhythm is controlled by an electrical innervation. I can only surmise that when the Bible refers to the 'heart of man' (for example, 'Above all else, guard your heart, for it affects everything you do'), it is a metaphor for feelings and emotions that mainly occupy the amygdala within our brain.

To state that the brain is an incredibly complex organ itself, with only a small amount known about its function and operation, is an understatement. To control the whole body by intricate electrical pathways is itself difficult to understand, but the added specialised features of emotion, memory, rational thinking and consciousness to name a few is near beyond comprehension – at least to the state of medical science at present.

I believe men and women have a 'soul'. Where our soul or spirit is located and how it works is again unknown. How does that inner being connect or relate to God's spirit and the supernatural? I don't know, but I accept the thought that 'emotions are the language of the soul' and are vitally important and essential to who we are.

'Our mental health requires the balance between heart and head' (subjective and objective). Neither purely analytical and intellectual, nor relying on feelings to interpret people and life. It can be unhealthy to just do emotion-directed reasoning, that is, if you feel it, it must be true.' – David Ridell.

The Bible recognises this when it talks about the need to renew our mind in Romans 12:2: 'Don't be conformed to the patterns of this world, but be transformed by the renewing of your minds so that you can figure out what God's will is – what is good and pleasing and mature.' This is very relevant when it comes to faith. It is not just about our emotions being moved as some critics would suggest, when they claim faith is just 'mystical thinking and loss of intelligence'. There is much rational reasoning and evidence that faith in a supernatural God should be considered. Faith has been described as believing in things unseen. There are numerous examples around me that I need faith to interpret since they are unseen, including wind, electricity, electromagnetic radiation and many other examples. I can, however, clearly see the effects and consequences of these, just as I can see the changes in the lives of those who have come to faith.

'Faith is different from proof; the latter is human, the former is a gift from God.' – Blaise Pascal

# Health and societal benefits of faith

Despite loose criticism by some that Christian faith is just a 'crutch' for the weak, there is historical, anecdotal and observational evidence that faith can improve and benefit our individual health and that of society in general.

I lived through the Billy Graham crusades of the latter half of the 20th century and read about and observed personally the transformation that took place in individuals, families and even society. One-third of the entire population of Australia in 1959 attended these crusades, heard the message that this evangelist brought about God's love and grace and the need to repent and receive His love and forgiveness.

One of the Billy Graham events, held at the Melbourne Cricket Ground, had the largest ever recorded crowd at 140,000. There was also a record crowd at the Sydney Cricket Ground. The response to the outcome of the crusades was enormous and many lives were transformed (including many people I knew then or have met since). There was a documented statistical reduction of alcohol consumption, extramarital births and reported crime in general in society.

Studies of young people have shown that those involved in church and possessing faith have lower incidence of depression, alcohol and drug abuse and lower suicide rates. Peer-reviewed research released in Norway in 2023 showed that faith contributes to good health in various studies. The research revealed there was a significant lower risk for various chronic disease such as cancer, diabetes and cirrhosis of the liver (due to lower alcohol intake).

Healthcare workers tend to compartmentalise patients. The lead investigator of the Norway research, Dr Hvidt suggested, 'Doctors, psychologists and pastors have their clearly defined roles and specialisation which is good, but it is important to remember that humans are not distinct parts, we are whole beings and need our spiritual dimension to be taken into account for wholistic healthcare.'

I have witnessed over my life, and have been involved personally, with the work of Christian communities expressing their faith in action, through such avenues as community care, care of orphans around the world, mission work in undeveloped countries, social welfare and counselling programs. The Salvation Army's work in this field is well known, particularly with their work during world wars. Ever since its commencement, the 'Army' has had a distinct reputation of service, especially during wartime where chaplains served tea, coffee and donuts on the frontline. One of these who served was my grandfather, Major George Franks.

The crisis support service Lifeline was formed by Reverend Alan Walker in 1960, helping countless Australians, especially through difficult times, via their 41 centres around the nation, and two and a half million calls per annum.

Our culture, and whole of Western civilisation, is based on Christian ethic. We are indebted to Christianity: for our laws, governments and justice systems; for the origins of our schools and universities; the development of science, medicine and hospitals; and for being instrumental in the development of human rights. I believe we are living in a present crisis in the Western world, largely as a result of materialistic atheism, which has sapped meaning and purpose from people's lives. I have personally observed this phenomenon expressed as reduced self-worth that has led to a deterioration of emotional and mental health.

## Culmination

Faith in God has accompanied my whole life, including my medical career, and it has been integral and important to me.

Blaise Pascal wrote, 'There are three means of believing – by custom, by reason and by inspiration.' Faith can only partially be handed down from our family of origin. Modelling can occur from what we may have observed from the example of others in the past (custom). However, there comes a time when a child becomes an adult and has to make up their own mind whether to accept the faith that was handed down to them.

At 20 years of age, I had my own personal realisation of truth (my moment of inspiration).

'What you care about is revealed in your priorities' – Matthew 6:21. I cared about my faith in God, so I intentionally put time and effort into growing and testing this over my life. In doing so, I believe the associated values and benefits of faith have offered me protection and freedom – not the reverse.

There is a difference between 'knowledge' and 'knowing'. I had knowledge of my wife Carol before I married her, but 'knowing' more about her came with time and the development of a deeper relationship. And there's still a lot more to discover. Many have knowledge of God, but it takes a personal commitment to know God and experience the lifetime relationship.

Over my lifetime, I've found a number of people who have decided to not accept the Christian faith personally until they fully understood all the facts and all the evidence related to their decision. Whether it be in ordinary aspects of daily living where we have faith in something or someone, or whether in the acceptance of the Christian faith, doubt will often be present and is understandable. It can be expressed as reservation, apprehension, or mixed feelings. Christian belief involves facts, faith and feelings in that order of priority. Our feelings can fluctuate and lead to emotional-based reasoning and so there is a requirement of facts and faith based on truths found in the Bible and in history.

For others, coming to faith in the loving God of the Bible is more an instantaneous experience and does not depend on full and complete understanding. People like Peter Hitchings (the brother of the well-known atheist Christopher Hitchings), whose life was changed as he stood in front of a painting of the Last Judgement. This brilliant man was suddenly reminded that he would come face to face with the risen Christ, and his life was transformed. He says in his book *The Rage Against God* that he should have been ashamed that 'fear' played a part in his conversion, and although he could have made up some credible story, he realised that his feeling of proper fear was an important gift that helped him to think clearly in moments of danger.

My personal conversion experience was a mixture of a sudden realisation at the age of seven of a simple truth that God loved me, then years of 'marinating' and progressive understanding. Another definitive moment for me as a young man was when I decided faith in God was real, based on reason, and I needed to do something about it for the rest of my life.

I have come to accept Christian faith, not just because I believe that it works, but that it works because I believe that it is true. Because of the consequences, I believe that having this faith is the most important decision that I or anyone else will ever make. To me, this is certainly worth investigating.

# CHAPTER ELEVEN

# MARRIAGE AND FAMILY

'Train up a child in the way he should go, but be sure to go that way yourself.'
— Charles Spurgeon

'In spite of all the scientific advances and great improvements in our material welfare, the family remains as the focal point of our existence.'
— Queen Elizabeth II

James Taylor has been an artist I've admired since the 1970s, writing many famous songs and being a magnificent Blues guitarist and singer. One of his well-known songs states 'Shower the people you love with love, tell them the way that you feel.'

Telling your family that you love them may sound straightforward and relatively easy to do, but it is not always so. I found it easier when my children were younger to say how much I loved them, but more difficult as they became adolescents and seemed to resist affectionate actions and words. This experience is not uncommon. As a grandfather, it now just rolls off the tongue to the grandkids, especially when leaving them, to say 'love you'.

This love, which was my desire to show and shower on my wife and family, has evolved and changed over the years, as I came to understand that people need to be loved differently. My children would probably acknowledge that I was not good at expressing my feelings verbally, rather I was better at showing my love by what I did for them. But that for some may not suffice, as was the case for my daughter, who later in life mentioned it was not what we did for her that showed her love, it was what we said that made the difference.

In 1992, Pastor Gary Chapman first introduced the concept of love languages to the world with his seminal book *Five Love Languages: The Secret to Love that Lasts* describing that people have different ways of expressing and understanding love. Needless to say, it's not just understanding our own preferred love language but more importantly the language of others closest to you in your life. The five primary love languages that have been labelled include physical touch (affection), words of affirmation, acts of service, receiving gifts and quality time. Each is important in expressing love in a different way. It is one thing to learn and understand the theory, it is another to put it into practice.

I have had to learn over the years what my wife's and my children's love language are because it is important for them to feel loved. I encourage parents to try to learn their partner's and their children's 'love languages' early because it will strengthen their relationships. It should be obvious that one does not just provide the 'primary' love language to those we love, and neglect the other four. We usually all need some of each, but we feel particularly loved when our main love need is met.

A time that I observed the impact of love languages and being showered with love came when Carol suffered significant depression at the age of 54, and which lasted three years. Having not suffered depression previously, it was a sad and difficult time to watch Carol go through many days of not being herself. Our children, who had all left home, were so encouraging to her through this time. Justin, our oldest son, came and sat with her and she was comforted by his presence. Racquel (my daughter) showered Carol with flowers, cooked meals and tidied up the house, which brought beauty into her days. Luke reminded Carol of who she was and how she could rely on her past life experiences (before the depression) to be a foundation for the present and her future.

Carol was unable to take medication due to adverse reactions, so she did what a woman of faith does – she prayed and asked God to heal her. This came slowly and through a few means simultaneously – body, mind and spirit. Carol and I drove to Cronulla beach regularly to go for long walks and she loved being near the ocean. She attended a suitable psychologist for insight and management, which gave her clarity of thinking. She met up with a loyal Christian friend (Julie) every few weeks for two years. We are indebted to Julie who took the time to care for Carol. Carol's faith in God is not just important to her, but it is a stronghold in her life. Carol recovered slowly through a process of holistic healing.

Her depression has not returned and since that time she has used her experience to encourage and help other women in similar predicaments.

## Marriage and motherhood

'God promised men that good and obedient wives would be found in all corners of the world. Then He made the Earth round… and laughed and laughed and laughed!'
– Author unknown

I first met Carol, through our church youth group. I was attracted not only to her physical beauty, but also her inner qualities. Like myself, she loved adventure, enjoyed outings to the beach and, particularly, dinner at the new Beverly Hills Pizza Hut!

Carol has a very quirky sense of humour and she can laugh at herself, an important trait to have in life, and something I think all our children have inherited.

I must have had some unusual patience of youth during our courtship, as I taught Carol to drive in my blue Cortina. On hindsight, Proverbs 21:23 was a relevant reminder during that time: 'Watch your words and hold your tongue; you'll save yourself a lot of trouble'! Perhaps humorous when thinking about driving lessons, this proverb is much more serious when entering into a long-term relationship. When I (or anyone else for that matter) stops and thinks before they speak, it can save a lot of grief for all involved, especially when we might be feeling angry or frustrated. It is impossible to take back words said in anger, and it takes a lot of work to repair the damage caused to another.

Proverbs also does not mince words when it comes to understanding a prospective wife before getting married: 'It is better to live alone in the desert than with a crabby, complaining wife.' – Proverbs 21:19

I don't remember this being raised in pre-marriage counselling classes, but I would think it should be applied equally to husbands as well! Fortunately, I did not end up in the desert, and I counted my blessings to have a wife who had a wonderfully calm nature, and whose occasional grievances about me were most times justified.

The name 'Carol' means 'song', and Carol's middle name 'Ann' means 'full of grace' so I've actually been married to a woman who embodies being a 'Song of Grace'! A book twice the length of this one could be written about the influence she's had on numerous people, especially in their times of hardship or personal trials. I love the way she exudes 'faith' – the strength to believe in God for unseen supernatural results in every area of life.

Carol has received reciprocal care from others during particular trials during our married life. One of these times was when she was depressed and another was when she had a miscarriage during our second pregnancy, when Justin was about three years old. Lack of assistance and personal care at the hospital she was admitted to aggravated the trauma she went through. Carol and I accepted that this trial was part of an unknown plan in our lives and, afterwards, Carol started to look forward to another pregnancy, but it did not come quickly. Her specialist suggested she had secondary infertility.

As Carol and I desired a sibling for Justin, we explored adoption and applied overseas – in particular in South Korea. After many interviews and visits, we were ready to proceed with adoption, but this coincided with an overseas trip to the USA. While we were there, we discovered Carol was pregnant. Understandably, it was a time of mixed emotions in our lives, where we had to let go of our adoption plans. But we were thrilled when our own little girl Racquel finally arrived, five years after Justin.

For those who know her well, Carol has a wonderful gift of discernment. Something I've forgotten at times at my own peril. This could include a discernment about who to employ, doctors to work with, or other important decisions in our lives. Her administration gift was highlighted when she began the BeYoutiful Girls mentoring program for adolescent girls. She began this in 2012. BeYoutiful Girls was born out of a visit to Rwanda after hearing Headmaster Fred Buyinza speak of his vision for his students. I have nothing but admiration for all Carol has achieved over the years with these various groups. I've been privileged to observe and share in the positive stories of the outcomes of young women, who have been given important life skills to take on the many obstacles life will throw at them in our ever-changing society.

At the end of 2019, Carol was presented with a community award by the then Prime Minister Scott Morrison, who was our local federal MP. She was presented with the award for everything she and her team achieved in mentoring girls from our local schools. Although not the reason for her voluntary work, it was lovely for her to be encouraged and I was proud of her.

Carol has always felt that motherhood was underrated and unappreciated in society – and I agree. She's been the manager of our home and the many tasks and roles she's taken on is exhausting to contemplate. A worthy description on this subject is 'Motherhood is like a heavy winter coat, you have to wear it whatever the season.' Our family has benefited because Carol took motherhood seriously and wore that coat for many years. Especially in the early years of our family, when the children were young, she chose to be a mother at home. When the children were all eventually at school, she obtained employment around the children's school hours so that she could be with them at the end of their day.

I have learnt from life in general and as a family doctor that there is no perfect marriage. My marriage was no different, in that 'perfection' was not a realistic expectation for myself or Carol. But I have also never forgotten the wise words of my friend Ian Grant from New Zealand: 'You marry the one you love, then you learn to love the one you marry,' - reminding me that falling in love can be easy - growing in real love takes time.

Marital fatigue is real and should be acknowledged, but it can be minimised and counteracted. For us, this has always meant dedicated time together, while at the same time allowing the other person freedom to do what they are passionate about. Carol allowed me to continue practising medicine way past the retirement age considered normal, while I have encouraged her to stay active in the things she's passionate about. We have always made sure we prioritised and planned common interests that led to pleasurable activities such as holidays, travel, walking and trekking and, more lately, swimming – now in heated pools! Time together should always be prioritised, whether that be simple coffee dates, a dinner or a movie. This can create romance and space to enjoy the moments together without any other distractions.

Marriage and families come with stressors from within and from outside the marriage (such as work, financial and health issues). When the stress levels build, they can lead to increasingly difficult times and emotional dysregulation, with resultant poor choices and behaviour. For men in particular that may mean counteracting unrestrained personal gratifications - a deception all men (myself included) need to be aware of.

When marriage difficulties arise, we can say and do things we regret, and most couples would have experienced this. Although normal in its commonness, there is an absolute, non-negotiable need to do something about our mistakes if we are not going to erode our relationship. One of the things Carol and I have found helpful is the need to frequently press the 'reset button', by saying sorry, and accepting each other's forgiveness, and moving on.

I am immensely thankful that being mindful, with some of the above choices, have helped our marriage to not only survive but become healthier. I will always acknowledge the influence of our common Christian faith, which is greater than the two of us. Irrespective of the circumstances we face as we journey through life together, exclusivity and faithfulness to each other has to be above them, and upholding the commitment given to each other in our wedding vows in 1975. As we grow older, we continue to be thankful for the joy of loving, and we remember that being loved is a gift that we give and receive.

## Illawong (1980)

As a young couple with one child, and after completing my hospital work, Carol and I decided to move from Baulkham Hills. Desiring to enter general practice at Lugarno, and not being able to afford a property in that suburb, we explored the new and growing development of Illawong, where land was still affordable. Purchasing our block in a new subdivision, isolated and surrounded by bush, we proceeded to design and then build our new house. Justin loved the bush setting and the outdoor activities this area provided.

The cul-de-sac was a safe street for our growing family and the children all enjoyed riding their bikes and playing with the neighbour's children, as well as exploring the back creek. Not long after being in our home, we built a swimming pool and the children loved having their friends around for a swim in summer. Over the years, a number of renovations allowed us to keep our home modern in appearance and functionality. It was certainly a wonderful family home we appreciated and enjoyed for 38 years.

We sold our Illawong house in 2018. It was sad to be leaving because we had a treasure chest full of memories and wonderful neighbours that we had the privilege to live alongside for nearly four decades. Carol and I both knew it was time to downsize, with only the two of us in a large house, and because of increasing maintenance of the pool and gardens. We were blessed to be able to obtain a duplex at Caringbah South, a delightful home, where we lived for three years until deciding to move closer to two of our children and seven grandchildren on the Sunshine Coast.

# Children

We dearly love each of our children, especially as we've watched them become mature and responsible adults. We've always said to each other that we did not want our children to be clones of us, but to grow up and fulfil their own individual potential.

# Justin

Being placid in nature means being calm, composed, easygoing, and even-tempered. Anyone who knows Justin would understand and agree that this is an apt description of his nature and attitude to life, both as a child, a young man and now as a middle-aged adult. He was an easy child to raise. We could take him anywhere, even out with friends to dinner, and he would entertain himself quietly, read a Little Golden Book or have a sleep on the floor. He loved helping outside around the house, and playing with his yellow Tonka truck to help dig trenches for electrical and plumbing pipes, and moving sand and dirt indiscriminately from one place to another. He just loved the outdoors.

Justin enjoyed playing cricket in the rumpus room as a toddler, using a 12-inch bat and me being the bowler. His favourite pastime as a young child was building Lego –

he became a specialist in all models and designs. Keeping his large collection meant that he could pass them down to his three boys, and this also allowed him to brush up on his skills as an adult. Justin would have made an excellent 'Brickman' on the TV show *LegoMasters* with his skills and personality.

From an early age, Justin enjoyed soccer, but as an adolescent this was replaced with wakeboarding, surfing, rock climbing and tight-rope walking. It is fascinating to observe his sons having similar sporting interests.

Like his mum, Justin was a fast runner, and soon did so well in school races that he made it to state carnivals, becoming state age champion. Again, it is a delight to observe some of those skills (and maybe genes), being passed down to his second son, Bodhe, who is a fast long-distance runner.

When he was about to enter adolescence, I took Justin on a three-day canoe and camping trip to Kempsey. The intention was to give me an opportunity in an adventure setting to explain to him the changes that would be occurring to his mind and his body in the following years, and it also gave us a chance to have fun and create lasting memories.

At school, his main interests were technical drawing and woodwork. His carpentry skills were honed as he approached the HSC, and for his major project he built a treated pine deck on the rear of our house, for which he won an award and was placed in the first 10% of the state. We were proud of his achievements. We enjoyed that deck for many years until we sold the house.

Finishing his schooling, Justin obtained a carpentry apprenticeship, but after two years we were surprised to find that he desired 'to run away with the circus'. In actual fact, he obtained a position with Cirque du Soleil, travelling to all capital cities of Australia, then Japan and then to Quebec, Canada, mainly in the catering department. He became friendly with the top acrobats, and he resurrected his previous balance and rope skills in the practice tent.

After a year working with the circus Justin settled down. This was influenced significantly by his girlfriend, Katherine (now his wife), who we love being part of our family. Ja and Katti (as they are affectionately known) have a love not only for each other but also mutually for the world's peoples and the desire to make a difference for those living in poverty in undeveloped countries. After marrying, they both worked for Katherine's father, who was the CEO of Every Home/Global Concern, a Christian not-for-profit organisation that supports projects in overseas undeveloped countries. This gave them opportunity to check that funds were being spent appropriately and to encourage workers in India, Bangladesh, South Africa, Zambia, Zimbabwe and Malawi.

Carol and I visited Justin and Katherine in Chennai, Southern India in 2004 to support and observe their work, which at the time was a long-term project building a school. Although a wonderful experience for them both, there was a price to pay by them while on mission. They were both persecuted by leaders of another religion who did not agree with their work. Ja's health suffered from repeated infectious diseases and Katti was injured when hit by a speeding motorbike.

Justin and Katherine's family now includes three boys. They made the life-changing decision to move to the Sunshine Coast in 2015. They were looking forward to a new lifestyle with less financial burden. The whole family have settled well into Queensland, establishing new friendships. The boys are enjoying their new school. Justin is employed by Tourism Sunshine Coast, working in IT and web design, which is so suitable with his love of the outdoors. Katti is studying psychology, also appropriate with her natural gift of caring for others.

Justin and Katti are such supportive parents of their three growing boys, and Carol and I enjoy observing this and participating in the life of their family and cheering them all on.

Justin and I have a number of common interests (surfing and water sports) and convictions (parenting and faith) and also some weaknesses especially when it comes to vanilla slices. In our travels we both look out for the best vanilla slices, rate them and then send a photo to stir the envy of the other!

# Racquel

As a child, Racquel was a bubbly and happy daughter, and a daddy's girl. Everything she did was with gusto, such as sports like surfing, swimming and netball. Racquel had many friends, but she attracted a few teachers who didn't appreciate her sometimes adventurous and forthright behaviour, especially as a young adolescent. School was somewhat a challenge for her at times, but when she later became a florist she shone in her creativity.

We enjoyed going together to watch the Sharks' football games, dressing up for the occasion in supporter fan gear. Racquel was so enthusiastic at these games that she often drowned out the cheerleaders!

Musically, she was a clever keyboard player after having lessons, and her piano teacher commented that she was naturally gifted. She wrote a song when her cousin Pete passed away at the age of 18. This song came from her place of grief. She enjoyed involvement in Sunday school musicals, music camps and also loved triathlon weekends with her friends.

As a young girl Racquel was so outgoing that she applied and auditioned for the *Hey Hey It's Saturday* Red Faces segment, playing a tambourine to a song from *Sister Act*, dressed as a nun. Carol and I sat in the audience, amazed at her confidence.

Life goes so fast. Before long, I was walking Racquel down the aisle at her wedding. Jack was Racquel's firstborn and our first grandson. The birth of grandchildren is always an exciting time in a grandparent's life. Lilielle, our first granddaughter, was born 19 months later and also brought great joy into our family. She was a precious little girl – now a precious adolescent.

Racquel's marriage ended soon after Lili was born, and this was a sad and difficult time for everyone. It's through these times that you realise there's no handbook for every situation in life – everyone's life is unique and complex. Being present at this time, in this situation, was the best thing we could do.

Racquel and her children stayed in their home until there was a need for them all to move in with us, to allow Racquel to save for her future and to have a rest from the busy-ness of being a single parent. We had daily contact with her and her two children, doing our best to normalise life for them all, and support them through this time, as any parent would for their child.

This was a time of reflection and personal growth for Racquel. We took pleasure in being active parents and grandparents during this period, showing love, having fun and undertaking daily activities such as school drop-offs, homework and kids sports. I taught Jack to play Chess and we relished the game we made up called 'Masai' marbles. We also enjoyed learning geography together as part of his bed-time routine.

Kintsugi is the Japanese art of restoring broken pottery by mending the areas of breakage with lacquer mixed with gold. It treats breakage and repair as part of the history of an object, rather than something to disguise. It allows you to see that being damaged is not a sign of failure or defeat, rather a sign of change, progress and improvement. It's the practice of self-love, allowing failures to be accepted. This analogy is what I observed in my daughter's life after the difficulties that she and her young family went through.

Forgiving yourself first allows you the opportunity of forgiving others. God can repair the brokenness in our lives and make us more beautiful through the process. Racquel has had her fair share of trials over the years, but to her credit, she slowly overcame these difficult years. These experiences have helped her become the strong and mature mother and daughter that she is today.

Racquel has many skills and qualities, including being a creative trained florist, a netball manager for her club at Coolum and a dedicated and protective mother and homemaker. Her sensitive caring and generosity towards friends, and anyone in need, is well known and admired. When she makes a decision, she carries it through with diligence and leaves no stone unturned.

Racquel later reconnected with Joel, who she knew as a child. Joel had been through his own trials, and they found that they had much in common, and had similar carefree personalities, a love of their families and Christian-based values. Carol and I sit back sometimes and just dwell on God's goodness in bringing Joel into Racquel's life, loving her children as if they were his own, and bringing so much joy and laughter into their whole household. Joel has his own two beautiful daughters (Unity and Maddie), allowing their blended family to extend to six children. When we see the girls visiting, we're encouraged as we witness the positive outcome of their coming together.

Racquel takes motherhood seriously, meeting the needs of all their children, while working to support the family income. In 2020, desiring to work towards purchasing their own home and own land with some space, they investigated properties on the Sunshine Coast and together bought a property online and sight unseen during COVID-19. They lived in a shed that they built on their land while slowly planning and supervising the building of their own home. This was a time of character-building and family unity. Like Justin and Katti, Racquel and Joel have settled in well, have quality neighbours and friends and are enjoying their new life on the Sunny Coast.

# Luke

At Luke's birth, Carol and I were thrilled to welcome another son into our family. He had a difficult start to life when I found he'd developed pyloric stenosis at six weeks of age presenting with increasing projectile vomiting. He required life-saving surgery at the Sydney

Children's Hospital and Carol and I took turns being alongside his cot 24 hours a day to help where we could until he was discharged.

Luke's hobbies and interests as a child included drawing, board games and Matchbox cars, visiting the park, and later beating me at mini-golf, despite me even building a putting green on our front lawn to practise. He loved swimming and having pool pony fights with Justin and Racquel, riding bikes and building cubbyhouses. He played soccer, basketball, tennis and now excels in running and trekking. I thoroughly enjoyed my involvement with him in these sports, attending matches and practice times, setting up soccer nets in the backyard and attaching a basketball ring to our back deck. In later years, despite a muscle disorder, he developed a love and skill as a mountain climber. I recall with pleasure the time I took him trekking (in lieu of his Schoolies trip) to the Northern Territory and in particular Uluru, where we both enjoyed and valued this time together.

He studied psychology at Wollongong University for four years and organisational psychology at Macquarie University for three years, after excelling in his HSC. Luke undertook an exchange student opportunity to study at the University of Colorado, Boulder in the USA for a year, which also gave him time for trekking and snowboarding in the surrounding mountains. Carol and I were excited to visit him there and enjoy sightseeing in the surrounding Rocky mountains of Colorado.

After Luke's graduation, which we proudly attended, we observed him put what he'd studied into practice as a HR (human resources) practitioner in large companies in Sydney, Melbourne and Christchurch, which was a great sense of achievement for him and delight for us.

Luke has always been a deep thinker, and as a teenager he wrote his own poetry and his artwork was inspired. Similar to his brother, he has a sincere concern and compassion for those affected by poverty in Africa (in particular Kenya). He observed personally on his two visits children living in overt poverty on garbage tips in Nakuru. Not being satisfied to just be 'concerned', Luke and his friends founded a not-for-profit organisation called OnCourse, that provides vocational training to young adolescents and women, and much needed schooling support for children. His fundraising is ongoing, with organising annual trivia nights to help keep the charity viable.

For anyone, overcoming trials in life is an ongoing process that can involve complexity, confusion and struggle. Carol and I realised this personally in 2008 when we discovered that Luke had same-sex attraction.

Luke was very active in the church, had a strong Christian faith and believed he had a life calling to be youth pastor, so this revelation suddenly and profoundly changed his life trajectory. He'd quietly realised this truth for a number of years, and was silently suffering significant depression to the point of thinking about self-harm. We did not realise the extent of these feelings until he shared poems he'd been writing about his predicament and his inner life secret.

There are many theories about why an individual becomes same-sex attracted and many I have read, but I'm still not confident that anyone truly knows. These different hypotheses are beyond the scope of this book, but a few pervasively kept me awake at night. There were a number of questions any dad might ask himself in response to this revelation. Had he been a victim of child sexual abuse? Had I developed a strong enough emotional father-son bond with him? Had I been a failure as a father? What had I done wrong and how could I have prevented this outcome for him? Was he born with, and has always had, his sexual orientation?

At first this revelation shocked Carol and I both, as Luke definitely did not fit the stereotypical appearance, idiosyncrasies and behaviour that I (and probably most of society) had developed in my thinking and experience over my lifetime. It challenged us both in a number of ways, perhaps myself more since I sought a reason and then a solution. 'Shame' never entered our psyches. We have never had been ashamed of our son, and we never will be. He is too loved for that to be a relevant feeling.

Together Luke and I visited a psychologist and a counsellor – to try to find answers. I was slow to learn that this so called 'problem' I was trying to solve was not able to be changed by me. Carol and I reassured him that we would always love him just the way he was. I realised that the 'problem' was more my thinking, opinions and attitudes, all of which are changing with time, and that is still an ongoing process.

It did cause Luke and us a degree of grief for the losses he was experiencing, and knowing the challenging road ahead. Being a close family, when someone goes through any challenge, all are affected. Our other children had to process this grief for their brother and came to the same conclusion. Luke is just as much loved and accepted as anyone else in our family.

The thought of trying to help him 'change' was sensitively and wisely challenged by Luke when he said: 'Hey Dad, for me to change my sexual orientation to heterosexual is as hard as it would be for you to change yours to being a homosexual!' That was a challenge I've never forgotten.

I realised that this 'trial' was not necessarily one we had to overcome, rather, one in which we continue to live in the ambiguity of. Even the term 'overcoming' is actually incorrect, it is more about adjusting to how we continue to love our son and his partner unconditionally.

Unlike some parents I've met in similar situations, we have not abandoned our son because of his sexual orientation. He knows who he is, and that he is loved and accepted by us, his whole family, extended family and friends, and by the God who he knows and believes in, and who has not abandoned him. We also have learnt to accept and love his partner Travis, whose surname ironically is 'Franks'! Our grandchildren adore their uncle Luke, who continues to be affectionately referred to as 'Chem' or 'Poochie Flynn' for their own peculiar reasons.

We continue to hold onto our Christian values and worldview, which Luke respects. We continue to enjoy our times with Luke and Travis, and taking an interest in their lives. Since their move to New Zealand, trekking has become a frequent pastime of theirs, taking in spectacular scenery, especially during COVID-19, and with the company of their adventurous greyhound Barkly, a much loved rescue dog.

Carol and I celebrate and give thanks for our son for all he is, particularly Luke's compassion and generosity in his work with the underprivileged and marginalised in Kenya. As it should be for everyone, our life should not just be defined by colour, race, religion or sexuality. It certainly isn't for Luke.

God continues to challenge me, and I have much greater love, awareness, empathy and understanding for same-sex attracted people. I am not a fan of the term 'gay', as I feel it is too restrictive and can adversely stimulate discriminatory perceptions that are actually misperceptions wrongly applied. Some of the most pleasant, intelligent people I have met have been many of Luke's friends. I've had the privilege of counselling parents struggling with their children's sexuality, emphasising to them to not break relationships with their child, and love their children for who they are irrespective of their sexuality.

In this whole process, I have again been aware of God's goodness – protecting my son when he was depressed before coming out, and helping me love all types of people who I wrongly had judged.

How hard it is to change one's opinions and attitudes that have been moulded by numerous influences over decades – family, societal, religious and political. But how refreshing and freeing it is to be able to admit being wrong in attitudes and allow change to occur – albeit slowly.

At the time of writing, Luke and I acknowledge that we have a much closer, open and enjoyable relationship than we've ever had. We also enjoy that we can have robust and challenging conversations where the two of us are willing to alter our beliefs and views if we feel that's applicable, whilst importantly maintaining mutual respect and love.

With Luke's interest in poetry earlier in life, it seems appropriate to refer to a poem 'Welcome to Holland' by Emily Peal Kingsley, written to help herself understand how to appreciate the positives, in times where life leads us on a different path to our expectations. (Refer to Appendix F 'Welcome to Holland'.)

Needless to say, Carol and myself have learnt much from observing our children as they've journeyed through their own individual personal struggles. We've observed their growth, becoming stronger and more mature individuals, maintaining their internalised sense of worth, while balancing their needs and wants with others. Parents are allowed to feel proud of their children and, although we usually keep these feelings to ourselves, as a proud dad I'm taking the liberty to put it clearly in writing in a book for all to read.

## Grandchildren

Grandchildren are just the best, and bring so much joy as one ages. It has been said rather cynically that if you knew how good grandchildren were, you would have bypassed having children and gone straight to grandchildren! More serious is the comment: 'Grandchildren complete the circle of love.'

Carol and I have seven grandchildren, ranging at present from 5–16 years in age. Not surprisingly, they are each unique in their personalities, interests and temperaments, but the shared features are their love of life and the God who gave it to them, their love for their parents and, fortunately for us, their nan and pa as well. We treasure their company, participate in their individual interests and laugh a lot when we're together. We have enjoyed travelling with them, taking them with their parents to places that create memories of exciting holidays and adventures.

From oldest to youngest, there is Jack, Jai, Lilielle, Bodhe, Lakyn, Pearl and Alaska.

Jack loves learning practical skills in building and wants to become an electrician. He's studying through distance education and is self-motivated, also a great baseball player and is a skilful fisherman. I remember taking him fishing at a very young age, when he caught his first fish, a small fish we called 'Barry the Bream'. His knowledge of all kinds of lures now allows him to catch much larger fish, including a monster called 'Barry the Barramundi', much to his pa's envy. He has a good sense of humour and a gentle nature. He is at present keenly preparing for his boat and car driving licences, exciting memories of which I also have.

Jai, on the other hand, loves surfing as well as filming his achievements using his mouth-held GoPro. He's an avid rock climber and also a skilled artist. We value Jai's paintings along with our other grandchildren's art, all of which we have framed. These take pride of place in our home. Jai is an avid reader and his love of books is commendable. Like his brothers, Bodhe and Lakyn, Jai loves his food, is a master builder of Lego, and a youth leader at his church. He thrives in the company of his school and youth group mates and is enjoying his teenage years while earning pocket money as a 'check-out guy' in Kmart.

Lili is an absolutely delightful young lady who has learnt the meaning of generosity and puts it into action with her friends and family. She adores working with horses, especially miniature ones, having won many award ribbons at horse shows throughout Queensland, and has been chosen to represent in the nationals. As a competent representative netball player and umpire, Lili now attends a high school that specialises in this sport, after having won a scholarship. I enjoy standing on the sidelines of her many games, cheering her on and also teaching Lili to surf (as I did with her mum many years ago). She loves family time, is affectionate and loves tickles from her nan.

Bodhe, at the time of writing, is the most musical of our grandchildren, learning the saxophone at school and thriving in the 'big band', as well as earning pocket money busking especially at Christmas-time. He also plays drums and guitar. Bodhe is a competent soccer player, and an accomplished long-distance runner, making it to state levels like his dad and nan, and even further to National level. He believes he can always beat his pa at one-on-one basketball, to which I suggest 'keep dreaming'! He's a very sensitive young man and wonderful friend to his mates, which in 2024 naturally led him to the leadership role of Vice Captain of Middle High School.

Lakyn is a real socialite, a gregarious young man who can be the 'life of the party'. He's also a skilled soccer player and loves fishing, especially with his dad and pa. Being the youngest in his family, he has learnt how to balance involvement in activities and independence when called for. His musical skills are developing on the trumpet (which his great grandfather would have been thrilled about), but also on the piano. He is also doing well at school in his subjects and is popular amongst his peers and teachers, becoming Captain of his Junior High School in 2024. He has an adventurous spirit, will have a go at a variety of sports and loves life.

Dear Pearl is the cutest little lady with a sense of humour that is mature for her young age. She loves playing with all things girly and with her sisters Lassie and Lili. Having a love of animals from chickens to guinea pigs, she can even get crows to answer her calls. She has an attractive personality and she makes friends easily at school. Swimming, trampolining, running, gymnastics and netball all appeal to her. She's also a fan of her nan's tickles. Pearl's prayers at the dinner table are sincere and loving. I enjoyed visiting her playgroup to teach the children about visiting the doctor and when we gave her a toy doctor's kit, it was my turn to be bandaged by 'Nurse Pearl'.

That leaves 'Lassie' (Alaska Rose), our youngest grandchild, who was born prematurely and spent her first weeks in the special care nursery. She has an outgoing nature and larrikin behaviour. She can also be the 'life of the party'. Lassie knows what she wants and at the same time she likes all the things her big sister (Pearl) likes. Lassie loves the aeroplane ride where she balances on Pa's knees. She's a clever girl with a cute smile and a love of nature and the outdoors. Like her sister Pearl, she enjoys reading, learning to swim and playing in the sand and water at the beach. She loves helping with washing up, setting the table for dinner and any activities outdoors on the family property.

Playing and enjoying time with grandchildren as a grandparent is a gift that should never be taken for granted. There is a continuum of giving and receiving – from them and from us. As one ages, the joy experienced as a result of our relationships with our grandchildren is appreciated and valued, making that ageing process all the more bearable and satisfying.

Like our three children and their respective partners, we are so proud of our seven grandchildren, and adore them each dearly. They are such a blessing to us. We love that they are all different and appreciate all their differences. Our desire is to be there for them, share life experiences with them, and support them as best we can in our remaining years in all their endeavours.

'Growing older is one of the facts of life. Watching one's children then one's grandchildren, we can't be certain what lies ahead of them. All we can do is try to set them on the right path and help them learn from the experience of those that have gone before.' – Queen Elizabeth II

# CHAPTER TWELVE

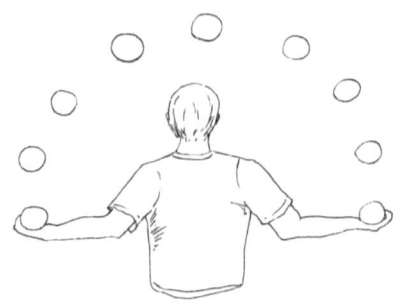

# BALANCING LIFE WITH MEDICINE

'Mental health is properly caring for our bodies which are the overcoat to our souls and our right to live on Earth.'
– David Riddell

'Rest when you're weary. Refresh and renew yourself, your body, your mind, your spirit. Then get back to work.'
– Ralph Marston

# Juggling

Since my early days in medicine, I've been asked on many occasions to give voluntary medical talks to all sorts of groups – mainly men's groups and, on some occasions, mixed audiences (men and women). Rather than making the presentations just about medical information and advice, I preferred to try to go deeper and discuss issues other than just health. Issues that I struggled with personally, and therefore assumed others did as well, such as balancing life's pressures as a young man and as a dad. I tried to cope with all the demanding and competing pressures: work and financial stress; family demands and involvement; time with my spouse; quantity and quality time with my children; and at the same time trying to exercise, enjoy sports and hobbies, and maintain other helpful relationships with friends.

Balancing these responsibilities and demands is not easy with the finite hours in a week, and like a 'juggler' throwing too many balls into the air, eventually some will be missed and dropped. It is a universal experience for all of us at different times in life, where we seem to have too many pressures and responsibilities to cope with.

I discovered in my life that there are certain situations where I had to prioritise my time and availability. I realised that there would be undesirable consequences if I had not made Carol and the children a priority, and I put aside other demands less important, even if only for a temporary period of time. Needless to say, like many times in life, it is one thing to think through the issues at hand and have good intentions, but it's never simple to take action. Like most other busy young men, I made mistakes that gave me the insight to make the changes needed.

Although juggling life's issues is common to each of us, my vocation as a GP did add another dimension – that of being on call 24 hours a day most days of the year. In earlier years, it meant literally being available for all patients of the practice to make contact after-hours for urgent needs. For a number of reasons in later years, my availability had to be reduced especially with the introduction of after-hours and online medical services. In earlier times it required setting boundaries, but also sacrifice – mostly by Carol, and my children when they were younger. I recognised my work was more than a nine-to-five job, it was a calling that I had a responsibility to uphold, but it could not have been achieved without Carol in the background managing the demands of our home.

From the first week I started in general practice at Lugarno in 1980, I decided to work a four-day week for the duration of my career so as to be able to devote at least one weekday (as well as the weekend) to my family and other interests. Otherwise, I knew the demands of medicine would have overtaken me and robbed me of the choices that I attempted to prioritise. This was, on hindsight, a preventative decision that was worthwhile persevering with in my career. There are a number of disadvantages in being self-employed, but the freedom to make this decision was one huge advantage. I'm so grateful, because my family and I have benefited from this. This choice gave me additional times to travel to and from school with my children and to take them to sporting activities, as well as having outings with my wife and even getting in some exercise, all of which I valued.

I knew I was fortunate when it came to the pressure of trying to maintain my health, because I had the opportunity of accessing medical care when required from other colleagues.

I encourage all men – whether young or old – to have at least a yearly health check-up. I challenge them with the example that they do not think twice about booking their car in for a regular service. But many men avoid seeking preventative medical attention for a variety of reasons. The main reasons being they do not prioritise the time for this, or assume wrongly that if they 'feel' well then they don't require a check-up. For far too long I have witnessed many men neglecting their health due to prioritising their work, and then attempting later in life to try to regain their health, which can be a lot more difficult and sometimes unsuccessful. As stewards of our bodies, we must personally see that we protect it by having regular medical check-ups.

## Family holidays

Holidays are an essential means of balancing the pressures of life. My holidays with family and, later in life, with just Carol, had to be planned and diarised since otherwise they might not have happened. For close to 20 years we regularly booked two separate holiday times at South West Rocks (SWR), one in April and the other in December. We holidayed with Robyn, my wife's sister, and our friends Denis and Bev from Taree – and both their families.

Our children in those formative years made wonderful memories from their holiday experiences and developed lifelong friendships as a result. The families stayed in the same unit block but in different apartments since we valued our own family times. Together we have loved our opportunities to relax with experiences such as deep-sea fishing, surfing, windsurfing and enjoyed the company of friends and family. Carol and I now can only travel to SWR on occasions but, 40 years on, some of the children of the three families still meet at the 'Rocks' for their own annual family holidays.

Holidays have given us and our children unhurried time to enjoy each other's company. In later life, what a joy it is to know that they have now placed time away with their families as a priority. It's also of interest for Carol and I to watch our children and their families do things differently to what we did, and be adventurous by undertaking holidays such as caravanning, trekking and camping.

## Sports

Over the decades I've tried a number of sports. This has helped me to discover the ones I enjoyed the most and give me a positive sense of achievement, as well as the obvious physical and mental health benefits.

In younger years, I was keen on rugby league and this was followed by social tennis and soccer. One year, I played two sports simultaneously with the intention of improving my basic skills in both cricket and golf. At the end of the year, summaries were sent out to help inform me on how I was progressing. When I read that my cricket scores were the lowest of the team, and my golf scores the highest of the group, it did not take much time for me to conclude that these two sports were not my forte!

After this realisation, I returned to water sports such as skiing, surfing and windsurfing, which I've enjoyed for years These have slowly mellowed into swimming laps, kayaking and fishing, but I still look forward to going to the beach early in the morning. Not so much to surf myself due to knee arthritis, but rather to watch (and photograph) my grandchildren. The sports I grew to love are rather isolating since they're usually done alone as compared to group sports.

To use my time wisely, I learnt to build relationships with surfing mates, and many a good surf was followed by coffee and a good chin wag.

## Travel

One of the blessings in my life has been the ability to undertake something I'm passionate about and that is learning more about the world in which we live through travel opportunities. I've been privileged since my teenage years to travel widely, and this has impacted my life in a positive way. I've grown through the experiences and the people I have met along the way.

Much of this travel has been on mission, some at medical conferences with opportunities to explore and update my medical knowledge in other countries. Early mission trips were to Zambia and, later, with a Salvation Army band in 1986 called 'Mission to China'. The reason behind this latter two-week visit was that China had been a closed country to the West for nearly 40 years following the communist post-war uprising by Mao Zedong in 1949. All missionaries were forced to leave. One of these missionaries was Wilbur Walker, a child of Salvation Army missionaries. For the next four decades, no-one in the West really knew what happened to The Salvation Army officers and millions of other Christians who had been persecuted and punished for any attempt to gather together or express their faith. It was unknown then whether they'd been able to preserve and maintain their faith in God while living under such hardship.

During the mission, we had to remove any labels on our caps and uniforms that referred to the word 'Army' since it was thought this could be an inflammatory word. The visiting band of nearly 50 people was led by our pastor at the time and Wilbur, a close friend of my parents and by then a much older man, was the driving force to re-establish connections with these brave, loyal men and women. Little did I know then that some 30 years later I would find myself in the company of Wilbur's grandson, Sam, on one of my Rwandan mission trips.

Our plane was late and we were exhausted after our night flight; however, the scene we met was a poignant one. There was a group of mainly elderly Salvation Army officers dressed in old and tattered uniforms along with their adult children waiting to greet us at 3 am at Beijing airport, singing hymns and sobbing as they realised they had not been forgotten. Over the ensuing few weeks, we witnessed how the church, which had been forced underground, had in fact thrived and grown substantially in numbers – a reminder of their incredulous commitment and faith, but also a reminder about a God who had been faithful through their unfathomable situation. As a young man at the time, it was a powerful demonstration to me of persevering under adversity.

Another experience with this Salvation Army band to the USA in 1983 was different in nature. I was able to enjoy quality time with my dad who I was billeted with. We were also in Newport, Rhode Island, when Australia won the America's Cup in sailing – a very patriotic experience.

Visiting various countries in Africa was always a joy: to reacquaint with friends, marvel at the landscape and be amazed at the wildlife. Carol and I have sponsored a student whose family was living in poverty, through the School of St Jude in Tanzania, for the duration of his schooling and it is an exciting opportunity to try and not only support one individual student, but contribute to the bigger aim of combating poverty through education. The school's goal is to allow one child from a family to gain a tertiary education and assist the whole family to escape from poverty, which is such a worthy desire. The school was founded and still run by an Australian school teacher (Gemma Sisia) and visiting the school and observing the life changing work undertaken for thousands of school children is a moving experience.

For over a year in 2004, my son Justin and his wife Katherine went to work on mission in Southern India in Chennai. They went to supervise the building and administration of a primary school in a small village – Annapompatoo – an hour or so drive from Chennai for the not-for-profit organisation Global Concern. Carol and I visited them to support their work, undertaking medical consults medical consults for some adults from the community. Carol encouraged ladies in the vocational centre. We observed their successful achievements and their passion for their village. India is a country of contrasts and sensory stimulation. From the time of arriving at the airport, every bodily sense is awakened from the colourful sights, the cacophony of sounds and the smells of spices and smoke. We both had an acute awareness of the degree of poverty that was obvious - similar to Africa. I found the words of one of Colin Buchanan's songs appropriate to reconcile this experience: 'You need to smell the poverty, to put wealth in its place.'

Europe was another place in the world that Carol and I had the pleasure to experience together, with its wealth of history and personal relevance to my ancestry and we enjoyed our travels to this continent. We also both wanted to bless Carol's parents and my dad by taking them on a cruise to Alaska and to travel the Canadian Rockies. We had a memorable adventure together, one that our parents reminisced about for the rest of their lives.

Our family also enjoyed other holidays together, including trips to New Zealand. We were blessed to have our parents and friends of our children with us. Travel has broadened the minds and lives of our children and ourselves. Carol and I have been fortunate in later years to be able to take our children and grandchildren on family holidays to Fiji, Alaska and Disneyland (USA), which have allowed us all to experience new places that have created amazing memories.

One holiday our families enjoyed in particular was Alaska. So much so that the next year the Maxwells (Joel and Racquel) chose that name for their newborn daughter in memory of the trip – Alaska Rose. On reflection, it was perhaps prudent that we did not take them to Afghanistan!

## Relationships – mentors and friends

I was aware early in my adult life that finding male mentors was a wise and worthwhile pursuit. Someone older with more life experience is often preferable, but not essential. Over my life I've had different mentors at different times. For a period of a few years, I was privileged to have been mentored by John Mallison, who has written many books on the subject of mentoring and regularly challenged me in different areas of my life – mentally, physically and spiritually. John was an experienced mentor who encouraged me to be a mentor to other younger men. I've tried to do this over the years in my medical practice and in my church arena.

Another mentor I valued was Ian Grant, a delightful Christian teacher, preacher, author and presenter. I valued and appreciated Ian's wisdom, help and guidance in issues to do with parenting and marriage over many years. His book *Fathers Who Dare Win* helped me to be a better dad and husband. Carol and I facilitated many seminars on parenting and marriage in our local community in Menai, where Ian and his wife Mary presented valuable insights and wisdom that influenced numerous attendees.

Over the years I've been privileged to have some close friends who I also call mentors. These men are so important in my life, and two proverbs in the Bible emphasises this truth: 'One who walks with the wise will become wise, but a companion of fools will suffer harm,' and 'The wise are glad to be instructed'. These close and trusted people offer a listening ear, can bring challenge, advice or wisdom from their own experiences – all of these in a comfortable and confidential relationship. My mentors have also helped me to see things that I sometimes haven't seen myself – blind spots and incorrect perceptions.

A few years ago, I purchased a pair of spectacles that I thought were a clever invention, but maybe on hindsight not so clever. They had magnetic frames with the idea that when outside in sunlight, or when driving, I was able to clip a UV filter on the outside of the frame. One morning at work, I was wearing these particular new trendy specs, and took them off for a brief time and laid them down on my desk, not realising I'd put them on top of a pile of paperclips that immediately became attached to the frame in the upper right corner.

Unaware of what had occurred, I wore these for the rest of the day and I kept observing an odd vague shadow in the upper right corner of my visual field and thinking that I had what is medically called a 'floater' in my vision. I kept flicking my eyes and head to try and remove this foreign intruder. It was not until the end of the day when I looked in the mirror, I was shocked to observe a line of paper clips like an antenna protruding from the frame of my glasses.

The humour and embarrassment of the finding was overshadowed by the thought that the 20 or so patients I saw during the day had not commented or asked about my peculiar appearance. I reflected later about this bizarre experience and thought that we all need at least one trusted person who can speak truth into our lives and challenge us when needed – and, of course, reveal obstacles that are hidden to us!

A friend has been described as 'someone who knows all about you – yet still loves you' – Elbert Hubbard. A friend is someone you can also have a good laugh with. Over my life I've found that it's relatively easy to develop superficial friendships, but deeper friendships take much more intention and effort and increases vulnerability. Because of the confidentiality in patient relationships in my work life, I became a much more private person in my relationships.

The mentors and close friends in my life have been men who I have grown to trust and as that trust has been earned I can be transparent with them. Mentoring from those who have grown into friends has been a process that I've valued, especially when these men have different expertise and life experiences. I believe it's important to have people in your life who commit to being a friend, but who will also pray for you when you ask (or even when you don't ask), when you're facing challenging circumstances, or when there's something to celebrate. Not surprisingly, when it comes to friendships of value, researchers are finding that electronic communications and social media can have potentially adverse effects on relationships. Face-to-face friendships can have elements of depth and reflection as compared to the delete and edit components of quick and easy, superficial electronic communications.

One particular relationship with a patient (and also friend) has resulted in reciprocal commitments since 1980. My support for Andrew Scipione intensified when he became the NSW police commissioner where for his eight years of competent (but stressful leadership), I was able to offer medical and practical support to him and his family, as well as rally around him through prayer when I was aware there was a crisis he was facing. Our mutual friendship has so far lasted 45 years.

Later he arranged an enjoyable opportunity for me to be involved in CAPP (Community Awareness of Policing Program), a time whereby for a month, I personally observed the roles and challenges of our police force. This gave me a new appreciation for police and the stressful situations they find themselves in. This gave me perspective for my patients who are police officers and the awareness of the importance of all countries' need to uphold law and justice. It also eased the long-held tension of a previous court attendance as an innocent witness way back in 1978.

Understandably, friendships in one's chosen profession are also moulded with time, and medicine is not exempt from this. There are many respected doctors and nurses that I've had the privilege of working with and befriending over my career in medicine – some of whom I work alongside in general practice, and others over the years who I've referred patients to and have learnt so much from. Specialists such as Dr Adrian Knox, who is foremost a delightful man and, secondly, a highly regarded plastic surgeon who has helped many of my patients over the decades, and who introduced me to the fun of kayaking (especially in a Hobie). Dr Robert Rosen, my dermatologist, has become a good friend also, who shares with me common interests outside medicine such as photography.

Other Specialist friendships have logically occurred with time, such was Dr Manoharan (aka 'Mano'). Respected personally since I was a medical student, and he was a medical registrar at St George Hospital, right up to the present time. He is one of the most knowledgeable, yet gentle professional doctors I have known. As well, Dr Carl Bryant, a clever, hard working interventional radiologist, who has served patients and GP's from 'The Shire' for all of my career in medicine.

I have come to trust and professionally relate to many other specialists I have had the privilege to work alongside in General Practice, sharing patient care with confidence and simultaneously developing trustworthy relationships.

The present supporting GPs and staff in my medical practice are among the people who offer daily support, encouragement, humour, wisdom and friendship, and make going to work on a daily basis enjoyable.

It used to be thought that there were significant different functional roles for the right and left sides of the brain – the right supposedly being more creative, the left more logical. To try to stimulate my creative right brain, I intentionally became interested in photography (in particular, landscape photography). After mainly living a cognitively objective-driven job in my life, I thought photography would assist the subjective creative side, which had been mostly under-utilised.

Research has now shown that the divide in function between the two sides of the brain is not always that straightforward. However, to improve my talents I set about buying a quality camera and taking a few photography courses. As a reputable landscape photographer, Ken Duncan's tuition was a logical first choice. I attended a photography retreat 'Rainforests and Waterfalls' in the Gold Coast Hinterland. The days spent learning techniques on composure and camera skills were invaluable and enjoyable, especially in such a pristine environment. Within a relatively short period of time, I was able to use what I learnt in Africa on safari and also on a Kimberley cruise in northern Australia.

Another especially close friend, Rob, equally developed an interest in this type of photography, and his skills advanced exponentially. He has had extra knowledge we both used to good effect in seeking to acquire unique shots. He has abundant awareness of locations throughout our beautiful country. This had come about due to his other passion of long-distance motorbike riding, which allowed us to travel to special places to visit on weekend trips. We visited and photographed remote locations such as Lake Mungo, a dried-up lake with eroded, moonlike craters and hills of soil due to wind weathering. Another location included the worn and dilapidated timber railway line and bridge in Gundagai, shot at dawn in winter with eerie, enveloping fog. The heritage stairs and stone buildings, and old lampposts shot at night, at 'The Rocks' at Circular Quay was also another great opportunity. We challenge each other with the thought that our best photograph is yet to be taken!

Overall, we've been happy with the results of our photography. And with how we've improved in our skills. On another level though, the outcome has been the deep comradeship that sharing with a loyal friend produces. More imagining of places to visit and people to photograph are discussed when we meet over breakfast. It's important to have goals to look forward to because planning pleasurable activities has been found to be helpful in maintaining a positive mood, but it is also produces enjoyable experiences and memories.

Pastor Rick Warren wisely says in his book *The Purpose Driven Life*: 'Relationships must have priority in your life above everything else –because life without love is really worthless. Often we act as if relationships are something to be squeezed into our schedule. We talk about finding time for our children or making time for people in our lives. That gives the impression that relationships are just a part of our lives along with many other tasks. But God says relationships are what life is all about – not achievements, or the acquisition of things.'

It was Jesus who stated what was most important to God – (firstly) love God and (secondly) love people. However, the busy-ness of life usually gets in the way – making a living, doing our work, accomplishing our goals – as if these tasks are more important. But the point of life is learning to do what Jesus taught – learning to love God and love people.

Relationships (those we love, spend time with and work with) are important, even when they change with time. I have realised and tried in my life to make time and nurture such close associations with God and with others, often needing to be much more intentional when life became too hectic or I became too self-absorbed – and only to my detriment.

# Retirement

I've come across the adage that as people get older they can 'feel the fragility of age'. It is actually an unsurprising statement, with the awareness of the issues that age brings, and which I observed in my parents, my patients and, in later years, myself. Ageing unfortunately brings along its degenerative effects in most of the organs and systems of our body, including skin, heart, brain, joints, eyes, ears and immune system. It's even harder bending down to pick something up, you have to think about how to do it carefully! It's not as likely that you will run to catch the bus. Carol and myself are already experiencing a number of these conditions and inevitably will face more. As Colin Buchanan sings, 'If you don't get the sickness, being well means nothing' – a heartfelt truth. There can be an occasional bright side to ageing, in that at the same time as our skin is wrinkling, our 'cataracts' are growing, making it somewhat blurry to see ourselves accurately in the mirror each day!

On a serious note, ageing is usually associated with the shrinking of the brain and not uncommonly mild cognitive impairment. This can result in varying degrees of short-term memory loss. You can forget the name of that TV show you have recently viewed. Younger generations need to try to tolerate and be empathic towards this reality. This is a normal part of life of getting older. On the contrary, it is important for those of us who are ageing to be aware of, and reflect on, the development of rigidity of thinking and inflexibility of attitudes we may have acquired.

A positive can be that past life experience allows you to take mental shortcuts and make quicker decisions. With ageing, there should be the benefit of wisdom that can be shared with future generations, but this is conditional on learning from our own mistakes, gaining insight from these and then using them to help others when the opportunity arises. As best we can, we should strive to stop, think and adjust our behaviour and pick our battles accordingly. That does not mean, however, that we have to minimise the virtues and values we've developed over our lifetime that mean so much to us and are part of our DNA.

There is much that can be done to minimise, or slow, the inevitable effects of ageing. Since our brains are still malleable, we can stimulate them by activities that help our memory such as social engagement, memory games, stimulating conversations and relationships, exercise, a healthy diet, adequate sleep and rest, and thinking about what can be done instead of what can't.

Having purposeful activities as you get older is important and worth getting excited about: your job (if you're still working), your family, your holidays, your hobbies, a social life and, lastly but importantly, any volunteer work – something that can be beneficial to us and to others. Striving to act happy and not just thinking about it, as well as counting our blessings (gratitude) rather than our problems, can help our emotional and mental health. Good intentions are one thing, but habitual actions in what I've mentioned above is the essential thing, and I hope to be working more towards them in my own life in the future.

Moving into retirement has often been described by some as moving from 'hero to zero', with the assumption that one was a hero and is now moving to another identity of being a 'zero' with no perceived worth. This description, and implied assumptions, I think is rather pretentious. The term 'hero' has become a cliche that is often overstated and embellished. This title obviously is open to personal interpretation and can be applied to an idol or a superstar, but I prefer the application meant for someone who was brave and took a risk – such as my dad. My medical career gave me opportunities to be involved in saving patient lives, mostly indirectly by my clinical decisions and occasionally by direct involvement in acute care, but I don't consider that this deserves the application of the adjective 'hero'.

The descriptor 'zero' suggests that one loses all self-esteem and worth on retirement. But if you know where your true self-worth comes from, it can be helpful when moving through the many changes that retirement and ageing brings. Although I know I will have to make adjustments because of the loss of my role in medicine as a doctor, I'm confident that I know where my ultimate self-worth comes from. I believe that I was called to medicine by God, and I personally know that He was the one who wired my brain for my vocation and clearly guided me into the positions of influence and experiences I've been privileged to enjoy.

Rick Warren also suggests that 'The purpose of life is living a life of purpose.' This resonates with me because it implies life is not all about me. Living intentionally, in a way that helps others, is not necessarily easy to do, rather it is the opposite. We all have inherent attributes such as self-importance and self-indulgence that conflict with this desire.

For myself, other opportunities to lessen the impact of a sudden retirement will include slowly reducing my working hours and keeping my medical registration as long as possible so I'm able to consult and continue to be available to my family and friends.

Hobbies and other interests that will also take my mind off the cessation of work will include increased involvement in my family's lives, involvement in voluntary work, and recreational activities and hobbies such as photography and gardening. I'm hoping to learn (perhaps miraculously) some cooking skills, and have opportunities for ongoing involvement in music. Who knows, this may be with the 'old boys band' who meet up at Coolum Beach regularly to play songs and tunes from the 1960s–1970s. Most of these guys have long white hair or mullets, beards and wear thongs – so maybe I will have to grow a ponytail and join them with my congas!

As I enter retirement, I think of the wisdom from a verse in the Bible that gives me some challenging values to strive for, and a legacy to leave: 'Older men are to be self-controlled, worthy of respect, sensible, and sound in faith, love and endurance.'

# CHAPTER THIRTEEN

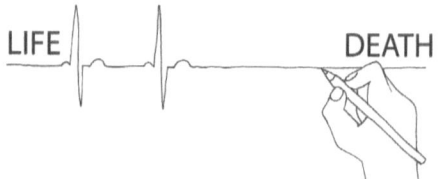

# THE GOODNESS OF GOD

*'Surely your goodness and unfailing love will pursue me all the days of my life, and I will live in the house of the Lord for ever.'*
**– Psalm 23:6**

*'All my life you have been faithful, all my life you have been so so good, with every breath that I am able, I will sing of the goodness of God.'*
**– Bethel Music**

# Coincidence or providence?

## Justin and Katherine's story

On Christmas Eve 2004, Carol and I were watching the traditional Melbourne Christmas carol service when there was a knock at the door. We were so surprised to find the unexpected sight of Justin and Katherine who were supposed to be in India.

The day before, they were preparing to pack and leave for a short holiday that had been booked on the coast of Southern India. The previous year, they had been serving on mission for the non-government organisation (NGO) Global Concern in Chennai, supervising the construction and functioning of a school in a village outside the city.

Early on Christmas Eve morning, they were prompted to return to Australia as a 'surprise' for their family and friends – a major change of plans. To their astonishment, they were able to purchase the last two seats on a flight to Sydney. It was a delight to see them again and hear their stories.

After a full day catching up with friends and family on Christmas Day, we all went to bed unaware of the news circulating around the world early the next morning – Boxing Day, 2004. At 7.59 am a large earthquake measuring 9.1 on the Richter Scale had occurred on the northern tip of Indonesia, and its power had generated the largest and deadliest tsunami in modern history. It spread to 14 countries in South-East Asia killing 230,000 people. Sadly, the tsunami reached the shores of Southern India killing 18,000. In particular, the seaside area where Justin and Katherine were planning to holiday had been badly affected and many lives lost.

Was this coincidence or God's provision of His goodness?

There was little doubt in all our minds that this incredible story was the working of the goodness of God in their lives and ours. Looking back on this event, Justin and Katherine were aware that they'd been guided by God-prompted to return home and a circumstantial sign that there had been available tickets to travel home to safety.

## Luke's story

Rhabdomyolysis is an uncommon medical condition caused by the breaking down of skeletal muscle as result of a direct or indirect muscle injury. If not treated immediately, it can lead to kidney damage. Luke, my youngest son, developed this condition in 2012 after heavy exercise at the gym. The rise in the enzyme creatinine kinase was so high it posed a threat to his kidneys, and he needed intravenous fluids in hospital over five days. Further investigation from a speciality clinic could not identify a definite cause, but he was advised to avoid repeated or strenuous muscle straining.

Maybe Luke did not quite hear that part of the advice from the specialist because within the next year he decided to climb Mt Kilimanjaro – the tallest mountain in Africa. Luke's new interests, hiking and mountain climbing were not inherited from his parents (with our idea of scaling mountains being via a chair lift or a gondola).

He started climbing different mountains around the world and often accompanied this with associated fundraising for a charity he was involved in. After the successful African mountain climb, Luke followed it with Aconcagua in Argentina's Andes Mountains in 2015, and later again Mt Everest base camp, which he attained with a climbing group he led, including with his older brother Justin.

Aconcagua, with an elevation of 6931 m, is the highest peak in South America, and highest in the world outside of Asia. Only 60% of the thousands of annual climbers summit successfully. Luke's planned climb under the supervision of trained guides was for a nine day climb with his friend from work, Huan Chan (HC), and a group of strangers, making up the party of 15. The party reached the last camp before the summit called Plaza Colera or High Camp Three, appropriately named since it was 6000 m in altitude.

That night, HC developed abdominal cramps probably from contaminated mountain water, and by the morning it was obvious she could not proceed with the last summit. This meant she had to stay alone in her tent at the campsite (which was on a flat, narrow and exposed section of the mountain). That left Luke with a difficult decision – attempt the summit with the rest of the group or stay behind and look after his friend. He chose the latter.

The morning on the mountain was nighttime in Australia. Carol woke in the middle of the night and felt prompted to pray for the safety of Luke not knowing what was happening on the mountain. We both prayed together for him, trusting that God was looking after him at that time.

When Luke was able to make contact a few days later, he was still in a state of shock. We were astounded to hear what had happened. After the group left to summit, a strong gale suddenly tore through the camp. It was so strong, it blew all the other tents and gear off the side of the mountain. Luke and HC were in their tent while it shook violently, trying to hold the upright posts in place to avoid being blown off as well.

Luke was in fear for both their lives as they hung on for hours. After a prolonged period of time and through the howling wind, Luke heard a voice outside the tent. Peeking outside, he saw an unidentified figure of a man who offered to take them down the mountain to the camp below. Luke and HC left their tent, which then blew off the mountainside. They slowly followed this man down to the safety of the camp below. They did not know who this man was and never saw him again, but they did eventually discover that the remainder of the party had not reached the summit and, sadly, another person in the other climbing party died that day in the gale.

Both of our children's stories could have had different outcomes and with traumatic consequences. I believe God had a plan for our children's lives through these experiences and we were grateful for God's goodness to us as a family.

## Liz's story

It could be argued that it is relatively easy to appreciate or claim the goodness of God with the above two stories when their results are so positive. It is not as easy, however, when the outcome is tragic or not what is hoped for, but God's goodness can still be seen and felt in these situations if we are mindful of it.

While writing this final chapter (mid-2023), Carol and I travelled to western NSW to visit interesting locations from my family's heritage. On a Sunday morning, we were driving to Dubbo when I received a distressing call that caused me immediately to pull off the road.

Liz, a good friend of ours, was terribly upset and said to me, 'Gary, I need your help. Ivor has died and the police need a death certificate.' Ivor was Liz's husband, a trusted friend and patient and a pastor in our church. He was much loved – as was shown by the attendance of 500 hundred people at his funeral a week later. Although shocked at hearing the news, I had to compose myself to understand what had happened and what was required to help our friend.

Ivor had been doing what he loved, walking in the countryside, in the Warrumbungles, enjoying the company of his wife and God's creation around him when he suddenly collapsed. Despite being in an isolated location, Liz was soon accompanied by another woman who had been walking the track and together they performed CPR. With no phone signal other than for emergency, Liz had been able to call the police and ambulance services who immediately came and did what they could to help. Despite the help given, Ivor had passed away.

Liz needed to contact her family and friends from Dubbo two hours away to come and pick her up, and also myself. Liz briefly had phone service, but enough for the few minutes to be able to make those calls.

Incredibly, I was able to explain that we were also travelling to Dubbo (a town we'd only visited on one occasion 30 years ago) to stay for one night. After conversing with the police, Carol and I kept travelling and arrived at our hotel within a short time of Liz arriving. In the meantime, I arranged for one of my receptionists to go to my surgery and email the necessary medical records required. It was an honour to be with Liz in her time of need and to comfort her and pray with her. This is something Ivor had done with so many others over the years in their time of distress. After arranging the paperwork and legal certificates required by the police, Liz was able to drive back to Sydney with her son Matt, who was able to secure a seat on the only flight to Dubbo that day from Sydney. What a privilege it was to be there, and to observe how providential God's care was to provide for Liz at a time when she needed this the most. We all experienced the goodness of God, revealed so clearly in such a tragic circumstance.

## Overcoming

In the Bible it says 'In this world you will have trouble. But take heart for I have overcome the world.' Are these words of Jesus who suffered undeserved 'trouble', relevant and helpful to a believer in modern day life? My experience has been that they are – but sometimes only evident in hindsight. With God's help, overcoming troubles, struggles and difficulties in life is possible. Some of my troubles I have outlined in this book, to remind myself and others how good God has been. The same truth in this verse is available to any person who reaches out to God.

A life knowing God is a life aware of His goodness and abundant blessings, irrespective of the circumstances. This does not mean that being a Christian results in an easy, trouble-free life – far from it. Nor can God be treated like a genie in a bottle that is activated for any desire when you have the need. It is an awareness of a supernatural strength that is not easily explainable solely from a human perspective. A strength that can even help us cope and eventually overcome the troubles we all face in life.

With death, it does not take away the human grief and loss, but it can ease the degree of pain by bringing a sense of peace as a result of the promise that God is always with us and offers us (and our loved ones) the hope of eternal life. We may not always feel His presence during these circumstances but promises from God's word (the Bible) such as 'You are with me…' (Psalm 23) can reassure us that He never leaves us and so bring great comfort. I have witnessed this eventuate on numerous occasions in people's lives in my lifetime – even in my own.

I heard these statements when I was younger and thought they were hackneyed phrases and expressions about false hope and a crutch to cling to, but in my life they have become an experience that cannot be erased by argument, ridicule or persuasion. A person's story is their own experience that no-one can take away from them, as they know it is true and that they are living in it. Similarly, in medicine, I cannot deny the truth of any patient's account of what is happening to them as they share it with me. Their story needs to be listened to and accepted because they are the ones experiencing it.

When I turned 40 years of age, I decided to go for a routine optometrist appointment. I knew that vision often deteriorates around this time and may need correction, but I'd overlooked that it could happen to me since my vision seemed fine. Despite my initial delusion that I would not be one that needed to wear glasses, I discovered that my vision had deteriorated in one eye, and I had compensated for this in my other eye for a number of years. The lens in the reading spectacles I required brought everything into focus. The result was improved clarity, less eye strain and headaches. One of the means of understanding and experiencing God's goodness is to intentionally focus on it, and on who He is and what He has done for us. As well, it can assist us to 'count our blessings'. A song I've always admired and that provides insights on this truth is simply called 'The Goodness of God'. (See Appendix G 'The Goodness of God'.)

## Life and death

The final book of the Bible, Revelation, describes an unknown time when Jesus comes again, and it paints the picture of what is called the 'Book of Life', which simply means a list of names of those who have placed their trust in Jesus. This may be for some as a seven year old, as it was for me, or at any other time in someone's life, even in their final years. As Christians, we have an assurance of a place in Heaven. That is our hope.

In a purely secular world the word 'hope' inherently involves uncertainty, e.g. *I hope the weather improves.* In contrast the Biblical use and the Christian understanding of 'hope' involves certainty – the promise of eternity with God.

One such verse in the Bible states the hope of our inheritance. "God has given us eternal life and this life is in His Son. He who has the Son has life. He who does not have the Son of God does not have life.'

In my years of work as a GP, there were a number of obligations I've had that were not so pleasant. One of these was having to visit patients who had just died, to write the necessary public health certificates, as well as to comfort their grieving families. Some of these deceased patients had already been taken to the funeral parlour, where I visited to identify their bodies, to write their death and cremation documents. When looking for their name in the deceased records held by the funeral parlour, it was like looking at a 'Book of Death' – just depressing and surreal. I also stopped and reflected and hoped that their names had been written in another book – the 'Book of Life'.

It was just a few centuries ago that death was something that people used to observe up close and frequently in their lives. The life expectancy of all people in those times was 40 years – half of what it is now. Many lost their parents when they were still children. In the harshness of life, nearly everyone grew up witnessing death and watching family and other relatives die young and old. Tim Keller, a well-known Christian author, when he was diagnosed with a terminal malignancy wrote a book called *On Death*. He correctly commented that medicine and science have relieved us of the many causes of early death, and today the vast majority of people die away from everyone except their close family in hospitals and hospices. Other than doctors and nurses, it is normal to live to adulthood and not watch anyone die or even see a deceased person unless a viewing is requested.

'This hiddenness of dying in modern society means that we of all cultures, live in denial of our impending death. We know intellectually and rationally that we are going to die, but deep down we repress it, as if we are going to live forever. Death is the one absolute inevitability, yet modern people don't plan for it and don't live as if it's going to happen. We avoid doctors out of fear, denying the mortality of our bodies and assuming they will just go on forever. And yet in the face of imminent death some people demand unrealistic and extreme medical procedures.' – Tim Keller

I have found in my dealings with patients that it is rare to find those who are reconciled to their own mortality, even in very old age or facing conditions that are usually terminal. Sadly, this appears to me that people these days are unprepared for death more than any previous generation and do little to think about or prepare for the inevitable.

Scientists have compiled a list of 1000 exotic things to do before you die. Without wanting to seem morbid, from a Christian perspective, the most important thing to do is to prepare for one's death – yet this did not appear on the list. It seems to me a sensible way of approaching this is to at least be ready for the inevitable and consider the relevance of God's promises because death is an absolute in life we will all face.

Although I've spent most of my life trying to keep people alive, it is important to be reminded that life is finite. It is also important to remember that life goes quickly and is short. Life needs to be cherished and lived well. Even the Beatles in some of their songs, wrote lyrics that touched on this reality: 'When I'm Sixty Four' and 'We Can Work It Out' – ('Life is very short and there's no time for fussing and fighting').

All of humanity will have a 100% fatality rate. Author Anthony Ackroyd wrote about the attitude changes he needed to make when he realised this fact. He said, 'Time is indeed precious and not be wasted and that this includes not wasting it by pursuing fabricated urgencies that rob us of the richness inherent in every moment.'

Karl Faase says about this statement, 'This is a positive insight. You and I won't last forever, so make good choices, enjoy the richness in all of life and get right with God. That's an important eternal choice.'

Over the next few years, I will be entering retirement, something I'm not particularly looking forward to because it will be difficult to accept after a lifetime of caring for others. I realise that change is an inherent part of everyone's life. I will need to adapt to the idea that good can come out of any change. The enjoyment that we may have been afforded in life in various ways are not permanent.

Despite progress in my lifetime in many areas – especially in healthcare – we will never create a perfect world. For all the gains, we will not see utopia on Earth, and we are left with a question to answer, 'Where do we place our hope for a future beyond this world?'

My belief is that one day I will find myself in Heaven, not having to overcome difficulties, or living in a world where we have to endure troubles, illness and suffering. Because of my faith in an extraordinary God, I will find myself out of a job for the first time in my life. I will discover what it means to be completely and forever 'refreshed'.

I commenced writing this book with the goal of handing down a legacy and knowledge of my life to my family and to my grandchildren in particular. The main goal has not shifted, but it has been added to. The writing of this book has become a task that involved numerous hours of candid reflection, reading and soul searching. I have enjoyed the creative part of writing, irrespective of whether it is ever published or read by only a few. The only thing I have control over is the joy of finishing the writing and the creation of something that did not exist in the world previously. I pray that it will bring honour to my family despite the sensitive stories and honour to God in the overall theme and content.

Finally, I desire for those reading this book to be personally refreshed when caring for others out of love - as this can bring profound satisfaction. My other desire is that you may personally experience the goodness and presence of God in your life that I have been privileged to enjoy in mine. If this has not been your experience it is never too late to discover it. C.S.Lewis challenged us all when he stated: 'You can't go back and change the beginning, but you can start where you are and change the ending.'

James Bryce says, 'The worth of a book is what you can carry away from it.' My hope in the reading of this book is that you can take something away with you.

# Appendix

## A.
### The anatomy and physiology of the ear

The outside ear and its profile has a function to make sure the shape of the actual soundwave going into our ear is appropriately positioned. Soundwaves travel into our outer ear canal and then hit the eardrum (the tympanic membrane), which is about one square centimetre. It reverberates with very fine vibrations, which moves three tiny bones, the ossicles, in the sealed middle ear. The ossicles then move up and down on the cochlea fluid in the inner ear, which in turn moves hair cells. These hair cells in the cochlear are like coral at the bottom of the ocean, swaying back and forth. Soundwaves move these 24,000 hair cells in a cavity the size of our small fingernail. The soundwaves 'type' in different patterns and tones and then send via electrical impulses in the acoustic nerve to our auditory centre of the back of the brain called the occipital lobe, which finally interprets the sound in different ways for us all.

# B.
## 'The Boy and the Starfish'
## - original story by Loren Eisley

An old man was walking along the beach one morning when he spotted a young boy crouched by the water, scooping something up from the sand and throwing it into the sea.

The beach was normally empty at this time of day, and so the old man stopped to watch for a while.

He noticed that the boy kept on shuffling a little further down the beach, then repeating this same action again and again – stopping, scooping, throwing, moving.

'What are you doing there, boy?' the old man asked, walking closer.

'I'm saving these starfish that are stranded,' replied the boy. 'If they stay on the beach they will dry out and die, so I'm putting them back into the ocean so they can live.'

The old man was silent for a few seconds.

'Young man,' he said, 'on this stretch of the beach alone, there must be more than one hundred stranded starfish. Around the next corner, there must be at least one thousand more. This goes on for miles and miles and miles – I've done this walk every day for 10 years, and it's always the same. There must be millions of stranded starfish! I hate to say it, but you'll never make a difference.'

The boy picked up another starfish, threw it into the ocean and replied, 'Well I just made a difference to that one' and continued with his work.

## How often do you make a small difference?

If everything you did had to have a huge, immediate impact before you gave it a little of your time, then you'd end up doing very little with your life. And, sometimes, the little things we do can add up and turn into big things – they make ripples that spread further than we can see.

Those starfish that the young boy saved may have gone on to produce thousands more.

The story above is a message of hope reminding us that every single person can make a difference, even if that difference impacts just one person.

# C.
## COVID-19 facts

TGA: Therapeutic Goods Administration

ATAGI: Australian Technical Advisory Group on Immunisation

NCIRS: National Centre for Immunisation Research and Surveillance

*Vaccine safety monitoring:* The TGA monitored vaccine safety and side effects, seeking information and reports from healthcare workers and patients. An independent group called AusVaxSafety conducted vaccine safety surveillance of the COVID-19 vaccines in use in Australia to ensure ongoing safety. They have done this by sending thousands of confidential surveys to patients vaccinated at all ages and with different vaccines. The evidence accumulated by AusVaxSafety and the TGA showed that COVID-19 vaccinations are considered safe and most side effects are mild and transient. The research is still ongoing and the evidence is available to anyone. As is the research into the consequences of natural infection and Long Covid, both of which are showing significantly more morbidity than any of the vaccine-related consequences.

*Vaccine myths:* With so many millions of people vaccinated against COVID-19 there were common medical complaints still occurring at similar frequency. Patients were concerned when they developed various symptoms around the time of vaccination and decided that there must have been a causal link, and so the vaccine was to blame for these symptoms. Associations (symptoms and complaints around the time of vaccination) are not necessarily proof of causation or evidence. In some rare cases, there may have been a previously unknown adverse reaction caused by COVID-19 vaccination but associations are not the same as proof of causation of adverse events.

Another mistruth circulating suggested that the vaccines caused heart attacks. In the fourth year of the pandemic, deaths from ischaemic heart disease were 17% higher than in a normal year. Although cardiologists have been concerned about this increase, they were not surprised. Rather than wrongly blaming the vaccines, the association was due to the delayed diagnoses, and prevention and treatment strategies throughout the pandemic, as well as the damaging effect on the heart directly from COVID-19 itself.

*Vaccine effectiveness:* It was initially hoped that the COVID-19 vaccines would be similar to the measles and the hepatitis A vaccines, preventing transmission between individuals. The reason for this not occurring was that the virus was initially thought to only enter the cells of victims via the spike protein attaching to receptors called 'ACE receptors', but it has now been suggested that there may be other means of entry to cells. Additionally, variants have continued to mutate and escape vaccine protection.

Vaccine efficacy so far has been shown to wane after about six months, as seen by falling antibody levels, so new and bivalent boosters have been required to continue to reduce the impact of COVID-19 symptoms, including severe forms of the disease and death. This waning of protection over time also occurs in cases if natural infection.

The next generation of vaccines need to be able to stop transmission of infection, just like the measles vaccine. Future vaccines should achieve this more effectively and so produce the desired 'herd immunity'. Future vaccines are likely to be multivalent vaccines against all COVID-19 strains, influenza and potentially deadly RSV, given annually.

# D.
## Textural criticism

There is vast evidence outside the New Testament for the existence of Jesus in ancient historical writings and no historian would deny this. But most information about Jesus comes from the New Testament. But how do we know that what was written has not been changed over the years?

We know this because of the science called textural criticism. This technique examines the number of copies of early texts that we have today, and the time gap between the original document and earliest copy that we have. The more manuscripts we have and the earlier they are written the less doubt there will be about the original manuscript. Other texts on ancient history widely used and accepted as authoritative in schools and universities, such as those written by Greek historian Herodotus and the Roman historian Tacitus, show a large time gap between the original and the first copies of the manuscript of which there are only few copies.

When it comes to the New Testament, it is very different. The New Testament was written in a short time gap between 40–100 AD and we have manuscript evidence as early as 130 AD, and full manuscripts by 350 AD. We have more than 5300 Greek manuscripts of the New Testament, 10,000 Latin translations and 9300 others. We can therefore be confident in the accuracy, authenticity and integrity of the New Testament scriptures that have been passed down to us today, compared to other alternative historical texts.

# E.
## Bible verses

**Psalm 19:1–4a**

'The heavens tell of the glory of God.

The skies display His marvellous craftsmanship.

Day after day they continue to speak; night after night they make Him known.

They speak without a sound or a word; their voice is silent in the skies; yet their message has gone out to all the Earth.'

**Romans 1:20**

'From the time the world was created people have seen the Earth and sky and all that God made. They can clearly see His invisible qualities – His eternal power and divine nature…'

# F.
## 'Welcome to Holland' poem
## - Emily Pearl Kingsley

'It's like planning a fabulous vacation trip – to Italy. You buy a bunch of guidebooks and make your wonderful plans: the Colosseum; Michelangelo's David; the gondolas in Venice. You may even learn some handy phrases in Italian. It's all very exciting.

After months of eager anticipation, the day finally arrives. You pack your bags and off you go. Several hours later, the plane lands. The stewardess comes in and says, 'Welcome to Holland.'

'Holland!' you say. 'What do you mean Holland? I signed up for Italy! I'm supposed to be in Italy. All my life I've dreamed of going to Italy.' But there's been a change in the flight plan. They've landed in Holland and there you must stay.

The important thing is that they haven't taken you to a horrible, disgusting, filthy place, full of pestilence, famine and disease. It's just a different place. So you must go out and buy new guidebooks. And you must learn a whole new language. And you will meet a whole new group of people you would never have met.

It's slower-paced than Italy, less flashy than Italy. But after you've been there for a while and you catch your breath, you look around... and you begin to notice that Holland has windmills... Holland has tulips... Holland has Rembrandts.

But everyone you know is busy coming and going from Italy... and they're all bragging about what a wonderful time they had there. And for the rest of your life, you will say, 'Yes, that's where I was supposed to go. That's what I had planned.'

And the pain of that will never, ever, ever go away... because the loss of that dream is a very significant loss.

But... if you spend your life mourning the fact that you didn't get to Italy, you may never be free to enjoy the very special, the very lovely things... about Holland.'

# G.

## The Goodness of God – Bethel Music

I love You, Lord
For Your mercy never failed me
All my days, I've been held in Your hands
From the moment that I wake up
Until I lay my head
I will sing of the goodness of God.

I love Your voice
You have led me through the fire
In the darkest night You are close like no other
I've known You as a Father
I've known You as a Friend
And I have lived in the goodness of God.

And all my life You have been faithful
And all my life You have been so, so good
With every breath that I am able
I will sing of the goodness of God.

www.ingramcontent.com/pod-product-compliance
Lightning Source LLC
Chambersburg PA
CBHW030107100526
44591CB00009B/307